JEWISH WRITING IN THE CONTEMPORARY WORLD

Series Editor: Sander L. Gilman, University of Chicago

Contemporary
Jewish Writing
in Austria 🍀
An Anthology

Edited by Dagmar C. G. Lorenz

University of Nebraska Press : Lincoln & London

Acknowledgments for the use
of copyrighted material appear
on pages 359–62, which constitute an extension of the copyright page. This volume was
published with the support of a
generous grant from the Cleve-
land Foundation to the Department of Religion at Case Western Reserve University, as part
of a project on Jewish-Christian
relations directed by Professors
Susannah Heschel and Eldon
Jay Epp. © 1999 by the University
of Nebraska Press.
 Manufactured in the
United States of America ☺

Library of Congress Cataloging-in-Publication Data
Contemporary Jewish writing in Austria :
an anthology / edited by Dagmar C. G. Lorenz.
p. cm. – (Jewish writing in the contemporary world)
Includes bibliographical references.
ISBN 0-8032-2923-2 (cloth : alkaline paper). –
ISBN 0-8032-7983-3 (paperback : alkaline paper)
1. Austrian literature – Jewish authors – Translations
into English.
2. Austrian literature – 20th century – Translations
into English.
3. Jews – Austria – Literary collections. I. Lorenz,
Dagmar C. G., 1948– . II. Series.
PT1109.J4C66 1999 830.8'08924'09436 – dc21
99-13472 CIP

In memory of Charlotte Lorenz (1913–1998)

Contents

2. The Interwar Generation

3. The Generation of Austrofascism, World War II, and the Shoah

4. The Post-Shoah Generation

5. The Generation of the Second Austrian Republic

Introduction

Disruption and Continuity:
The Situation of Jewish Writing
in Contemporary Austria

The volume at hand presents texts by Jewish and Jewish-identified Austrian authors of several generations, all of whom are distinct in their basic experiences and outlook. The works reflect in a multitude of ways the respective eras that shaped the authors emotionally and intellectually and influenced the aesthetic sensitivity and quality of their writings. Works are included from authors born before World War I; the interwar generation; the generation of Austrofascism, National Socialism, World War II, and the Shoah; the post-Shoah generation; and the Second Austrian Republic. All of the authors discuss their experiences or write about their visions from a Jewish point of view. Of course, the events that shaped twentieth-century history have affected Austrian society as a whole. However, the degree to which a group or an individual desired to or was able to identify with the majority experience of this predominantly Catholic country that at times displayed a strong German nationalist, even fascist and National Socialist, predisposition and the degree to which a person was excluded or discriminated against because he or she was perceived as "other" determined the way in which these authors experienced, assessed, and transposed events into writing.

Alluding to a street between the former Jewish quarter and the rest of Vienna's Inner City, the Tiefe Graben, Hans Thalberg states in his autobiography that in postwar Austria the intellectual and emotional spaces of Jews and non-Jews were separated as if by a deep moat.[1] Until 1938 this quarter, which is close to the Stadt-tempel, the only synagogue that survived Kristallnacht (Night of broken glass), had been replete with businesses owned by Jews. After the so-called Anschluss and the pogrom of 9–10 November 1938, the Jewish community was destroyed, and the Shoah ended what little continuity there had been in Vienna's Jewish history – a history marked by persecution, expulsion, emigration, and re-migration. The rebuilding of Austrian society after World War II did not include an invitation to Jewish exiles to return. Those who did were expected to conform to the dominant culture. Ruth Becker-mann writes in Unzugehörig (1989; Not belonging), her account of the formation of a Jewish community and her own Jewish child-hood in post-Shoah Vienna, that Jews were allowed to live in Aus-tria again, provided they were discreet and quiet and did not em-phasize their Jewish identity.[2] The Austrian chancellor Julius Figl demanded that they assimilate to Austrian society as a whole. Con-sidering the obstacles young Jews faced in developing cultural ex-pressions of their own in a generally repressive climate, the com-plexity of the new Jewish culture and literature in Austria today reflects, as Sander Gilman notes, "a 'real' Jewish cultural presence. 'Real' in the sense that the debates, the schisms, reveal a living and breathing cultural entity."[3]

After 1945 some Jews did settle in Vienna. The majority of them came from eastern Europe. They founded businesses and took up residence, often in neighborhoods where Jewish life once had pros-pered: the Inner City, the adjacent Leopoldstadt, and as did Hilde Spiel after her return from England, in the suburbs where their families had lived prior to the Nazi era. Spiel reflects on her tenuous situation as a former Jewish exile who returned to Austria in her essay "I Love Living in Austria," which is included in this volume. Her experience was exceptional: few of the Viennese Jews who had survived the Shoah, exile, or both returned to postwar Austria.

The newly emerging Jewish community established itself despite predictions of doom and disaster and in disregard of objections on the part of anti-Semites in Austria and the international Jewish public. Surprisingly, however, the Jews who came to Vienna from different countries and cultures forged a new Jewish discourse with specifically Viennese characteristics. In "The City and the Self: Nar-ratives of Spatial Belonging among Austrian Jews," Matti Bunzl argues that the diverse postwar community developed a Viennese character and a " 'Viennese-identified' Jewish self."[4] In his auto-biographical essay "From Kreisky to Waldheim: Another Jewish Youth in Vienna," Bunzl also traces the process through which he and other Jews of the postwar generation constructed their identity in opposition to the latent anti-Semitism of the Austrian public and the positions articulated by members of the older generation. His views correspond to those of other intellectuals of the postwar generation. "In Vienna I know every stone and every star," Robert Schindel writes in his poem entitled "Vineta 2." The sentiments he expresses are similar to those stated in Ruth Beckermann's film Die papierene Brücke (1987; Paper bridge).[5] In both cases the audience draws the conclusion that the speaker does not mind living in Vienna.

In the mid-eighties the Austrian presidency fell to a man who gained the approval of a large percentage of voters when his involvement with the Nazi regime became public and drew the attention of the media worldwide. At that point, silence and assimilation ceased to be options for the children of Holocaust survivors and exiles. Yet their disappointment with their fellow Austrians, including the seemingly progressive ones, which is so convincingly expressed by Doron Rabinovici in "Der richtige Riecher" ("The Right Nose"), neither affected their fondness for Vienna nor stopped them from trying to come to terms with the galut, their Austrian existence. Most younger authors acknowledge and embrace their central European Jewishness. For many Jews from eastern Europe, Vienna represented an alternative to the anti-Semitism they confronted in their native countries – the Polish Jew-hatred, well documented in Claude Lanzmann's Shoah, the brutality of the Rumanian Iron Guard, and Stalinist anti-Semitism.[6]

According to Bunzl, Vienna's emerging Jewish culture (re)invented itself before the background of the Jewish literature and culture of turn-of-the-century Vienna. The younger intellectuals derived from this era discursive and ideological components for self-expression. Other models were available through the literature of the interwar period in so-called Red Vienna.[7] Among the recently reprinted and rediscovered authors is Veza Canetti, whose promising career as an author began in the early 1930s and ended abruptly

soon thereafter because even a Social Democratic editor such as
Otto König of the *Arbeiter-Zeitung*, where Canetti had placed most of
her publications, considered a Jewish woman writer a liability. Veza
Canetti's works, including "Der Neue" ("The New Guy"), remained
inaccessible to the general reading public until the late 1980s. However, writers and intellectuals seeking alternative models to mainstream postwar Austrian literature had familiarized themselves
with the traditions of the Left already much earlier.

Contemporary Jewish writing in Austria establishes intertextualities with Jewish and non-Jewish Viennese authors; the allusions to Robert Musil in Elfriede Jelinek's *Die Ausgesperrten* (1980;
Wonderful, Wonderful Times), Ruth Beckermann's use of the title as
well as of concepts of Arthur Schnitzler's famous *Jugend in Wien*
(1920; *My Youth in Vienna*), an account of growing up Jewish in turn-
of-the-century Vienna, and the critical references to the bona fide
former Nazi Heimito von Doderer in Robert Menasse's network of
novels, including *Selige Zeiten, brüchige Welt* (1991; Blissful times,
brittle world), are only a few of the many examples. Beyond the
Austrian frame of reference, the larger German-speaking cultural
code, most notably Hegel, plays an important role in Menasse's
works.[8] Other members of the contemporary Jewish intellectual
community in Vienna, among them Robert Schindel and Doron Rabinovici, blend Viennese literature of different periods and movements with post-Shoah literature and historiography. There is a
clear connection between their own perspectives and experiences as
Viennese Jewish writers and the accounts, histories, and fiction of
the Holocaust. Rabinovici's most recent novel, *Suche nach M.* (1997;
In search of M.), is a compelling example of the blend of styles,
genres, and traditions present in the most recent prose works of
these writers. All of them use the concept of Vienna and the corre-
sponding associations of a complex central European urban culture
and a rich Jewish past as a communicative device and an arsenal of
images, names, characters, topoi, attitudes, and, of course, language. Rather than being an empirically or historically verifiable
entity, their Vienna is constructed from historical and contemporary discourses.

The majority of Jewish writers born after the Shoah turned to the
literary production of the pre-Nazi era, particularly to works and

authors outlawed under Nazi rule, to establish an oppositional or at least alternative Austrian discourse distinct from the mainstream. By doing so, they avoided the dilemma of having to deal with a language corrupted by Nazi thought, which was a major concern of West German authors or writers who published predominantly in Germany, for example, Paul Celan. Celan's "Todesfuge" ("Death Fugue"), one of the most widely known Shoah poems, was written during or around the time the poet lived in Vienna, or even earlier. Compared to his later, much more cryptic texts written in Paris and published in the Federal Republic of Germany, "Death Fugue" is an accessible representation of the genocide committed in the Nazi death camps. In none of his later poems did Celan represent the Shoah so directly. Silence as a recurrent theme and a literary practice is characteristic of Celan's later works, which, similar to the poems of Ilse Aichinger, demand of the reader a great deal of attentiveness to the text and the willingness to participate in the creative process.

The works of many contemporary authors suggest continuities between the pre- and post-Nazi era, which historically do not exist. Most contemporary Jewish authors have no biographical ties to and certainly no personal knowledge of Vienna before the Anschluss, Austria's annexation by Germany, but their attitudes were shaped by those of older Jewish and Jewish-defined authors who were concentration camp survivors or exiles. Whether the older authors returned to Vienna or continued to write and publish in the Austrian context, younger Jewish intellectuals read and examined their works with regard to their own situation. Thus Hans Weigel, Friedrich Torberg, Albert Drach, Elias Canetti, Hilde Spiel, Georg Kreisler, Hermann Leopoldi, Erich Fried, Jakov Lind, and Elisabeth Freundlich provided directly and indirectly patterns for the following generation. The literary and artistic creativity of Holocaust survivors who came to the fore after 1945, such as Paul Celan, Ilse Aichinger, Jean Améry, Simon Wiesenthal, Ernst Fuchs, and Friedensreich Hundertwasser, also played an important role in shaping the young generation's understanding of the Shoah and their relationship to Austria. So did the narratives as well as the silence of their own relatives. Although Erich Fried, Jakov Lind, Georg Kreisler, and Elias Canetti resided outside of Austria, their works

were read, listened to, and discussed by the Austrian public, and
they established a prominent Viennese presence. They became the
center of symposia and gala events. In the 1980s Elias Canetti, who
was awarded the Nobel Prize in literature in 1981, held frequent and
highly acclaimed readings from his works. His aphorisms, of
which some taken from the Das Geheimherz der Uhr (1987; The Secret
Heart of the Clock) are included in this volume, reveal Canetti's extraordinary breadth and depth of thought. His brilliant aperçus and
puns are reminiscent of his former idol Karl Kraus. Indeed, Canetti
provided an important link between authors of the interwar period
such as Karl Kraus and Hermann Broch and the postwar generation
of Viennese Jews.

The younger generation owes the ease and astuteness with which
they articulate cultural criticism to their fin-de-siècle models and
the interwar satirists, philosophers, poets, cabaret artists, and
scholars. Robert Menasse writes in his essay on Austrian identity,
Das Land ohne Eigenschaften (1992; The land without qualities) that
Austria may be a nation, but not a homeland. He scans the cultural
terrain to show the inner tensions in Austria, a country that has a
critical Jewish and anti-Fascist presence but also associations of
former SS members that are enjoying the sympathy, if not the support, of the conservative media and some leading politicians.[9]
These inconsistencies prevent, according to Menasse, the construction of a positive national identity. Robert Schindel's novel
Gebürtig (1992; Born-Where) also traces a wide spectrum of attitudes
toward the past. On the part of his non-Jewish characters, they
include denial, repression, and at times shame, whereas his Jewish
characters often identify themselves as victims because they identify
themselves through the victims of the Nazis. Some reject the notion
of being Austrian altogether, while others do not, and some manipulate and exploit history for personal gain. By differentiating between the reactions of young Jews and non-Jews, the children of the
perpetrators and those of the Nazi victims, Schindel acknowledges
the dualistic model of Jews and Nazis expressed in Thalberg's metaphor of the "deep moat." In the prologue of Born-Where Robert
Schindel introduces the metaphor of the "double lamb," which is
illustrated by the characters of rather dissimilar twin brothers of
Jewish descent; in this part of the novel they function as ciphers of

the multiple levels of confusion and schizophrenia in contemporary Austrian society and their effects on the Jews living there.[10]

Some exceptions notwithstanding, during the early 1980s most younger Jewish authors adopted the position that a normal interaction between Jews and non-Jews in Austria was impossible. They had grown tired of explaining and justifying their existence to latently or blatantly anti-Semitic fellow citizens. The Jewish intellectual elite began to set itself apart from non-Jewish Austria, discouraged by the official stance taken by the Gentile majority that their country had been the first victim of Nazism. Becoming increasingly aware that their perspective and sense of self could not be reconciled with the majority point of view and version of history, they began to pursue their own cultural agenda. Bunzl writes: "Most Austrian Jews readily disavow an Austrian identity, seeking instead to differentiate themselves from (imagined) Austrian traits. In doing so, Jews often use the term 'Austrian' in constitutive opposition to a Jewish self."[11]

The postwar-generation authors of Jewish background were aware of the impact that the Shoah and the Nazi legacy had on them, and they recognized their long-term effects in their country of residence. Sensitive to these issues, they realized that among many non-Jews their age, knowingly or unknowingly, the attitudes of the Nazi generation, authoritarian patterns and proto-Fascist gender, race, and class stereotypes were reproduced. They record these phenomena with an outside observer's detachment, as in Elfriede Jelinek's novel Wonderful, Wonderful Times. Her protagonists, the Witkowski twins, display the same mentality and psychological characteristics as their parents, former Nazis. Without the political structures of National Socialism, their resentments, feelings of inferiority, and lust for power remain unchanneled. Rather than in party activities and organized mass murder, they manifest themselves in random acts of brutality and uncontrollable, chaotic emotions that culminate in the young man's killing his entire family. Nadja Seelich and Robert Menasse likewise deal with aggressive and self-destructive tendencies among non-Jews. In addition, they explore the broken-down lines of communication between Jews and non-Jews.[12] In the essay "Film, Staat und Gesellschaft in Ost- und Westeuropa und ich" (1992; "Film, State, and Society in East-

ern and Western Europe – and I'") Seelich includes her memories as
well as her impressions of the new Prague, her native city, without
synthesizing the discrepancies between her own two languages,
Czech and German, and her background. All of these are reflected
in her films.

Most Jewish authors who grew up after the Shoah wrote about
the effects the Shoah had on themselves and their peers. Their
works record their insecurity, disorientation, mistrust, and an almost neurotic hypersensitivity, as well as feelings of being marginalized and of belonging to a vulnerable minority. They often discuss
their futile attempts of reaching out to the larger society and con-
solidating their fragile sense of self. Nadja Seelich's film *Kieselsteine*
(1982; Pebbles) represents a landmark in the search for a new Jewish sensitivity and self-expression. Released at the beginning of
the 1980s, the work reveals in a private setting a modern Jewish
woman's inability to conform to the standards of the conservative
Jewish community and her incompatibility with Austrian and German non-Jews. Other works contextualize this core conflict in
terms of politics. Many authors discuss the failure of young Jews to
align themselves with the political Left during the 1960s and early
1970s. Even among the self-proclaimed non-Jewish anti-Fascists,
whom many Jews had considered their natural allies in confronting
the past, there was no forum to discuss the Holocaust. From their
disappointment with what Jean Améry calls the self-alienated Left,
which "in the guise of anti-Zionism" had made anti-Semitism respectable,[13] the new Jewish discourse emerged.[14]

Contrary to the profound personal involvement with Austria on
the part of older authors such as Hilde Spiel and Hans Weigel –
Weigel was one of the first to call for a normalization of the relationship between Austria and Germany in his essay "Das verhängte
Fenster" (1946; "The Draped Window") – the families of the
younger authors felt aloof vis-à-vis Austria and its future. Already
Ilse Aichinger, who grew up in Vienna under the Nazi rule, signals a
markedly different reaction in her 1946 essay "Aufruf zum Mißtrauen" ("A Summons to Mistrust"). She calls for introspection and
self-criticism on the part of all those who survived the war and the
Nazi dictatorship and strongly suggests that the time to conduct
business as usual has not yet come, if it ever will. For the following

generation, emotional ties to Israel, cultivated in the circle of family and friends, were more common than loyalty toward the Austrian legacy. Sander Gilman is correct in pointing out the multifaceted, in many ways problematic effects of the existence of a Jewish state on the European Jewish experience: "It is possible to have a firm, meaningful cultural experience as a Jew in the Diaspora or to feel alone and abandoned in the Galut (and vice versa) – two people can live in the very same place and time and can experience that place and time in antithetical ways."[15]

During the postwar era the emotional bond with Israel was stressed in Jewish families. These ties were strengthened by vacations and study abroad. Later, however, many Austrian Jewish intellectuals began to reexamine the values conveyed to them on these occasions. In particular, they questioned Zionist ideals and Jewish nationalism. Robert Schindel, Ruth Beckermann, Anna Mitgutsch, and Doron Rabinovici consider Israel one of the options open to them. In contrast to some former West Germans such as Lea Fleischmann and Henryk Broder, who moved to Israel in protest, most Viennese writers disagreed with Jean Améry's assessment that Jews had only two alternatives: "the freedom to assimilate in their host countries under the aegis of the Enlightenment, and the freedom to emigrate to an Israel that even within the pre–1967 borders would have enough room to receive a flow of immigrants that most likely would not be particularly large."[16] Rather, they envisioned a Jewish life, however defined, in Austria and an Austrian-Jewish identity configured in a larger international context. The scenario of Viennese cosmopolitanism involves a high degree of selectivity and individual choice as far as religious, national, and cultural paradigms are concerned.

The literature and films of the 1980s and 1990s reveal the process involved in the formation of a contemporary Austrian Jewish identity. Ruth Beckermann, for example, points out that Nadja Seelich's Kieselsteine was the first film to deal with the relationship of "Jews and non-Jews of the second generation."[17] Beckermann's own film trilogy Wien Retour (1983; Return to Vienna), Die papierene Brücke, and Nach Jerusalem (1990; Towards Jerusalem),[18] Anna Mitgutsch's novel Abschied von Jerusalem (1995; Lover, Traitor), and Robert Menasse's and Doron Rabinovici's prose works are part of a new tradition produced by a small, close-knit, and highly visible group of intellectuals.[19] Seelich's film *Sie saß im Glashaus und warf mit Steinen* (1992; She sat in the glasshouse and threw stones) was one of the first to establish a connection between Kafka's pre-Nazi, pre-Stalinist Prague and the post–Cold War landscape and to situate Vienna in the multicultural landscape of central Europe.[20] Rather than promoting a common ideology, these works evolved in an ongoing search that requires positioning and repositioning from one work to the next. Taken in their entirety, they are a body of texts that configures Jewish space as evolving similar to concentric circles, with Vienna at the center of the inner circle, and with wider ranging circles encompassing central Europe, eastern Europe, the Middle East, North Africa, and western Europe and finally embracing the world. This spatial model also reflects the global parameters of post-Shoah Jewish history.

Seelich's *Kieselsteine*, Beckermann's account of Jewish life in Austria, *Unzugehörig*, and Peter Henisch's *Steins Paranoia* (Stein's paranoia) show how Austrians of different Jewish backgrounds establish themselves in a sphere apart from Gentile society physically, emotionally, and intellectually.[21] Their sense of difference is the force that drives their writing. At the same time, the Jewish sphere configured in their texts as well as in their social environment is permeable and accessible to non-Jews. Like the Jewish salons of the eighteenth century and later the coffeehouses, it is a Jewish-defined space where non-Jews, for the most part intellectuals, come to visit.

Contemporary Jewish writing communicates dissenting views and opinions about social developments and everyday life in Austria. The distinct views within this minor or subculture also involve particular modes of expression and aesthetics, none of which are entirely new.[22] Detachment, a penchant for satire, particularly when portraying Austria and Austrian society, have traditionally been a part of Jewish writing. In that sense Jakov Lind's biting satire *Eine Seele aus Holz* (1962; Soul of Wood), Elfriede Jelinek's *Wonderful, Wonderful Times*, and Nadja Seelich's *Kieselsteine*, as well as Robert Schindel's *Born-Where*, Robert Menasse's *Selige Zeiten, brüchige Welt*, and Doron Rabinovici's *Papirnik* (1994) and *Suche nach M.*, are integral to Viennese Jewish literature.[23] Satire calls for intimate knowledge as well as detachment on the part of the author. Writing as an outsider who is intimately familiar with the mainstream point of view had long been a characteristic of Jewish writing of the interwar period, the Jewish cabaret, and the works of Jewish journalists. This tradition is associated with names such as Karl Kraus, Jura Soyfer, Hermann Leopoldi, and Karl Farkas. Friedrich Torberg in *Die Tante Jolesch* (1977; Aunt Jolesch) and Georg Kreisler in *Worte Ohne Lieder* (1986; Words without songs), which contains "Bundschuh the War Criminal" and "The Unknown Nation," carried these expressions and forms into the postwar era.

Elfriede Jelinek, in a 1993 interview, discusses the achievements of the Jewish interwar satirists, their "work with language and criticism of existing conditions with the help of language" as a fundamentally Jewish undertaking.[24] She stresses her own affinity with Kraus, Farkas, and the Waldbrunn cabaret. Positioning herself next to Edgar Hilsenrath and Robert Schindel, Jelinek defines herself through the tradition of Jewish writing and, identifying herself as the daughter of a Jewish victim of Nazi persecution, as an Austrian Jew.[25] Jelinek's identity construction in terms of her family background, literary tradition, and politics is paradigmatic of the public position assumed by many other Jewish authors in contemporary Austria.

Elias Canetti, whose novel *Die Blendung* (1935; *Auto-da-Fé*) appeared briefly before the Nazi takeover, Hugo Bettauer, and Veza Canetti had been masterful literary satirists who, directly or indirectly, became models for the following generations.[26] The sense of the grotesque and the high degree of disassociation in the works of Jakov Lind, who critically and irreverently wrote about such sensitive issues as the Nazi "euthanasia" program and the Shoah, satirizing at the same time the post-Shoah discourse of *Vergangenheitsbewältigung* (coming to terms with the past) is reminiscent of Elias Canetti. Lind exposes the callousness of the perpetrators and the double victimization of Jewish Nazi victims. With a similarly sardonic humor Jelinek shows that repressive social dynamics were perpetuated from the interwar period through the Nazi era into the 1950s and 1960s. She depicts the history of victimization and brutality as ongoing. Similar views are expressed by Nadja Seelich, whose film *Kieselsteine* is replete with funny and shocking episodes that deal with the failed attempts of young Austrians, Germans, and

Jews to overcome the past that divides them. The point of view in the film is that of the Jewish protagonist.

Disappointment with Austrian society and their parents' solutions to the problem of marginalization caused many of the younger authors to question the positions espoused by Jewish and Jewish-identified authors in the postwar era. They shared neither the radical distrust of ideology and group identity that the previous generation had embraced nor its belief in the autonomous, nonconformist individual, an ideal informed by existentialist philosophy. Indeed, individuals holding such ideals are satirized by Jelinek in *Wonderful, Wonderful Times* and by Menasse in *Selige Zeiten, brüchige Welt*. In the light of contemporary writing, Hans Weigel's emphasis on the individual and individuality in *Man kann nicht ruhig darüber reden* (1986; It is impossible to speak about it dispassionately) seemed anachronistic, if not revisionist, at the time it appeared. Weigel's disavowal of a Jewish identity, his careful approach to issues such as the Nazi past, Zionism, and anti-Semitism, avoids confrontation and is to a certain extent palatable even to deniers of the Holocaust. On the other hand, the younger generation had also become critical of Marxist anti-Fascism and the New Left. Certain views of the New Left are represented in Erich Fried's works, which at the same time express the grief and sensitivity of someone who had a narrow escape from the Holocaust. As a young man, Fried lost friends and family members in the death camps. This experience informs his poetry. At the same time Fried considers Zionism a form of racism. In his answer to Jean Améry, "Ist Antizionismus Antisemitismus?" (1982; "Is Anti-Zionism Anti-Semitism?" he characterizes Israel's political agenda as expansionist and imperialist. Fried's criticism of capitalism and the Fascist structures he associates with it is carried even further in the works of Elfriede Jelinek, who grew up in postwar Vienna and associated herself with the German New Left. *Wonderful, Wonderful Times* is paradigmatic of her assessment of Austria's failure to deal with Fascism. Jelinek interprets the categorical rejection of ideology and the predilection for existentialism on the part of former Nazi sympathizers and the children of former Nazis as class-specific. She portrays the outlook of the lower middle class, the social stratum that had been Hitler's stronghold, as reflecting an unwillingness to confront Austria's collective guilt. Moreover, she asserts that the focus on the individual conceals the actual powerlessness of this class. Jelinek's satirical portrayal of members of the working class reveals the decline of the revolutionary movement. Similar perspectives emerge in Robert Schindel's *Born-Where*. Jean Améry, on the other hand, raises doubts about the agenda of the Left in "Der ehrbare Antisemitismus" (1982; "Antisemitism on the Left") and its appropriateness for Jewish survivors and their children. Contrary to Fried, he views anti-Zionism as a variant of anti-Semitism. His opinions had a widespread resonance among Jews who previously had sided with the revolutionary movement of 1968. Seelich, Beckermann, and many of the interviewees in Peter Sichrovsky's *Wir wissen nicht was morgen wird, wir wissen wohl was gestern war: Junge Juden in Deutschland und Österreich* (1985; *Strangers in Their Own Land: Young Jews in Germany and Austria Today*) share Améry's point of view.[27]

In contradistinction to the voluntary or involuntary, not necessarily positive, group identities established in the works of Jelinek and Fried, Seelich's and Menasse's semiautobiographical Jewish characters appear isolated and alienated. The portrayals of specifically Jewish, albeit individualistic, experiences by Beckermann and Rabinovici likewise reveal a disinclination to conform to traditional Jewish roles and expressions of Jewish identity. Although for some authors, among them Anna Mitgutsch, who converted to Judaism, religion is an important aspect of being a Jew, religion is not foremost in contemporary Jewish writing.

The memory of the Shoah, Nazi racism, Jewish stereotypes, and the relationship with the non-Jewish, rather less than more Christian majority, which, as noted by Hans Weigel, is likewise defined by its relationship to the Nazi past, are far more important.[28] Jewish history and customs are represented in Jewish texts and have a primarily cultural significance. Beyond these specific topics, an important textual marker is the control of the Jewish voice. *Die Galizianerin* (1982; The Galician woman) is an example of a cooperative effort between the privileged, non-Jewish author Brigitte Schwaiger and the Holocaust survivor Eva Deutsch. The role of the former is that of the editor; the latter acts as a resource person and informant. The result is an ambivalent, albeit fascinating, text that conveys neither the Jewish nor the Austrian feminist point of view.

By its fragmentation the text itself becomes an illustration of the barriers and the lack of a shared point of view between a Jewish survivor and a mainstream Austrian author. The situation of the two collaborators is paradigmatic of the difficulties that exist between Jews and non-Jews in present-day Austria.[29]

Like Eva Deutsch, most of the younger authors do not consider assimilation an option because they lack the necessary trust in Austria and the German-speaking cultural sphere in general. Whereas Hans Weigel, a former exile and one of the most influential figures of postwar Austrian cultural life, continued to plead for the reconstruction of traditional cultural values and an Austrian culture consisting of non-Jews and Jews, the younger authors do not share his optimistic view of a better, morally upstanding Austria with which a symbiosis would be possible. Hence their critical attitude toward Weigel's conciliatory essay "The Draped Window" and their outrage at his views in *Man kann nicht ruhig darüber reden*. The latter, although it was written before the Waldheim scandal, reads like a condemnation of Israel, the Jewish World Congress, and the anti-Waldheim activists. Ironically, there was greater agreement between members of the older generation, regardless of their specific ideology – Weigel, a conservative, Fried, a leftist, and the former chancellor Bruno Kreisky, a Social Democrat – than between them and Jews born after 1945, as far as key issues such as Zionism, the Nazi legacy, and Jewish identity were concerned.

Weigel's staunch individualism and his adamant opposition to collectivism, regardless of what kind, are products of his conservative, Austrian middle-class background, the social stratum to which the Jews of Vienna had traditionally belonged or aspired. An Austrian patriot who refused to let himself be marginalized as a Jew, he defines himself through the German language and the culture represented by Goethe, Beethoven, Stifter, and Mozart. Although Weigel's anti-Israel position, similar to Fried's Socialist-inspired position, was based on different assumptions than those of the Nazi sympathizers and right-wing Waldheim supporters, the larger Austrian public had little objection to it. In a certain way it seemed to exonerate them from criticism and self-criticism. For this very reason most younger Jewish authors found it objectionable. For them the Shoah was not a tragic, but atypical, incident; much less did they believe, as Weigel did, that the potential for right-wing radicalism was effectively curbed.

To be sure, there were dissenting voices from the very beginning. As early as 1946, Ilse Aichinger in "A Summons to Mistrust" called for continued critical introspection on the part of all Austrians who had survived World War II, and in her novel *Die größere Hoffnung* (1948; *Herod's Children*) she describes the devastating effects of Nazi racial politics and of the public support they had enjoyed.[30] By dealing openly with the Nazi crimes and the anguish as well as the courage of the persecuted, works such as Aichinger's novel, her poem "Mein Vater" (1978; "My Father"), and her short story "Rahels Kleider" (1976; "Rahel's Clothes"), Paul Celan's poem "Death Fugue," Jean Améry's essays, and Albert Drach's novels, including *"Z.Z." das ist die Zwischenzeit* (1990; "M.T.": That is the meantime) established an alternative discourse. This discourse, however, did not flourish in Austria: Celan lived and wrote in France, Améry in Belgium, and Aichinger for many decades in the Federal Republic of Germany.

These authors' works explore the closeness as well as the distance between the victims and the perpetrators and the interconnectedness between past and present. Aichinger's "Rahels Clothes" and "My Father" reveal the rift separating neighbor from neighbor and parents from their children. With a keen awareness of the fact that the Holocaust had destroyed the public that would have been receptive to her views, Aichinger opts for silence as the only possible expression for the Holocaust experience. Her silence is not an absence of words and meaning but the absence of words and communication. This silence, caused by the insurmountable communication barriers left by the Shoah is central to Paul Celan's works as well. Both authors' poetic styles evolved from the realization that language has no words to express extreme situations such as the Holocaust. Ruth Klüger Angress, in her analysis of Claude Lanzmann's documentary film *Shoah*, "Lanzmann's *Shoah* and Its Audience" (1986), as well as in her poetry, validates the insights conveyed in the works of Aichinger and Celan.[31] The realization that the larger society had no desire to come to terms with the Holocaust in an atmosphere of openness contributed to these authors' sense of isolation. Like many survivors, Aichinger, Celan, and Améry found themselves more closely engaged with the human beings and the culture destroyed by the Nazis than with their contemporary society.

Celan's "Death Fugue" remains one of the most acclaimed poems about the death camps. Indeed, it has repeatedly been used as an icon in the works of the younger generation of Jewish writers. Likewise, Simon Wiesenthal's accounts and fiction dealing with the Holocaust have become part of the canon read by authors of the younger generation, and his voice has been heard, if not always acclaimed, in historical situations such as the Waldheim election, as seen in his essay "Der Fall Waldheim" (1988; "The Waldheim Case"). Important in this body of literature are also the works of exile authors who wrote about their experiences and their memories, such as Jakov Lind, Jean Améry, Albert Drach, Elias Canetti, Manès Sperber, Hilde Spiel, Friedrich Torberg, and Elisabeth Freundlich, particularly the works they devoted to the memory of the Austrian-Jewish past and Jewish tradition; among them are Torberg's Die Tante Jolesch, Freundlich's Der Seelenvogel (1986; The soul bird), and Lind's short stories, including "The Story of Lilith and Eve" (1983). Although many of Lind's prose works were originally written in English, they were translated into German and reached the Austrian public as well.[32] In recent years, this has also been the case with the Vienna-born Shoah survivor Ruth Klüger Angress. Her essays, including her review of Lanzmann's Shoah, and her poetry, written at different stages of her life, and some of which reflects her rediscovery of her native city, belong in the larger context of Austrian Jewish writing. Klüger's autobiography, weiter leben (1992; Continuing to live) is told from the point of view of a survivor and a literary and cultural critic.[33] The work reviews in bold strokes the author's memories of Nazi-dominated Vienna and the concentration camps Theresienstadt and Auschwitz, her experiences as an émigré in the United States, and her life in contemporary Germany.

Post-Shoah Austrian Jewish literature establishes its major issues, concerns, and perspectives through culture-specific themes, images, and modes of expression. An anything but homogeneous body of literature, it stands apart from the literature of non-Jewish authors. Internally, it is characterized by marked generational and political differences. Inasmuch as most writers of the immediate

postwar era cast themselves as individuals, exclusive of group con-
texts, they had difficulties in articulating their experience of the past
and problematized their own silence. They configured their Jewishness as the remnant of an irretrievably lost past. Their views reflected the notion that after the Shoah there would be no future
Jewish community in central Europe, hence the existentialist outlook that many of them adopted. One of the few authors of the
older generation who did envision a continuity of Jewish life in the
German language and in Europe was Friedrich Torberg in *Golems
Wiederkehr* (1981; Golem's return).[34]

A new Austrian Jewish discourse evolved in Vienna in the early
1980s, spearheaded by John Bunzl and Bernd Marin's *Antisemitismus
in Österreich* (1983; Antisemitism in Austria), Nadja Seelich's *Kieselsteine*, Hans Thalberg's *Von der Kunst, Österreicher zu sein* (1984; About
the art of being an Austrian), and Ruth Beckermann and Josef
Aichholzer's film documentary *Wien Retour*.[35] The new discourse,
firmly situated in the present, opposes the co-optation of Austrian
Jewish intellectuals by the majority culture. The works of the post-
Shoah generation reveal fundamentally different attitudes toward
the past and Austria than those of non-Jewish writers, regardless of
their specific political outlook, and they differ from the writing of
the previous generations. Most contemporary authors consider
Austria their country of residence, but not necessarily and not exclusively so. Many of them were born outside of Austria: Seelich
was born in Prague, Bunzl in England, and many of them lived
outside Austria for extended periods of time. For example, Menasse
lived in São Paolo, and Beckermann in Paris.

A pervasive sense of exclusion and self-exclusion permeates the
works of the children and grandchildren of exiles and Holocaust
survivors because of their foremost internal reference point, the
Shoah. Unlike the postwar writers, they are outspoken about it:
they name the death camps, reveal the details of the persecution,
and do not shrink from discussing what the previous generation
conveyed to them through their words and actions. They connect
the memory of the Holocaust and Jewish exile to that of a larger
Ashkenazic and Austrian Jewish culture; thus it entails a global
sense of geography. Their inner landmarks reflect both their own
experiences and outlook and those of former generations: the sites

of Jewish geography, connected by routes of trade, migration, marriage, and, of course, escape. This network links Vienna to Jerusalem, Odessa, Czernovitz, Prague, Berlin, Paris, London, New York,
Los Angeles, Cape Town, São Paolo, Buenos Aires, Melbourne,
Montreal, Shanghai, Bombay, and all of them to Auschwitz.

The questions: Where is it safest for Jews to live? Where can they
best express their Jewishness? inform the global quest described in
all of these works and have given the examination of the relationship with Israel a special urgency since the intifada. The violent
conflict between Jews and Arabs brought latent points of disagreement, even conflict, to the fore, as shown in the controversy between Améry and Fried. For younger authors such as Beckermann,
Mitgutsch, Schindel, and Rabinovici, the political situation in Israel
led to an examination, including a self-examination, as to what it
means to be Jewish. In clear distinction to views held by some older
authors, they began to differentiate between the terms "Israeli" and
"Jew." They focused increasing attention on the legacy of the galut,
that is, European, particularly eastern European, Ashkenazic Jewry.
The ethical values they associated with the Yiddish-speaking world
were pacifism, love of education, and spirituality. Rather than the
misery of the ghetto culture and the victim status ascribed to this
lost culture by Zionists and westernized, assimilated Jews, the Ashkenazic tradition came to represent a commitment to peace and
humanity for many contemporary authors.

However, contemporary authors are also cognizant of the pogroms of the past. Skeptical of lasting arrangements in any one
country, they designed a discourse of destruction and survival that
is aloof vis-à-vis Austrian society. Paradoxically, though, it is coupled with a profound appreciation for certain aspects of Austrian,
in particular Viennese, life. Like many exiles, Hilde Spiel and Frank
Zwillinger, for example, they are fond of the city of Vienna and at
the same time suspicious of the Austrians. They tend to portray the
latter as distorted, cartoonlike characters, as does Seelich in Kieselsteine and Rabinovici in "The Right Nose." Current critical and
philosophical debates have also influenced these authors' writing.
The impact of feminism, for example, is obvious in discussions of
Jewish identity in gender-specific terms. Seelich, Beckermann, and
Mitgutsch approach the issue of contemporary Jewish identity from

the point of view of Jewish women, combined with the more general questions of where to live as a Jew, and how. Male authors, such as Schindel, Menasse, and Rabinovici, likewise construct new attitudes toward gender and sexuality in their works.

Although for different reasons and with different assumptions, most Austrian Jewish authors end up portraying Vienna as a viable, yet by no means ideal, option. Seelich, whose focus is central Europe, does not deal with Israel at all. Beckermann, like most of her colleagues, lacks an urgent existential affinity for Israel. Neither does she consider eastern Europe an alternative. She, like many, views it as the graveyard of Ashkenazic Jewry. Vienna is a default option, but in view of the problems associated with the United States and Israel and both countries' international politics, not an entirely distasteful one. In Mitgutsch's Lover, Traitor Israel becomes the testing ground of Jewishness and the concept of identity in general. The protagonist, an Austrian-born woman, is incapable of conforming to the ethnic, moral, and political codes of Israeli society, whether Jewish, Arab, or Christian. In Menasse's novel Selige Zeiten, brüchige Welt the choice is between Brazil and Vienna, and, like Schindel, Menasse also explores rural Austria as opposed to the big city.

From the identification through Jewish history, new topoi have arisen; one example is the debates between anti-Waldheim demonstrators and Nazi apologists and sympathizers in St. Stephen's Square. One particular encounter, recorded in Beckermann's Die papierene Brücke, is also portrayed in Rabinovici's "The Right Nose" and in Schindel's Born-Where; Beckermann's filming of the production of the Theresienstadt sequence in Herman Wouk's War and Remembrance likewise has become such an event. More generally, certain sites, such as coffee houses, parks, neighborhoods, and social milieus, provide unifying reference points in contemporary Austrian Jewish writing. So do certain core texts. Intricate intertextualities reveal close ties between the relatively few Jewish authors in contemporary Vienna and an intense involvement in a common discourse, filtered through the medium of traditional Viennese Jewish culture. The building blocks of the new Jewish writing are the events of the 1980s and 1990s. Processing and debating events such as the Waldheim affair, German unification, and the reorganization of Europe have strengthened the sense of community among Jewish writers and their resolve of defining themselves against the larger public.

The notion that Vienna is congenial to Jewish life seems to have remained constant over time; it had already been expressed by Peter Altenberg, Arthur Schnitzler, and, although coupled with a keen awareness of the social ills of the interwar period, by Hugo Bettauer and Veza Canetti. After the Holocaust, Hilde Spiel in "Ich lebe gern in Österreich" (1984; "I Love Living in Austria") and Hans Weigel in countless essays expressed "a love beyond words" for Vienna. Along with an unmistakable affection for Vienna, contemporary Jewish writing establishes positions similar to those discussed by turn-of-the-century and interwar authors.

Contemporary Austrian Jewish authors, because of their diverse culture and language backgrounds, need a common focal point. Vienna as a topos and as a geographic site fulfills this function for them, as it had for Jews of earlier epochs who had come from the outlying areas of the Austro-Hungarian Empire and had to negotiate different positions and internal reference points.[36] As a result, contemporary Jewish writers are faced with choices that resemble on the surface those of their predecessors. However, the experience of the Shoah, unforeseen and unprecedented, separates their mindset from that of earlier generations even if they appear to continue their predecessors' traditions.

With reference to Arthur Schnitzler's novel Der Weg ins Freie (1908; The Road to the Open), Egon Schwarz summarizes the attitudes among turn-of-the-century Viennese Jews: the "successful businessman's clinging to his Judaism in the face of his family's embarrassment," the "son who flirts with an aristocratic lifestyle and conversion," "the Jew who joins the Social Democrats," "the upright Jews without illusions." "But in the end," Schwarz writes, "it all boils down to a clash of ideas between those who would emigrate in order to establish a Jewish national home in Palestine and those who would stay where they are, namely in their beloved Vienna." As a last option, with Karl Kraus as his prime example, Schwarz mentions Jewish self-hatred and self-denial.[37]

All of these approaches to Jewishness are discussed in the contemporary literature and films produced by Jewish authors. Despite frequently made claims to the contrary, this suggests a continuity between yesterday's and today's Jewish discourse. Indeed, there is such a continuity, a textual one. Neither the book burnings and the suppression of Jewish literature nor the reservation shown toward Jewish Holocaust literature after 1945 prevented young Jews from familiarizing themselves with German Jewish writing and from building their works on the Jewish authors who preceded them; indeed, many of them would be forgotten were it not for the high intellectual profile of contemporary Jewish writing. Their connecting to a disrupted and defamed legacy helped them to formulate their own oppositional points of view, thereby validating on their own terms the disassimilation process that evolved from nineteenth-century anti-Semitism.

At the time of the Shoah an unprecedented degree of assimilation had been achieved between German-speaking Jews and non-Jews. It seemed a matter of time before the immigrants from eastern Europe, who had a deep appreciation for German and Austrian culture, would enter the mainstream.[38] Although Nazism put an end to the impending Austrian-Jewish symbiosis, it took more than a generation to acknowledge, comprehend, and articulate the finality of the destruction. For the most part, the prewar generations did not accomplish the intellectual and emotional break. Refusing to relinquish the values of their younger years, some of them tried to transpose them into postwar reality, or they looked back in mourning, doubting that a new beginning was possible for them. The post-Shoah generation, however, proved in its own way that it was, indeed, possible and forged a new textual tradition that reflects the past without the paralyzing guilt and mourning. Both aggressive and introspective, that tradition conveys the experience of a small community and the subjective insights of the individual. The writers of the post-Shoah generation participate in the larger literary production and shape it as well. At the same time, they are, and want to be, distinct and unassimilated.

Notes

1. Hans Thalberg, *Von der Kunst, Österreicher zu sein* (Vienna: Böhlau, 1984). See also Ruth Beckermann, *Unzugehörig: Österreicher und Juden nach 1945* (Vienna: Löcker, 1989), 10.

2. Beckermann, Unzugehörig, 65.

3. Sander L. Gilman, Jews in Today's German Culture (Bloomington: Indiana University Press, 1995), 69.

4. Matti Bunzl, "The City and the Self: Narratives of Spatial Belonging among Austrian Jews," City and Society (1996): 55.

5. Robert Schindel, "Vineta 2," in Ein Feuerchen im Hintennach (Frankfurt am Main: Suhrkamp, 1992), 18; Ruth Beckermann, Die papierene Brücke (Vienna: Filmladen, 1987).

6. Claude Lanzmann, director, Shoah (New York: New Yorker Films, 1985).

7. Red Vienna is the topic of Ruth Beckermann's film Wien Retour and a motif in Schindel's poem "Splitter Kindheit (Zum Fortgehn von Franz Bönsch)," in Geier sind pünktliche Tiere (Frankfurt am Main: Suhrkamp, 1987), 116–19: ". . . meiner Jugend zauberwilder Demiurg / Bist du mir worden dieses lachende, dies rote Wien" (118).

8. Elfriede Jelinek in Die Ausgesperrten (Reinbeck, Germany: Rowohlt, 1985; first published 1980) does so with Musil's Der Mann ohne Eigenschaften. Robert Menasse's narrative universe in Sinnliche Gewißheit (Frankfurt am Main: Suhrkamp, 1996; first published 1988); Selige Zeiten, brüchige Welt (Frankfurt am Main: Suhrkamp, 1994; first published 1991); and Schubumkehr (Salzburg: Residenz, 1995) is reminiscent of the vast network of narratives and characters of Doderer's extensive lifework. Occasionally Menasse makes direct references to names that occur in Doderer.

9. Robert Menasse, Das Land ohne Eigenschaften (Frankfurt am Main: Suhrkamp, 1995; originally published 1992), 103, 124–26.

10. Robert Schindel, Gebürtig (Frankfurt am Main: Suhrkamp, 1992).

11. Bunzl, "City," 64.

12. Nadja Seelich, Kieselsteine, directed by Lukas Stepanik (Vienna: Cinéart, 1982). See also Menasse, Schubumkehr.

13. Jean Améry, "Antisemitism on the Left," in Radical Humanism, trans. Sidney and Stella Rosenfeld (Bloomington: Indiana University Press, 1984), 45–46.

14. Sander L. Gilman assumes a later time frame, as the title of the collection of essays Reemerging Jewish Culture in Germany: Life and Literature since 1989, ed. Sander L. Gilman and Karen Remmler (New York: New York University Press, 1994) suggests. His cutoff point is the opening of the borders between East and West that preceded German unification. In the Austrian context, different historical landmarks apply.

15. Gilman, Jews, 6.

16. Améry, "Antisemitism," 50.

17. Beckermann, Unzugehörig, 17.

18. Ruth Beckermann and Josef Aichholzer, directors, Wien Retour (Vienna: Filmladen, 1983); Beckermann, Die papierene Brücke; Beckermann and Aichholzer, Nach Jerusalem (Vienna: Filmladen, 1990).

19. Anna Mitgutsch, Lover, Traitor: A Jerusalem Story (New York: Henry Holt, 1997), originally published as Abschied von Jerusalem (Berlin: Rowohlt, 1995).

20. Nadja Seelich, Sie saß im Glashaus und warf mit Steinen, directed by Nadja Seelich and Bernd Neuburger (Vienna: Extrafilm, 1992).

21. Peter Henisch, Steins Paranoia (Salzburg: Residenz, 1988).

22. According to Gilles Deleuze and Félix Guattari, three constitutional elements are characteristic of minor literature: "the deterritorialization of language, the connection of the individual to a political immediacy, and the collective assemblage of enunciation." According to these authors, the bond between the individual and the group is reflected on the literary level by the frequent references to "community" and "territory." Gilles Deleuze and Félix Guattari, Kafka: Toward a Minor Literature, trans. Dana Polan (Minneapolis: University of Minnesota Press, 1986), 16–17.

23. Jakov Lind, Eine Seele aus Holz (Munich: Knaur, 1962); Doron Rabinovici, Papirnik (Frankfurt am Main: Suhrkamp, 1994); Doron Rabinovici, Suche nach M. (Frankfurt am Main: Suhrkamp, 1997).

24. Sigrid Berka, "Ein Gespräch mit Elfriede Jelinek." Modern Austrian Literature 26, no. 2 (1993), 129.

25. Berka, "Gespräch," 137–38; Gilman, Jews, 3.

26. Hugo Bettauer, Die Stadt ohne Juden: Ein Roman von Übermorgen (Frankfurt am Main: Ullstein, 1988; originally published 1925); Elias Canetti, Die Blendung (Munich: Hanser, 1963; originally published 1935). Veza Canetti's novel Die gelbe Straße (Munich: Hanser, 1990) originally appeared in sequels in the Vienna Arbeiter-Zeitung in 1933 and 1934.

27. Peter Sichrovsky, Wir wissen nicht was morgen wird, wir wissen wohl was gestern war: Junge Juden in Deutschland und Österreich (Cologne: Kiepenheuer and Witsch, 1985); Strangers in Their Own Land: Young Jews in Germany and Austria Today (London: I. B. Tauris, 1986).

28. Hans Weigel, "Man kann nicht ruhig darüber reden," in Man kann nicht ruhig darüber reden (Graz, Austria: Styria, 1986): 117–41.

29. See Dagmar C. G. Lorenz, "Hoffentlich werde ich taugen: Zu Situation und Kontext von Brigitte Schwaiger/Eva Deutsch, Die Galizianerin," Yearbook of Women in German 6 (1991): 1–25.

30. Ilse Aichinger, "Aufruf zum Mißtrauen," *Plan* 1, no. 5 (1946): 588; *Die größere Hoffnung* (Frankfurt am Main: Fischer, 1974; originally published 1948).

31. Ruth Klüger Angress, "Lanzmann's *Shoah* and Its Audience," *Simon Wiesenthal Center Annual* 3 (1986): 249–60.

32. See Simon Wiesenthal, *The Sunflower: With a Symposium* (London: Allen, 1970); Friedrich Torberg, *Die Tante Jolesch* (Munich: dtv, 1977); Elisabeth Freundlich, *Der Seelenvogel* (Vienna: Paul Zsolnay, 1986).

33. Ruth Klüger, *weiter leben* (Göttingen, Germany: Wallstein, 1992).

34. Friedrich Torberg, *Golems Wiederkehr* (Reinbeck, Germany: Rowohlt, 1981).

35. John Bunzl and Bernd Marin, *Antisemitismus in Österreich* (Innsbruck: Inn-Verlag, 1983).

36. Marsha Rozenblit, *The Jews of Vienna, 1867–1914: Assimilation and Identity* (Albany: State University of New York Press, 1983), 1, writes: "Vienna has also become a symbol of the ability of Jews to participate in German culture, and to play a leading role in its avant-garde."

37. Egon Schwarz, "Jews and Anti-Semitism in Fin-de-Siècle Vienna," in *Insiders and Outsiders: Jewish and Gentile Culture in Germany and Austria*, ed. Dagmar C. G. Lorenz and Gabriele Weinberger (Detroit: Wayne State University Press, 1993), 60–61.

38. In 1921 Felix Theilhaber observed the almost complete absorption of western European Jewry into Gentile culture, which he considered tantamount to the destruction of German Jews. Felix Theilhaber, *Der Untergang der deutschen Juden* (Berlin: Jüdischer Verlag, 1921). As Josef Roth noted in *Juden auf Wanderschaft* (Berlin: Schmiede, 1927), 657: "The sons and daughters of the Eastern Jews are productive. While their parents barter and peddle, their children are the most talented lawyers, doctors, bankers, journalists, and actors."

1. The Pre–World War I Generation

Albert Drach

Albert Drach was born in Vienna in 1902. His family history is typical of Habsburg Austrian Jewry: His father was a Viennese Jew who taught mathematics at the Wieden college preparatory school and owned real estate. His grandfather had moved to Vienna from the Bukovina, and his mother's parents came from well-to-do Moravian merchant families. At the age of twelve, the same year that Austria's fin-de-siècle culture was about to be destroyed by the cataclysmic events of World War I, Drach began to publish poetry. He later studied at the University of Vienna and received a doctorate in law in 1926. While working as a trial lawyer in Mödling, he wrote plays, short stories, and poems. During the 1930s he faced increasing difficulties in publishing his work, as did most Jewish writers, because of rising anti-Semitism. Soon after the annexation of Austria by Nazi Germany, Drach, like his protagonist in the following text, escaped to Yugoslavia and fled to Paris. In 1940 he moved to southern France, where he was arrested and interned in several French concentration camps. Following his accidental release in 1942, Drach survived in hiding until the arrival of the Allied troops in France. He returned to Austria in 1947. Having regained possession of his family's residence, he married in 1954, and in 1964 his collected works appeared in eight volumes.

Drach is a major chronicler of Austrian Jewish memory from the last days of the Habsburg monarchy to the present. His work combines characteristics displayed in the works of other interwar authors, such as Doderer, Roth, and Canetti, but Drach's bizarre sense of humor and appreciation for the grotesque is unique in that he constantly contextualized his work with realistically portrayed events and refers to real-life situations. Drach's writing style also reflects the author's profession. It is fashioned after the highly stylized legal language of the late Habsburg Empire, whose bureaucratic tradition far outlasted the end of the monarchy. The influence of German and Austrian poets of the classical, romantic, Biedermeier, and realist eras is apparent as well, combined with expressionist and surrealist features. Drach is the author of poetry, *Kinder der Träume* (1919; Children of the dreams); novels, *Das große Protokoll gegen Zwetschkenbaum* (1964; The great protocol against Zwetschkenbaum), *Das Spiel vom Meister Siebentot und weitere Verkleidungen* (1965; The play about Master Siebentot and other masquerades), *Die kleinen Protokolle und das Goggelbuch* (1965; Small protocols and the book of Goggel), *Das Aneinandervorbeispiel und die inneren Verkleidungen* (1966; Playing past one another and internal masquerades), *Unsentimentale Reise: Bericht* (1966; Unsentimental Journey), "Z.Z." *das ist die Zwischenzeit* (1990; "M.T.": That is the meantime), and *Untersuchung an Mädeln: Kriminal-Protokoll* (1971; Experiments with girls); and plays, published in *Gottes Tod ein Unfall* (1972; God's death – an accident). Drach died in Vienna in 1995.

Albert Drach

EXCERPT FROM
"M.T."

That Is the Meantime

While the son considered himself safe for the time being, things were taking an entirely different turn as far as the mother's affairs were concerned. As soon as the son had left, she had to move her belongings from what had remained of the apartment she had been guaranteed by word of honor to the humid former office suite of the architect in order to surrender to the glazier-and-waiter couple, who had advanced to the status of members of the master race, everything that a certain undeserving great-nephew of an erstwhile deserving great-uncle in his capacity as a party member, if not mayor, had decided to transfer to those who enjoyed his favors at the expense of a Jewish mother. Not even her maid was available anymore to help her carry out this task. Because of the son's return the latter had to be given immediate notice and had no longer participated in the mother's and son's taking temporary shelter in the daughter's apartment. In fact, she had parted in tears. Her tears of gratitude, which time would undoubtedly dry before long, did not help the mother in the least with her third move, which was to precipitate her decline. She already looked like a mere shadow. Even if there was no immediately impending eviction date this time, an earlier date could be set any time, and it was unlikely that the son would be able to assist his mother to comply with it, should he still be around.

At this point the danger of being harassed in the streets of Vienna was not yet an issue of concern for mother and son. Although both were natives of this city, they had fallen into oblivion after their retreat to the suburbs. To be sure, the son was still known to the authorities, but they worked only during daytime hours. Although they had begun to keep an eye on unrests, they had for the most part not yet begun to take an active role in them. For members of the family that meant a respite and an opportunity to catch their breath. In addition, the son did not necessarily possess the kind of features that would immediately identify him as a Jew, and the mother, for her part, epitomized fading suffering royalty. The daughter, finally, eclipsed the female images attached to the billboards, one of which, incidentally, represented her body. An unlicensed commercial painter had sketched it during her only visit to a public pool without obtaining her legally required consent. He did not dare depict her face as well, as it could be seen in art gallery displays in paintings by the most avant-garde as well as more conventional painters. Even though there was little danger that mother and son would be baited in the City of Songs, and such danger could be excluded entirely in the case of the daughter, it was nonetheless not advisable for the three of them to make appearances together in public parks, theaters, and movie houses. They might run into trouble as a result of what they said, if not because of their demeanor. Restaurants were also already beginning to accommodate the new regime to a large extent, which they had apparently not even done in all parts of Berlin. But the genuine Viennese has never been able to conceal a certain propensity for crawling. For example, the well-to-do proprietor of an ostentatiously prestigious establishment wrote on the front door of his restaurant, in keeping with the spirit of the day: "Off-Limits to Dogs and Jews." Yet, in the Inner City another, genteel, and quiet hotel, which displayed a green anchor, did not join in the Jew baiting. Here, the family was able to take its last meal together before the son set out on his journey to at this time still uncertain exile, which nonetheless some of those interested in his immediate demise begrudged him. With him he took the state-approved sum of thirty reichsmarks in travel money.

That evening the mother was very quiet; so was the son. The daughter, in contrast, chatted, counter to her usual habit. She even made promises that she would never be able to keep. Thus she said, among other things, that she would take the mother to her husband's native country, where she herself intended to return. But aside from the mere fact that her passport lacked a necessary stamp that to obtain would cause major difficulties, and she could not take on the additional burden of assuming responsibility for a third person, the mother's staying was synonymous with her ownership of the house, at least according to the official decrees. Clearly, the woman forcibly anchored in this manner might probably have wanted very much to weigh anchor and follow the son. However, she could hardly warm up to the idea of traveling together with her stepdaughter to a country for which she felt little sympathy and that everyone, with the exception of the feeble-minded allied politicians, expected to become the second-next victim of Hitler's fight against the efforts to keep peace undertaken by a meritorious former British postal official and his French lackey. Yet, for the time being the son had deprived himself of the opportunity to have his mother join him. After all, he held only a questionable visa for a questionable state close to the African equator and, along with it, a transit visa for Yugoslavia. Yugoslavia, however, was a country where the mother would hardly have wanted to or been able to go. Moreover, she was afraid that the son would there resume the adulterous relationships that, she claimed, would be the cause of her untimely passing.

At the train station where the departure was to take place, a sleeping compartment had already been reserved for the son as it had been before and proven most useful for his trip to and from Berlin. The daughter, incidentally, had bribed the sleeping-car conductor this time so that he would exercise a proportionately moderating influence on the passport and train inspections, as the train was leaving the territory of the Reich. It so happened that only a single person who was not a family member had appeared at the station to offer his farewell, the young and otherwise shy colleague who, although afraid of a direct blow to his eye, had drafted the contract with the military authorities and managed to save the son several times as he was drifting amidst the rocks. As for the rest, the customary minutes of silence were observed, which in this country are scheduled at every memorial service. The friend and colleague was generally not talkative, but he tried nonetheless to introduce a few cheerful moments into the prevailing atmosphere of gloom and doom, as if the occasion at hand were not a burial, or as if in spite of the finality of the event the funeral guests had to be wined, dined, and entertained according to the custom in rural areas. The only result was the mother's complete withdrawal. The daughter displayed her ordinary, more cheerful disposition, and the son was completely silent in the end, be it that he had pangs of conscience, be it that he was already focusing on putting this interim period behind him. The truly good friend even carried on his back the son's heavy black suitcase filled with books to the luggage compartment, because no porter who could have taken care of it was to be found. The conductor took charge of the lighter luggage. In the absence of those preoccupied with the dispatched and carried-on luggage, the mother in a sudden inspiration gave the son a short embrace when the daughter looked the other way. Doing so she told him in spite of her restraint up to this point that she would likely not ever see him again. Although the son sensed that she said the truth, he resisted the unfamiliar kiss as if it infringed upon his masculinity. His gestures and facial expression did not give the slightest indication that the fate of those he left behind affected him in the least, let alone that he would reveal any such compassion verbally or even feign it.

Even crossing the state border did not awake him from his peaceful slumber, be it that he had actually fallen into a deep sleep, be it that he only pretended. Whichever the case may have been, the conductor, having received ample remuneration and become dependable, kept the luggage inspectors at bay and displayed the passport relinquished to him only partly opened, while pointing his head at the inadvertently or purposefully sleeping man. Obviously this gesture sufficed – the date was only 26 October 1938, and for a few more days the slogan "Juda kick the bucket" was still misinterpreted by lower-ranking officials to mean "Juda take a trip," although the authorities had declared beyond a shadow of a doubt that this interpretation was not the intended one. Moreover, they deterred possible countries of destination from admitting Jews knowingly and willingly by granting them no more than thirty marks of travel money. The son had strictly adhered to this rule, but the daughter, assisted by a Yugoslavian woman and paying double the amount, had transferred the exact sum of money that was to be granted a passport holder without the entry "J" (which the son had originally been, to be sure, but had ceased to be due to his own fault) to his intended place of residence. However, it remained altogether uncertain if he would reach his port of destination at all. As soon as the train arrived in Zagreb, the kindhearted sleeping-car conductor woke him up. Cars had to be changed, and a Yugoslavian control was imminent. Either it was impossible for the waker to influence the procedure, or this service was no longer covered by the tip.

Instantly a reddish-faced troll in uniform appeared, confiscated the son's passport, and announced to him, now that he was passportless, that men, women, and children with a "J" printed in their documents were kept in detention in Agram, that is Zagreb, where their future fate was to be decided. However, the son put up a fight against any further intervention in his future existence with unusual vehemence, be it that from now on he intended to make his own, autonomous decisions, be it that he wanted to reach the intended destination of his journey at all cost. For that reason he addressed the man in uniform gruffly and, since the latter did not allow himself to be impressed – either he did not comprehend what was said or was blindly following orders – the passport was not returned. Yet, even without it, the son ran after the train destined for Split, which was already leaving the station. He lugged his carry-on bag until he managed to throw it to a kind person on the train who assisted him and then jumped into the car, which was still moving at a moderate speed. Thus the zealous policeman could not catch up with him, even though he finally ran in spite of his obesity as if his and not only the life of the son were at stake. He kept custody of the passport of the escapee in effigy.

Nonetheless, perhaps because of his limited jurisdiction, the red-headed stooge must not have considered it worth his while to prevent the son from continuing his trip by having the train stopped somewhere or at least by having it searched at one of the scheduled stops. Whichever the case may be, the son was not bothered again, and his trip went according to schedule. And when the car and he in it pulled into the final station, the bald-headed medical specialist and the blond woman wrestler were already expecting the escapee with a hearty welcome. He was led immediately to his future abode through a labyrinth of steps and dark underpasses inside of what had remained of Diocletian's fortress. Here he was supposed to stay for as long as he was tolerated in the country. The large suitcase, which weighed easily a hundred kilograms and had been carried on the back of his shy friend, had remained on the train uncontested. Without a passport being presented, it was handed over to two stocky men, who struggled to haul it away. Astonishing as it was for the huge piece of luggage to have come along at all, notwithstanding the son's arrest in Zagreb, and for it now to be handed over to him without any formalities, it was even more astonishing how much money the two men intended to collect for transporting the luggage, considering that all he had was thirty marks. Three hundred marks at the most would be added later to this amount, provided they were transferred in the correct manner. Yet, as far as all this was concerned, the medical specialist filled the breach for the time being. He already knew the local rates, whereas the son, despite his earlier trips to this country, did not remember them.

Thus they arrived at the archaic house, which might well have dated back to the era of the early Roman emperors. The son was accommodated in a stately room with an adjacent storage space for the luggage and a large bed in the middle of the main room. Since a certain appliance, an electric conductor inside a heating pad, appeared to have been damaged, the medical specialist announced his intention of fixing the defect in the heating device after having checked out the plump, approximately sixteen-year-old housemaid. Having ascertained that no one else was around, he removed himself to the kitchen to this end, not without making certain that the housemaid was coming along. She was apparently needed for the repair. Meanwhile his wife and the son were busy unpacking. Their hair, as they engaged in the process, touched occasionally, but no further damage arose as a result of more intimate contact. When, however, the extensive work of emptying the suitcase and stowing the effects temporarily restored to the son was completed, he and the medical specialist's wife stood facing each other, with only the uncovered bed between them. At this point the woman, full of anticipation, explained to the hesitating man that one of her reasons for taking an older husband was that she had believed it to be more likely that she would be able to rely on such a man's loyalty in certain matters. Yet, he had already grossly disappointed her in Austria several times as far as that was concerned, and here he was taking up with every maid. She, on her part, had felt obligated to be faithful until she knew how things were with him. Now everything was again the way it had been in the past. The son reacted to her revelations with apprehension, rather than gratification. Indeed, the heating pad had to have been mended by now, or at least it should have turned out to be beyond repair. Moreover, there was no obstacle between him and the woman he desired but an open bed, and the latter is usually not considered an impediment in a situation of mutual consent. In addition, immediately upon his arrival the son had noticed that the steps of a third, currently uninvolved person could be heard long in advance because of the creaking, dry wooden floor; also, the luggage piled up in the entrance hall would delay a possible interruption and block the view of the bed offhand if perchance they should be surprised prematurely.

But although the son was already in the state that enabled him to take possession of a woman in the way nature intended, and even though the blond wrestler communicated her greatest willingness unequivocally in words, gestures, and even, as it were, through the expression of her body and face, no so-called fall from grace occurred between the two. Out of some superstition the son seemed to fear for his mother's safety, although he himself had left her in the clutches of his enemies and other blood- and loot-craving party agencies without providing for her subsistence in any way and even without exhibiting the appropriate remorse. Obviously it was not reality he was taking into consideration, but a mere miracle to which he wanted to reserve a right by way of his symbolic renunciation. However, a long time ago he had already forfeited any such right as a result of his actual omission and wilful abandonment – except if he were to lessen his crime (without being able to atone for it completely) by eliminating the fatal outcome it was certain to produce for his mother and by taking belated, albeit still timely and successful, measures. Instead, the only idea that came to his mind was that of a mystical renunciation. Moreover, this renunciation involved no more than things that were expected of him in the first place and that he was generally inclined and probably able to do. Meanwhile, a ghostly chill rose from the empty bed between the lovers. It intensified the longer the mutual state of desire continued without being satisfied and the longer it took for the husband to repair the heating pad in the presence of the plump, but only sixteen-year-old, housemaid.

Finally, after what seemed a very long time, definitely an interval sufficient to allow the ones who had left to partake several times in the pleasures that the ones who remained inside left unconsummated, the maid reappeared with the all too familiar circles around her eyes and the electric pad, which, in fact, was in perfect working order. No explanation was given as to how the correction had been effected and if it had to be undertaken at all, because possibly all the heating pad needed was being adjusted to the appropriate voltage. Instead, the doctor stopped in front of the untouched bed and inquired benevolently and amused if his wife and his friend had had a good time. This question, in fact, was answered by the immaculate linen sheet and the uncrumpled blankets.

When the husband and the blond woman left, the former satisfied, the latter disappointed, nothing could keep the son any longer in his temporary abode. Although he did not possess the required passport documents, he ran conspicuously out into the small square as if he hoped that from there he would get somewhere, be it to meet the person from whom he could collect the three hundred marks, be it to see one of the town dignitaries to whom his sister had recommended him in case he needed something from the authorities. And he did need both money and a passport, because in a foreign country without either a person can hardly expect any cooperation from the authorities. Nonetheless, it is also conceivable that at that time he had no serious desire of obtaining either money or a passport, but merely wanted to escape the thought of the medical specialist and his wife, perhaps also the thought of his mother, and more generally, anything that still reminded him of home.

During his search for the saving straw or nothingness he met a bespectacled young woman at the extreme end of the not too deep harbor that ocean liners could not enter at all. She stared into the water as if it belonged to her or she to it. When she turned around unexpectedly, perhaps to determine if someone observed her, he looked into an extremely ugly face for which even the glasses represented an improvement. Since neither her body nor her legs had a conciliatory effect, aesthetically speaking, he was faced with a case of perfect, Medusa-like ugliness such as was rare in this country. Moreover, the face, repulsive in itself, bore an expression of comical despair. Apparently this creature was unlucky in love and anything else as well. Everything corresponded to her unfortunate face, including the elements that served to support it and that, insofar as they might have produced a contrast, could have detracted from it.

Be that as it may, as soon as the son spoke his few words of French that, when they would still have been of use to him, he had been unable to summon at the consul general's office, but that he now knew how to pronounce, he received a most gratified answer in the same language. Yes, the girl, if that's what she was, even turned away from the interesting ocean toward him. She immediately knew where the lady lived from whom he intended to collect the three hundred reichsmarks, and she accompanied him to the very place, which was not far. For this reason he complimented the monstrosity on her language proficiency. Thereupon the eyes of the misshapen creature began to shine but she merely said that the members of her family were cultivated people and spoke French frequently. Meanwhile, they had already arrived at the house of the three-hundred-mark lady. She, a considerably nicer-looking woman, received the son with particular kindness, offering her apologies for still being in her negligee. In addition, she handed him the amount of four hundred reichsmarks, saying that it was the amount he could rightfully claim and the exact amount permitted. After that she made him take a seat and offered him some of her homemade pastries. Subsequently she engaged in a real German conversation, which transcended the realm of the merely conventional. Moreover, she reminded him phonetically, that is, in terms of the register of her voice, of conversations he had had with the wife of the medical specialist. After that he had enough, and although he was asked to return, he decided not to do so and took off as fast as possible. Yet, according to his watch, half an hour had already passed.

In the street – if the miserable alley deserved that name – the ugly girl was still waiting. The way she looked up at the son when she saw him again, so soon, as she said, had a certain spooky magic about it, so that he initiated a conversation in English, which he spoke better than French and which his present companion understood as well, which surprised him even more. She, however, simply stated that the local educated families spoke this language as well. The obvious thing to do at this point would have been to find out if the creature also knew German, but that was precisely what the son allegedly did not want to do, simply because he intended to suspend his memories as much as possible, most likely those of home, but also those of the blond woman and the medical specialist.

Nonetheless, he explained to the girl that they had quite a long walk ahead of them, namely, to the dignitary of whose protection he wanted to avail himself. Of course he did not state the particular reason he had for visiting him and only mentioned the name. At that point the miserable little person to whom he had appealed for help became extremely mirthful. She stated that the family in question enjoyed the highest respect and that their palace was indeed at a considerable distance and in a completely different neighborhood, but she would accompany him nonetheless.

They climbed steps, crossed alleys that in turn were bridged by other alleys located farther up, and went past fashionable new buildings and the gigantic statue of a Croatian bishop, cast by a local artist. Finally they arrived again at the pier, which they crossed in the opposite direction until they reached the palatial Venetian-style building where the dignitaries he planned to visit were said to live.

Full of gratitude the son took his leave from the girl, who stopped, however, as if she intended to watch if the son would actually be admitted. He entered in an entirely casual manner, but then, prior to climbing the marble stairs, he did reflect which phrases would be appropriate to be used upstairs.

An exceedingly dignified merchant of impressive stature and his equally statuesque, obviously honorable spouse received him. The two appeared so much like Renaissance characters that they were in perfect harmony not only with the house but also the portraits, which could well represent their own ancestors or their role models unless they had been acquired along with the palace. At any rate, at the time to which the palace and possibly also the originals of these paintings dated back – in case they were the originals – the merchant trade had not yet acquired bad connotations. And it seemed as if this type of mercantile activity was still practiced by the residents of the house. In addition, as has undoubtedly been the case during the Renaissance, the people in this palace were involved in politics. Their activities were in essence devoted to fighting the ruling prime minister, Stojadinovic, who was not only one of Hitler's lackeys but was also said to be an enemy of the Croatians. One leader of the nation in question was to be buried tomorrow; however, he had perished as a result of an illness, not assassination. Nonetheless the great deceased would receive a decorous funeral. The son, who was immediately treated as an old friend, was asked already at that point to participate in the event, seated in the grandstand. Afterward refreshments were served. At first he wanted to decline, but considering that he had had nothing to eat until now, not even breakfast, but only a few pastries, he ended up accepting.

All that benevolence elicited impertinence as its reward. This is why the son brought up the matter of his passport already at this point, although it would have been best if he had kept it to himself until later. Although the old gentleman and the equally old lady listened to him calmly, they did not respond at first. Then the honorable gentleman suggested that the son should perhaps take care of the matter at the police station and that he knew several people there. They were, however, he said, Serbs, and he was not overly fond of them. But his daughter-in-law, a native of Montenegro, where the Serbian script was also used but the people nonetheless had entirely different views – and she was truly an excellent person – made the authorities give the family the same respect they generally enjoyed.

No sooner had the words of praise begun to evoke the daughter-in-law's image in the son's imagination, than the surprise effect was considerably increased when she actually appeared soon thereafter. Since his childhood the son had known Czernagora to be a country of magic, and during his later trips in those parts this notion had been confirmed. The beauty of the women was so great that he understood why a small king of a large country had obtained his spouse in precisely that area. Yet, the woman so highly praised surpassed his imagination and any personal impression left by other members of a female population that was disgraced by the males of their mountainous nation by having to perform the hardest work.

The woman who had just now appeared in a pleated dressing gown had the face and demeanor of a Greek goddess, complemented by the perfect form of an antique statue that had lost none of its divinity by having turned flesh. Even the exposure of a considerable part of her physique, which her dress allowed for, seemed natural and was carried off with majesty. All in all, everything was so authentic that it was not subject to moral convention. Only the rulers of the heavens can assume such a pose, they who appear before human beings to shatter or to exalt them.

This at least is how the son thought his encounter should be described or confessed. But it could also be that his impression of the lady he had just perceived turned out so exaggerated because since time immemorial he had felt an enthusiasm, almost a love, for everything that came from the country of the Black Mountains, feelings that could be traced back to the notoriety and courage of the people and the bizarre landscape itself. In all likelihood it was a contributing factor that he had been accompanied to the house where he met this woman by a girl who was the exact opposite of any ideal of beauty. In any event, the son removed himself only after hours of immediate contemplation had passed. During this time he tried to make an impression, without being able to present anything to justify his presence. Yet he left with an invitation for tea the day after the next and another for a theater performance at a later date. Meanwhile he almost forgot that in the interim he was also expected to take part in the great Croatian leader's funeral ceremony at the request of the old gentleman and his lady.

According to his retrospective observation "inspired and carried by a smile," he left the antechamber of heaven where admittedly he had been invited only for tea and a theater performance, rather than nectar and ambrosia. As for the rest, and, by the way, prematurely, it seemed to him that he had overcome all difficulties regarding his passport and other matters. All of a sudden he found himself face to face with the ugly girl, who had waited for him for hours to hear his report and share his happiness about the friendly reception at the palace or, in the case of a shorter waiting period, to commiserate with him about his failure or at least to show him the way home, which, left to his own devices, he might not have found. He believed that he had to capitulate to so much affection on the part of a creature whom he had first addressed out of profound anger and who had taken him here and waited for him as the result of an unexplained misunderstanding or perhaps merely a wish to be helpful. In an obscure alley he therefore groped for her breasts, which, although they were not visible, could be suspected to be concealed by her nightmarish clothes. And because the woman did not seem to mind any of it – at least she did not fight him off – he also tried to approach her otherwise, namely, with respect to her lower regions.

At this point the accosted woman stated in perfect English that she was married to a professor, wherefore the street was not an appropriate place for such a mockery of her husband, particularly since it was possible to see a lot from all the windows without being noticed oneself. It so happened that she knew a young immigrant woman close by who had been disappointed by her husband and had just had an altercation with her lover. She was on very good terms with that woman. Thus, in the obvious absence of the other lady's husband the opportunity might well present itself to arrange for an intimate rendezvous of the three of them at the lady's house. This way none of them would be a loser. The lady, she said, was much prettier than she was. The son had never been made such an offer. Yet, he immediately considered it acceptable, even if only as a kind of hors d'oeuvre for future pleasures with a goddess who might well be within his reach. The immigrant woman could not possibly be more unattractive than the woman who had made him this generous proposal to share. She was obviously aware of her own ugliness.

The two finally arrived in a fairly dark alley at the house where the immigrants supposedly lived. This time his companion went first to see if her friend's husband had left the house. This she apparently determined right away, because even before she could have discussed her plan with the woman about to be visited, she already motioned to the son to follow. As soon as he entered, he found himself confronted by the wife of the medical specialist, who was standing in the doorway. Impossible to consider a retreat at this point, but the execution of the plan proposed by the professor's wife was out of the question. All he could do was to confess that the wife of the medical specialist and the man who had the legitimate claim on her had met him at the station before daybreak and that he was happy to know now her place of residence. However, he would return another time when he was sure to meet the so-called male half of the family as well. Regrettably for him, and perhaps for the latter, the other man arrived very soon, and the encounter immediately took on a completely conventional tone. In the process it transpired that the professor's wife spoke and understood also German, because the ensuing, albeit brief, discussion was conducted exclusively in that language. After all, in educated circles such as her family belonged to one was proficient in that idiom also, as the ugly woman stated with a broad grin. Leaving her behind, the son now decided to set out for home alone. Consequently, he arrived at his temporary abode not before the late evening hours. Part of the problem was that he kept losing his way, since the small alleys had become entwined as if in a Gordian knot, but also the fact that he did not even want to go home immediately and took both his lunch and his afternoon snack in remote inns along the way.

When he arrived home, the sixteen-year-old maid immediately proceeded to make his bed and, while doing so, exposed her thighs almost all the way up to her bottom, which was left unconcealed for lack of underwear. Moreover, she appeared a second time after having left and repeated her pose. Although the son made a bet with himself that the adolescent girl, whom he again let go without her having achieved her goal, would appear a third time, he engaged in masturbation in the meantime. At a later date he regretted his decision and searched for the girl, who for reasons unknown to him had been dismissed or had left her job in the house on her own accord. He went so far as to seek her out in a shady restaurant, her new place of work. She kept him waiting for a long time, and when she finally came, she merely laughed in his face. This was answer enough, and probably a fitting one.

Meanwhile, the memorial service for the Croatian politician took place, which was conducted with great splendor. A proud, mournful demeanor and a challenge to Serbian dominance were part of it. Although the noble deceased had died of a stroke, old age, or an illness, perhaps also as a result of the medical treatment of these, his transmission to the underworld was undertaken and celebrated no differently than if he had been a victim of the regime in power, in other words, Serbian domination over the Dalmatian Croats. Being an invited guest, the son, a refugee without a passport, was ushered to his seat in the grandstand, where he was seated next to the noble old gentleman who had provided him with the revelation. After all, he had the task to display silent grief and to display no less rigidity and pride than his host. The spies interspersed amidst the gathering stood out because of their stout, corpulent build atypical of this region. At most they were pointed out by a movement of the head, otherwise they were not paid much attention to.

Then a military display of the available forces was held in the square, during which those who owned them exhibited their respective robes and many ribbons with the Croatian colors, emblems, and banners. Speeches about the greatness and significance of the deceased followed, in which there was much talk of Croatia and occasionally of Dalmatia. This part of the celebration had to be whispered to the son in simultaneous translation, that is, such an immediate transmission seemed to be considered absolutely necessary, although for his part he could have dispensed with it. Then the clergy appeared, and since it was the intention to emphasize the Catholic faith – the Serbs after all were members of the Eastern cult – several clerical dignitaries had been produced in contrast to other memorial services. They murmured prayers and made the respective gestures with the props they had brought along. The coffin was virtually invisible. Either it had not yet arrived or its view was blocked by the military crowd. Toward the end, songs, apparently of the nationalist variety, were intoned, however, the lyrics were not sung. They were probably outlawed or not conducive to the silent protest, which only the monotonous speeches, the murmuring of the priests, and purely musical forms of expression were allowed to interrupt or, more correctly, underscore.

Only much later, when everyone was moving toward the cemetery, an object that looked like a coffin became visible. It was followed by the proudly mourning relatives, the occupants of the grandstand, including the son, as well as by two spies who were to observe and record the process. When the deceased was finally buried, the son ended up standing right behind the widow. Because he did not know how to behave, he kept an appropriate distance. The gentlemen following behind each kept the same distance from

him as well as from one another that he put between himself and
the widow. By virtue of his undecidedness the son had added a new
detail to the ceremony that the others could not help but imitate.

Meanwhile his mother had received a summons to the county
party headquarters. Apparently the issue was the son's where-
abouts. The daughter could not do much for her because just at that
time she was to hide a number of Jews in her husband's circle of
acquaintances who had received notification of their imminent arrest. She did not accompany the mother but advised her not to
comply with the subpoena. The mother, however, accustomed to
order, felt that it was impossible to stay away. Perhaps she also
considered it opportune to do her presumed duty at a time when the
stepdaughter was still delaying her departure until she would obtain
her stamp. This way she was still in the country and within reach.

When the mother entered the cold office where she had been
summoned to go, a piercing voice screamed at her from the background. Its hoarse, guttural sounds could make a person wonder if
their originator was a member of the human race. His pitch and
style of speaking were designed to call to mind Adolf Hitler, the
Führer, whom he imitated. The actual speaker was none other than
the crook in whose persecution the son had persisted until his
departure, despite his apparent lack of success. He had, however,
been prevented from becoming Gauleiter (district supervisor) of the
Lower Danube, formerly Lower Austria, because of a file copied by
the son's former office clerk, who was now a party secretary. The
hoarse voice commanded the mother to inform him where the son
was staying, otherwise they would catch him without her help; the
Führer's long arm reached far, even across the oceans, if need be.
Although the mother should have noticed how ridiculous the alleged proportions of the person in question were, she took the
threat very seriously as the red color rising in her cheeks indicated,
confirming the weakness of her heart, to which she usually did not
pay attention. Moreover, her blushing suggested that she already
feared the worst for her son, who meant the world to her. Therefore
she not only denied knowing his address but declared energetically
that there was no reason to persecute him other than his desire for
personal revenge, which had nothing to do with the cause of the
Führer and chancellor.

Barely had the crook with the blond crew cut registered her reproach when he was overcome with a kind of uncontrollable rage. In the process he grew even more pale, although this was hardly possible considering the newtlike pallor of the upper protuberance of his body that in the case of human beings is called face. However, since he could not think of a response, he only shrieked forth invectives, and his saliva added a moist element to his hoarseness, causing overhasty slurs. When finally he spouted forth what had accumulated in his throat it was expressions such as "miserable Jew whore," the announcement that her son would be shortened by the length of his masculinity and his behind would be perforated because he was a communist dog, an excrement Semite, and a lawyer thief; she however would be hung by the opening between her legs. None of these images became utterly conceivable to the woman at whom they were hurled, and they did not even reach her, because only when she had already left the room did she feel like holding on to the wall.

Elias Canetti

Elias Canetti was born in Rustchuk, Bulgaria, in 1905 into a large Sephardic family. His native language was Ladino, but in his multicultural environment Bulgarian, Romanian, and German were also spoken, and his education included modern and classical languages. In 1911 Canetti moved with his parents to Manchester, England, where his father died soon thereafter. With his mother, Canetti and his brother Georg then relocated in Lausanne and, in 1913, in Vienna. In 1929 Canetti received his doctorate in chemistry from the University of Vienna. However, as he reveals in his autobiography, his primary interest had been and remained literary and cultural. Influenced by Karl Kraus and Hermann Broch, Canetti began his writing career Vienna. Veza Taubner-Calderon, who later became his wife, was his first and most important critic, a role his mother had performed earlier. Canetti considered Vienna his literary home and made Austrian German the language of his choice, although he spent considerable time in Berlin and Paris. In 1938 the Canettis emigrated to London.

Elias Canetti's first novel, Die Blendung (1935; Auto-da-Fé) was published in Vienna in 1935. Under Austrofascism this avant-garde text received little attention. In 1965 it was republished in Germany. So were his numerous dramas. For his extensive and intellectually challenging oeuvre, most notably his treatise on mass psychology, Masse und Macht (1960; Crowds and Power), Canetti was awarded the Nobel Prize in literature in 1981. Canetti's autobiographical writings, including Die Stimmen von Marrakesch (1968; The Voices of Marrakesh), Alle vergeudete Verehrung (1970; All the misapplied reverence), Die Provinz des Menschen: Aufzeichnungen 1942–1972 (1973; The Human Province: Notes 1942–1972), and Das Geheimherz der Uhr (1987;

The *Secret Heart of the Clock*), as well as his three-part autobiography, *Die gerette Zunge* (1970; *The Tongue Set Free: Remembrance of a European Childhood*), *Die Fackel im Ohr* (1980; *The Torch in My Ear*), and *Das Augenspiel* (1985; *The Play of the Eyes*), are remarkable documentary and literary texts. Among Canetti's literary awards are the Büchner Prize (1972) and the Kafka Prize (1981). Canetti died in Switzerland in 1994.

Elias Canetti

The Secret Heart of the Clock

An insatiable politeness has taken hold of him, he feels like bowing over and over; everyone's gone, he keeps bowing.

It would have given much pleasure to some people who are no longer alive, but not so much as to enable them to come back to life.

Even *feigned* modesty is good for something: it helps others build their own self-assurance.

Now they make it a point of honor to ask you. Suddenly it looks as if you had something to say. But you have forgotten it.

There are people who hold it against him that he didn't throw stones as a child.
    They also mind his talking about himself without becoming shameless.

When he turned eighty he admitted his sex.

Since his hopes were false – were his fears false, too?

You can't make a fuss about the fact that you're coming to the end of the road. For a long time you've been making a fuss about the end in general, for some, for this one, for that one, for all.

You should not overrate the fact that you don't *see* the new form of life.
    If only others, later, find it and grasp it – it doesn't depend on you.
    It is difficult to accept that it doesn't depend on you.

People in another form, things that talk, is that what lies ahead?
    The creatures your foot has trampled.

Of all the poets I know, Büchner has the greatest concentration.
Every one of his sentences is new to me. I know each one, but it's
new to me.

His disintegrating knowledge holds him together.

Even though he no longer retains anything new – the movement of
learning does not let him go. As long as he persists in it, he does
not feel he has died.

From time to time, every few months, he receives a new book about
unknown parts of the earth. Then he feels hot all over, as though it
could still be saved.

The dangers add up, each one of them has become overwhelming.
Each one has been recognized and named, each one has been calcu-
lated. Not one of them has been tamed. Many people are well off.
Children are starving. One can just barely breathe.

That he owes thanks to his *own* early life doesn't mean that he finds
the early life of others worth thanking.

The Spanish element in Stendhal, his Italian life, in the French
language of the eighteenth century. More cannot be expected.

If things are the way they are in your life: that *nothing* is past and
gone – where does the human race put it?

What is the use of remembering? Live now! Live now! But my only
reason for remembering is to live now.

Increase of what is worth knowing, decrease of the capacity to
absorb it; every day he gains a drop less, more and more drips past
him and drains off, not into him; how he yearns for all the things he
would have liked to know!

He offers himself for poisoning, the experimental martyr.

Try *not* to judge. Describe. There is nothing more disgusting than condemnation. It's always this way or that and it's always wrong. Who knows enough to judge another? Who is selfless enough?

In the end he received everything in his own lifetime and was forgotten.

He surrounded himself with resuscitated people.

    ★

Pessimists are not boring. Pessimists are right. Pessimists are superfluous.

When I was in Geneva, I met a self-examiner. I did not know it yet, but his face was different. It was the way I would like to imagine a ghost: someone who doesn't put up with being dead.

" – si je ne suis pas clair, tout mon monde est anéanti."
– Stendhal to Balzac

The child, not yet ten years old, looking something up in a huge Chinese dictionary.

He thanks all who have released him from their hearts.
    He wants to be alone in the end.

Even in the midst of destruction he doesn't want to change so much as a syllable in his books.

Anger at those who predicted it. How easily it passed their lips!

Old age, if it is to deserve its name, should bring the best.

One repatriate returning to *many* countries.

So many who want to leave Europe. I want to increase my presence in Europe.

In five minutes the earth would be a desert, and you cling to books.

An evening of sorrow and herbs; in front of the window an egret.

Creatures whose life lasts no longer than minutes.

☆

Forgive less, it isn't good for them. They should be allowed to feel ashamed.

Piano music from the plane tree.

The word one reads most frequently today is "torture."

Feigned fits of rage, prehistoric.

Wilted by the daily newspaper.

Whom should one beat instead of oneself?

Cruel punishments back then. Mass murder today.
    Still, in "mass murder" the attraction of the crowd.

He has earned his misery by honest means and wouldn't dream of giving it up.

"Emli n mfas" – "Lord of breath," one of the names the Tuareg give to God.

"It was said that he forbade all singing except for religious chants. No drumming was allowed, and even the cries of donkeys were to be suppressed." – The Tuareg

"According to Aulus Gellius, there were families in Africa whose speech possessed a special power. When they praised beautiful trees, rich fields, lovely children, excellent horses, fat and well-fed cattle in extravagant terms, then all these things would perish as a result of this praise and for no other reason." – Noctes Atticae, IX 4

☆

To be able to hide so well that you would be the earlier one.

Longing for the time when you wanted *in vain* to be more highly regarded.

"Although Isaac did not die, Scripture regards him as if he had died and as if his ashes lay heaped upon the altar."

All contemporary writing makes fewer demands on the reader. It doesn't require any worship of the dead and it is not yet firmly established. Perhaps by tomorrow it will have evaporated, or be unrecognizable.

You are not at all a man of this century, and if there's one thing about you that counts, it's that you have never submitted to it. But perhaps you might have accomplished something if you had submitted to this century while resisting it.

Conscience-entrepreneurs.

As a kindly storyteller he acquired the confidence of the human race, two minutes before it exploded.

He mistrusts the answers of his life. This does not mean that they will turn out to be false.

The donkey as horse dealer.

Memory-acrobat as ruler.

The child passes its childhood on to smaller and smaller children.

A hut for the great, a shrinking-hut.

The pain of speaking. You speak at cross-purposes to yourself.

★

To reach people by way of enemies.

He is more attached to failures than to successes.

If gods exist, they are paralyzed: *our* curare.

The careless multiplication, nature's essential blindness, senseless, mad, brazen, and vain, becomes a law only by virtue of the declaration of hate against death. As soon as multiplication is no longer blind, as soon as it is concerned with each single thing, it has acquired meaning. The horrific aspect of "More! More! More! For the sake of destruction!" becomes "That everything be sanctified: more!"

Before it turns into decay, death is confrontation. Courage to face it, in defiance of all futility. Courage to spit death in the face.

His experience, from way back: always when his vilifications of death intensify, death takes a near one away from him.
    Is this anticipation or punishment? Who punishes?

Among the words that have kept their innocence, that he can pronounce without reserve, is the word "innocence" itself.

To disappear, but not completely, so that you can know it.

Everything you rejected and pushed aside – take it up again.

Explain nothing. Put it there. Say it. Leave.

Maybe you reinvested the details with dignity. Maybe that is your only achievement.

In order to exist *today*, one needs an intimate knowledge of completely different times.
    Mutual awareness of the ages.

        ★

To write in daggers or breaths?

Perhaps he is drawn to every faith and perhaps that's the reason why he has none.

The *grandiosity* of thinking, which he found suspect. Splendor and dialectics – words related to music.

What if God had not existed and had come into being only *now*!

Do you want to forget him whom you never found?

It is undeniable: what interests him most in the ancient cultures are their gods.

Astonishment of the deceived serpent: the apple's inextinguishable remains.

"Life experience" does not amount to very much and could be learned from novels alone, for example, from Balzac, without any help from life.

With the slowing down of memory you begin to lose all the things you invented for yourself. All that's left of you are the conventional generalities, and you take up their cause with vigor as if they were discoveries.

This trick of stocking up on reading matter for future centuries.

An animal that saves humanity from destruction. – An animal, and the memory it preserves of extinct humanity.

He refines his impressions until they are so thin that they can't apply to anyone else.

        ★

The destroyer of tradition who contributes the most to its preservation.

He has become more defenseless against death. The faith to which he was committed offered no protection. He was not permitted to defend himself.

But now others were there, with him. Did he not defend them either? Why is it that most of them have been cut down and he is still there? What secret, disgraceful relation prevails here, unknown to him?

If one has lived long enough, there is danger of succumbing to the word "God," merely because it was always there.

There is something *impure* in the laments about the dangers of our time, as if they could serve to excuse our personal failure.

Something of this impure substance has been present, from the very beginning, in laments for the dead.

There is more than one reason for working with *characters*. One of them, the important and right one, is directed against destruction. The other, the worthless one, has to do with a self-love that wants to see itself variously reflected.

There is an interplay between both these reasons; their relationship determines whether one's characters are universally valid or vain.

The heart has become too old and longs to go everywhere.

Your "definitive" statements are the least conclusive of all. But what's vague, even careless, acquires substance by virtue of what it lacks.

Someone who proves what he least believes.

       ★

Back to closed-off, clam sentences that stand securely on their feet and don't drip from all their pores.

What do you feel like when you close up the wall between you and the future?

Musil is my ratio, as many Frenchmen have always been. He doesn't panic, or doesn't show it. He stands up to threats like a soldier, but he *understands* them. He is sensitive and imperturbable. Whoever is terrified of softness can find refuge in him. One is not ashamed at the thought that he is a man. He is not just an ear. He can insult with silence. His insult is comforting.

Always occupied with the wrong things. Do you know the right ones?

The same fear for seventy years, but always for others.

Without reading, no new thoughts occur to him. Nothing connects with anything anymore. Everything totters in its separate domain. A loose landscape of stalks that stand far apart, not dense like grass.

He can't get it out of his head that *everything* might be useless. Not just he alone, everything.
     Nevertheless he can only go on living as if it were not useless.

PJ: I see the room. I see his bed, his rotting teeth. How did he manage to live so long. I have never asked myself that about anyone else. He nibbled at the necks of elderly women, they let him. In Paris I once saw him in the courtyard of the Sorbonne, mocking the students mercilessly, his only hardness, otherwise he was gentle and soft. I have not seen PJ. for at least ten years, maybe longer. But earlier, when I came to Paris, he treated me as if we were old acquaintances, he was the only one who called me by my first name. We had almost nothing in common, even though he treated me in such an open and generous manner. I knew he had been in the camps. He didn't mind accepting honors for that. But the real liberty he took was in refusing to fit into anything, any rule, any marriage, any course of events, any clothes. Everything he wore hung loosely about him, threadbare giveaways, and since one never saw him dressed in anything other than these wide flapping garments, there was something clownlike about this man who was always smiling.

He lived in Dostoevsky's "House of the Dead" but he lived alone. He knew that was a large part of his attraction. He had been released and was still there. He smiled and grinned at his freedom. He seemed happy to me. Perhaps that was why, after my brother's death, I could not stand him anymore.

You will not escape any signification. You will be distorted in every possible way. Maybe you only existed in order to be distorted.

A great many people can live only in names. They acquire the names of well-known persons and use them incessantly. Then it almost doesn't matter what they say about them, so long as they just mention their names. Names are their wine and spirits. They are not afraid of using them up, there's a steady supply of other names, they're always on the lookout for new ones, and in a pinch they'll take one from the obituary.

Pawnbrokers for fame.

Nations discover what they owe each other. Feasts of indebtedness.

A year of islands.

A place where no famous man ever set foot, a chaste place.

      ★

The treasure of the seen as the treasure of good works.

Justify memories? – Impossible.

"When a grape sees another grape, it ripens." – Byzantine Saying

"His face radiated the same kind of grave charm when he told with intense delight how he had once held a swallow in his hands, peered into its eyes, and felt as though he had looked into heaven." – Wasianski, *Immanuel Kant in seinen letzten Lebensjahren* (Immanuel Kant in the last years of his life)

The most difficult thing for one who does not believe in God: that he has no one to give thanks to.

More than for one's time of need, one needs a God for giving thanks.

A bad night. I don't want to read what I wrote during those hours. No doubt it was weak, it was *not permissible*, but it calmed me.

How much may one tell oneself for the sake of calming the mind, and what are its continuing effects?

You are not the only one who does not forget. How many equally sensitive people have you hurt, who will never get over it.

No one understands the subterranean spadework of anger.

They allowed him the choice of one limb that would not be eaten: grateful cannibals.

Each time, before every rebirth, he rebelled.

The ones who still interest him most among the ancient peoples are the Egyptians and the Chinese: the scribes.

Beauties, yes, but not in the language in which you write, in *other* languages.

He doesn't understand anyone he hasn't insulted.

He imagines how old he would be if no one close to him had died.

To live in secret. Could there be anything more wonderful?

A region, as large as Europe, inhabited by four people.

What is solitude, he asks, and how many people would one have to know before it would be permissible to be alone, and is it a reward one has to serve like a sentence, and will it be followed by one punishment among many?

It turns out that creation has yet to take place, and we, we seem to be there in order to prevent it.

At every feeling, he catches himself red-handed.

Don't sharpen your thoughts to a point. Break them off in their nakedness.

The great thing about Schopenhauer is the way he was formed by a very few early experiences which he never forgot, which he never allowed to be distorted. Everything that came later is nothing but solid decoration. He isn't hiding anything beneath it, consciously or unconsciously. He reads in order to confirm the early impressions. He never learns anything new, although he is always learning. Even in a hundred years he would not have exhausted the early material.

★

Every day someone else tries to bite off a piece of his name.
    Doesn't anyone know how bitter that tastes?

He recollects everything he hasn't experienced.

Say thank you? No. But shower them with thanks.

". . . and just as they went into raptures over the unconscious when that was fashionable, now they will go into raptures over aristocratism, because that is in fashion."
– Paul Ernst, Fr. Nietzsche (1890)

That those who understand the horror of power don't see to what extent power makes use of death! Without death, power would have remained harmless. They go on and on, talking about power in the belief that they're fighting it, and leave death by the wayside. They think it's natural and therefore of no concern to them. It's no great shakes, this nature of theirs. I always felt bad in the presence of nature when it pretended to be inalterable and I believed it to be so. Now that its alterability is showing up wherever you look, I feel even worse, for those performing the alterations don't know that there are things that must *never* be changed, under any circumstances.

Envisioning the threat does not diminish the significance of the past for him; on the contrary, he follows its traces back further, as if there one could find the rupture, the fault line, knowledge of which would enable one to meet the threat with good fortune.

But there are many fault lines, and each one proclaims itself the only one.

Juan Rulfo: "A dead man doesn't die. On All Souls' Day one talks to him and feeds him. The deserted widow goes to the grave of her dead husband, reproaches him for his adulteries, abuses him, threatens to take revenge. Death in Mexico is not a sacred and alien thing. Death is the most ordinary thing there is."

. . .

"And what, Mr. Rulfo, do you feel when you write?"
"Pangs of conscience."

If everything collapses: it has to be *said*. If nothing is to remain – let us at least not exit obediently.

I feel no weakness as long as I consider what I am still there for. As soon as I stop thinking of that, I feel weakness.

He feels violated by people, and animated by images.

Soutine: "I once saw the village butcher slit open the neck of a goose and let the blood run out. I wanted to scream, but his cheerful look throttled the sound in my throat."

Soutine observed his throat and continued: "I still feel that scream here. When as a child I drew a primitive portrait of my teacher, I tried to liberate myself from this scream, but in vain. When I painted the dead ox, it was still this scream I was trying to get rid of. I still haven't succeeded!" – Soutine to Emile Szittya

There is a terrible power in the intolerance with which one perceives people, as if one were shutting their mouth with both hands to prevent them from biting. But they don't always want to bite, how can one know what they want if one forces them to keep their mouths shut? What if they want to *say* something that can never be said again? What if they just want to moan? To exhale?

Everything is missed, the most innocent, the best, because one is afraid of their teeth.

He was proud of not knowing the way. Now he is weak and looks at the road.

★

What he most hated about history was its revenge.

No wonder you prefer the old chronicles – they know so little.

All the forgotten ones came to him to pick up their faces.

The words of praise that besmirch the purest things.

Should one from time to time commit treason against oneself, that is, acknowledge the impossibility of a beginning and draw the conclusions? Why does one like those people so much more who are not able to do that, who, as it were, believe themselves to death?

For some confusions there is no religion.

To stop biting down, to leave the mouth of the sentences open.

The poet whose art resides in his lack of detachment: Dostoevsky.

One expresses one's time most completely by what one *doesn't* accept about it.

He never asked God.

He wants clarity only where he means to offer a glimpse. Everywhere else a questioning darkness.

It's possible that the form of *Crowds and Power* will turn out to be its strength. By continuing the book, you would have destroyed it with your hopes. As it stands now, you force the readers to search for *their* hopes.

He wants to be selfless without denying his work. The squaring of the poet.

Veza Canetti

Veza Canetti, née Venetian Taubner-Calderon, was
born in Vienna in 1897, as the daughter of a large
Jewish family of Bosnian extraction. Taubner-
Calderon was an active participant in interwar literary
and intellectual circles in Vienna, most notably those
of Karl Kraus. It is here that she met her future husband Elias Canetti, when she was just beginning to
establish herself as a writer. Taubner-Calderon published short prose pieces under different pen names,
including Veronika Knecht and Veza Magd. Her story
"Geduld bringt Rosen" was included in Wieland
Herzfelde's anthology Dreißig neue Erzähler des neuen
Deutschland (1932; Thirty narrators of the new Germany), brought out by the prominent publishing
company Malik, Berlin. Taubner-Calderon's novel Die
gelbe Straße (The yellow street) came out in sequels in
the Vienna Arbeiter-Zeitung in 1933 and 1934. The National Socialist coup attempt and the radicalization of
the public sphere in Vienna, which caused even Social Democratic publishers such as Otto König of the
Arbeiter-Zeitung to sever their ties with Jewish authors
because of widespread anti-Semitism, ended
Taubner-Calderon's career. In 1934 she married Elias
Canetti, and in 1938 the couple emigrated to London.
Although Veza Canetti continued to write, she died in
London in 1963 without having published another
work. In the late 1980s, shortly before his death, Elias
Canetti edited his wife's forgotten works and pub-
lished them with Carl Hanser Verlag in Munich, his
own publisher: the novel Die gelbe Straße (1990), the
collection of short stories Geduld bringt Rosen (1992;
Roses reward patience), and the play Der Oger (1991;
The ogre). The latter, although completed before the
author's exile, had not appeared until that time.
Rather than emphasizing Jewish topics, Taubner-
Calderon's works reflect socialist views and deal with

the everyday lives and struggles of simple people. However, the neighborhood in which her novel is set is the predominantly Jewish Ferdinandstraße in Vienna's Second District, and the family history and background of many of her protagonists in both her novel and her play strongly suggest that they are Jewish.

Veza Canetti

The New Guy Edited by Elias Canetti

Seidler had such good references from his many years of loyal services as a cashier that he got a position in a factory as a supervisor. He was in charge of the department where thread was spooled and placed in boxes. At the end of the workday he had to search every worker for spools of thread. When he fingered the pockets of his fellow human beings and felt the resistance of a hidden spool of thread, he did not move a muscle and let them pass. The workers returned his love, which greatly displeased his superiors, and he was terminated.

His good references, in particular the reference of his honest face, helped him a second time. He obtained a position as a salesperson in an elegant jewelry store, and now his pockets were searched when he left the business at night. They adhered to several other strange practices at the jeweler's Kranz & Son. For example, his fingerprints were photographed, and he had to wear woolen gloves when he touched the jewelry boxes in the display cases so that in case of a burglary the fingerprints of the thief could be immediately identified.

After a short time his superiors realized already that it was not necessary to search his pockets, but they also realized that his honesty and goodwill were not enough for this position. Seidler did not know how to talk a customer into buying a particular piece of jewelry because he did not understand the value of jewelry. He considered the whole commotion ridiculous, the fuss the ladies made, bending for hours over chips of glass and examining them through magnifying glasses and the fuss his superiors made over this type of ladies, bowing and scraping before them and forgetting all about their usual dignity, and he himself felt ridiculous acting as if all this were of major consequence. He started out one day forgetting that he had to wear gloves while setting up the display (which fortunately nobody noticed) and ended up letting a customer walk out, which everyone noticed, and at that point he had to leave again.

Now he sat next to the desperate ones and waited for a job. A fellow worker from the factory, who was still grateful to him, alerted him to a newspaper that had recently started to be published. He immediately went to the editorial office, submitted his references, and got the best position in our entire city, right in front of our most beautiful church. Four salesmen representing papers of different orientations stood there already; the one with the small moustache under his nose and the brown suit sold the German papers, then there was the "Austrian" one, the *Extra* one, and the *Telegraph* woman. When she needed change, she called out "Hitler!" and the brown fellow gave her change. If he had none, she called "Extra!" and the man from the *Extrablatt* stepped forth. There was no political strife between them, there was only the hunt for customers, the hunt for bread, and their hatred was directed against the rain, which spoiled their business, and against a beggar, who knew how to distract the customers, and most of all they hated a new guy, who might become a competitor. And Seidler was this new guy. The four whispered and kept their distance when he approached them, and the next day the brown fellow brought along a pipe, stuffed it with wool, and blew the smoke into the "new guy's" face, so that his voice became screechy and he could not call out. An unnecessary measure. New papers don't sell, one has to persist until they succeed.

The "new guy" persisted and announced his papers with a hoarse voice and much too timidly. In the process he became as thin and resigned to his fate as a Gothic statue. Once he tried to help the *Telegraph* woman when she wanted to change a fifty-groschen piece, but rather than taking his money she preferred to let a customer go, and his hand dropped helplessly. Next to the self-confidence of the brown fellow, who arrogantly flaunted his broad hand full of German papers and yelled a momentous "Heil!" at every customer, the figure of Seidler looked so pathetic that the passersby became aware of him and bought his newspaper. Soon they also became used to it, and thus he was able to take home a small income faster than he had thought.

But one day two men stood before him. They identified them-selves as being officers of the criminal-investigation department. They took him aside and told him straight out that he was sus-pected of theft and was therefore being arrested; there had been a burglary at the jewelry store of Kranz & Son, and no fingerprints had been found besides his.

Someone who has fought all his life against the temptation to end his misery by reaching into the cash register – an act that would not have seriously harmed anyone – or by taking a piece of jewelry, whose loss would have hardly been noticed, someone who has resisted all these challenges feels so sullied by a false accusation that he blushes, stutters, and becomes teary-eyed, not knowing what to say, thus acting as if he were guilty. Seidler did precisely that. Although he solemnly declared his innocence before the ex-amining magistrate, he was taken into custody, because inquiries had been made among the newspaper sellers. It was the brown fellow who had alleged that the new guy had immediately seemed suspicious to him. He had acted fearful and timid like a guilty conscience personified.

Seidler sat in his cell as if lashed by invisible whips, but nobody understood his silent despair. Then the door opened and a man entered who seemed unfamiliar to him. Only when the man ad-dressed him did he recognize his fellow worker from the factory. "You're in a fine mess," his comrade said. "And I remember exactly that one time you set up the display without wearing your gloves. Instead of talking, you allow yourself to be incarcerated! However, I have testified on your behalf; this is not the right place for you!" Seidler was released that selfsame hour because there was not a single indication to suggest that he was guilty. He also was restored to his old position in front of the church, but the mood there had not become any more favorable. Moreover, his nerves felt badly strained because of the shock of the last few days, and for a long time his diet had not been such as to strengthen him. He called out his papers in a tired voice, but the corners of his eyes remained dull, as if he were trying to fight back his tears. Then suddenly the two policemen were back, and he stood there, defenseless and expect-ing to be seized harshly and unjustly once again. But what was that? They walked by, they walked up to the man with the German news-

papers, they pulled him aside, confiscated his entire wall of newspapers, and took him away. Excited, the three people began to talk
among themselves, looking full of misgivings at the "new guy" as if
he were the cause of these events.

The officers from the criminal police returned immediately, this
time without the brown guy. They walked up to the newspaper
sellers, and it turned out that the passersby had repeatedly complained about the brown guy because he acted so impertinently and
provocatively. Furthermore it turned out that during a house search
a great amount of explosives had been found at his place and that
he had been wanted by the police for a long time. When the newspaper sellers were questioned by the police, they did not betray him.
Dissatisfied, the two officers approached Seidler and looked at him
a little more friendly than they usually did. Of course Seidler had
good reasons to talk about his colleague's inflammatory speeches,
but he merely declared that as far as the others were concerned he
was an outsider and had no knowledge of anything. "But your
colleague did not behave all that well toward you," one of the officers said pointedly, but then he politely touched his hat with his
fingertips and followed the other officer.

"That was nice of him," the "Austrian" said loudly so that the
"new guy" could hear it, and the "Extra" positioned himself close
to Seidler. The Telegraph woman, however, was waiting impatiently
for the next customer. Then she called, slightly embarrassed, "Hey,
Red! Get me some change!"

Friedrich Torberg

Friedrich Torberg was born as Friedrich Kantor in Vienna in 1908 to a Jewish family. (He officially adopted the name Kantor-Berg in 1930.) In 1922 he moved to Prague, but his work as a journalist, critic, and author took him frequently to Vienna. Torberg was a prominent member of the coffeehouse culture in both cities, as is obvious from *Die Tante Jolesch*. He also wrote for newspapers in Leipzig and other German cities. His early novel *Der Schüler Gerber hat absolviert* (1930; *The Examination*, filmed in 1981), which criticizes the practices and biases of the educational system, was a major success. In 1938 Torberg sought exile in Switzerland and France. After having served for a year in the Free Czech Army, he escaped via Portugal and Spain to the United States. In the 1940s he worked as a screenwriter in Los Angeles. Later, in New York, he wrote for various papers, including *Time* magazine. When Torberg returned to Vienna in 1951, he had already begun to write about the experiences of European Jews, anti-Semitism, the Holocaust, and Jewish exile, as in his novel *Auch das war Wien* (1984; This too was Vienna), which he wrote between 1938 and 1939 and on which the Austrian film *1938* (1987) was based. Torberg was one of the most outspoken Jewish voices in postwar Austria and was often criticized for the public avowal of his loyalty to the victims of the Shoah, his indictment of the perpetrators, and his opposition to Communism. Still a controversial figure, Torberg died in Vienna in 1979 after a long and productive career as novelist and critic. His oeuvre includes twenty-one original works and twenty translations. As Ruth Beckermann states, Torberg, because of his autobiographical literature, his critical essays devoted to central European Jewish culture, and his novels dealing with Jewish history, was a major force in shaping post-Shoah Jewish literature.

Friedrich Torberg

Aunt Jolesch in Person

As far as Aunt Jolesch is concerned, I owe my knowledge of her existence and many of the statements attributed to her to my friendship with her nephew Franz, the beloved and thoroughly spoiled descendent of a family of industrialists of Hungarian extraction. Having lived for generations in one of the German-language islands in Moravia, the family had acquired considerable wealth. Franz, stunningly attractive and endowed with a strong talent for loafing (he only abandoned the latter for playing bridge and hunting), was probably twelve years older than I, for he had already taken part in World War I. In later years, the friends who were his age continued to refer to him jokingly as "His Majesty's most beautiful lieutenant." I frequently visited his family's Moravian estate – a cynical, self-ironical saying in those circles was, "Only a fool has no estate in Moravia" – and I remained close to him until his untimely death. In 1939 the German occupation forces had imprisoned him because he was a Jew, and in 1945 the Czech liberators had expelled him because he was a German. One might say that the transformation of the Star of David into a swastika took place without transition on his back. He spent some time in Vienna and finally relocated in Chile, where soon after he died as a result of his imprisonment in the concentration camp. Aunt Jolesch did not live to see any of this.

Franz was her favorite nephew, and by a lucky coincidence one of her most noteworthy statements relates to him – to him and two profoundly Jewish practices. One consists of invoking divine benevolence for a project about to be undertaken, such as for a trip, which one will start, "God willing," tomorrow and from which one will return next week "with God's help," except if something, "God forbid," were to prevent it, perhaps even an accident, from which

"God may protect us." No less ingrained, albeit lacking religious motivation, is the Jewish need to find something positive in a mishap that has already occurred. The phrase used in such a case is: "On the positive side . . ." The point of reference can be, for example, a sudden illness that did not lead to a catastrophe thanks to speedy medical assistance: "On the positive side, the doctor arrived immediately"; it could also be "on the positive side" that on this occasion another dangerous disease was discovered in its early stages and successfully defused.

On one such occasion Nephew Franz, returning home from a car trip, had had an accident on the road. Although he had had a narrow escape involving only the shock and minor damage to the car, the family discussed the accident extensively at the dinner table, partly because at that time both car ownership as well as car accidents were in their beginning phase and hence rare, partly because everyone was afraid for Franz's unscathed bones after the fact. Again and again people wanted to hear how he had averted the threat of danger – his car had started skidding in the rain on a wet bridge – and again and again Franz began to tell his story, embellishing it with ever new details and new analyses.

"On the positive side," he concluded one of his reports, "the car with me in it did not slide over into the opposite lane but against the railing of a bridge."

At this point Aunt Jolesch entered the conversation for the first time. Until then she had only listened, rather uninterested, without saying a word (because nothing had happened to her Franz and that was the main thing). Now she lifted her finger and stated the following admonishment with great emphasis: "May God protect everyone from all that is on the positive side."

All through her life she said many things worthy to be quoted and observed, our Aunt Jolesch, but never again did she say anything quite so profound.

Rumor has little to report about the uncle by the same name, and even those few things he owes to his wife, our aunt. He was, to avoid the High German expression "a dandy," someone who in Austria is called a fop. Even in his old age he valued fashionable, custom-made clothes and insisted that for that purpose the tailor come "to the house." When such an occasion arose once again for the purpose of having an overcoat made, Aunt Jolesch interjected with not altogether emotional determination, "A seventy-year-old man does *not* have an overcoat made for himself," she declared. "And if he does, have Franzl fitted for it at the same time."

For the sake of historical accuracy it must be noted that one of the customs that the nouveau riche bourgeoisie had taken over from the aristocracy was to have certain services performed "in the house" rather than to visit the place of production. One not only summoned the tailor and the dressmaker, the hatter and the shoe-maker, to one's home, but also the barber, even on a daily basis, Sundays included. Accordingly, he was paid well and treated pro-portionately poorly. Thorsch, a well-to-do industrialist from Par-dubitz, the father of the film scriptwriter Robert Thoeren, who was successful in Berlin and later in Hollywood, behaved especially badly in this respect. For many years he tormented his (of all things, Jewish) barber by the name of Langer with all sorts of moods and antics, and Langer put up with it for years – until one day he had had it. He was in the midst of lathering Thorsch's face when all of a sudden he stopped, packed up his things without saying a word, and disappeared. The promptly hired successor willingly and with-out opposition put up with the harassment of his new client, but he shaved him badly and was soon dismissed. His follower, on the other hand, was a master of his trade but not of himself: he reacted so violently to the first insult that his employment was immediately terminated. The fourth one Thorsch tried met all expectations, both as a barber and an object of insult, however, he did not meet them with the necessary regularity. Sometimes he showed up too late, sometimes not at all. Thus he also fell victim to dismissal. Thorsch was faced with the increasingly more conclusive realization that there was no acceptable substitute for Langer.

Around that time my friend Thoeren, as he occasionally did, came from Berlin to his parents' home for a short visit. It was no small surprise to him to meet his father on the staircase in an apparel fit for a formal visit: cutaway, bowler hat, cane, and gloves.

Astonished, he asked, "Where are you going, Papa?"

The following was delivered in a ponderous, almost solemn tone:

"Son – in every man's life there comes the day when he has to either apologize or do his own shaving. I go and apologize."

It is no coincidence that both phrases, that of Thorsch as well as that of Aunt Jolesch, deduce a general maxim from a personal situation. Both the warning allusion to the fateful day that will arrive in every man's life and the sober statement that a seventy-year-old man does not need to have an overcoat made for himself are conclusions that imply a claim of truth, independent of the specific situation. (For this very reason they are comical, if not intentionally, then at least by no means inadvertently.)

The aspiration to make insights that are specific to a certain situation universally applicable was a recurrent characteristic, as in Aunt Jolesch's following succinct statement: "A single person can also sleep at the couch."

Of course, an unmarried man's ability to derive benefit from spending the night in a rather uncomfortable position was not the point, but rather the question if it was an imposition to expect him to. In Aunt Jolesch's opinion it was not. The problem arose when on the occasion of one of the frequent family reunions at the Jolesch household so many guests had been announced that lodging was in short supply and every halfway appropriate piece of furniture was turned into a bed. At that point Aunt Jolesch decided that the makeshift beds were more appropriate for single people than for the male, and even more so, the female half of a married couple. A single person obviously can sleep on a couch, but a married one obviously cannot.

When at the end of such social gatherings, after opulent meals and extensive hours of conversation in the spacious "salon" the last visitors had finally taken leave, Aunt Jolesch roamed about for a long time, rearranging *fauteuils* and straightening table cloths, from which she removed improperly abandoned leftovers and carelessly strewn ashes, some of which had to be swept off the carpet as well. She shook her head over the spots caused by spilled wine or coffee, collected cigar and cigarette butts, which had burnt holes into many a crocheted doily, and muttered disapprovingly and repeatedly, "A guest is an animal."

To be sure, she did not pronounce these words in standard Ger-

man. She said, "Eh guest is eh animal." She used a casual, comfortable Jewish jargon with a regional flavor (far removed from real
Yiddish) that preserved certain remnants of the Jewish German
formerly spoken in the ghetto and for this reason was strictly taboo
in sophisticated circles and barely tolerated in the privacy of one's
own home. Its public use was limited to the jargon theaters that
flourished in Budapest and Vienna and until 1938 had quite outstanding comedians at their disposal. A revoltingly bastardized
version of this jargon was and probably continues to be spread to
this day in anti-Semitic jokes. As a means of communication it has
ceased to exist. For this reason it will be necessary for me to com-
ment on it occasionally in the following text. I also want to point
out at this point that I will have to rely to a considerable degree on
my readers' linguistic, even musical, intuition when rendering certain phrases, idioms, and intonations. All I can offer here is the
score; they have to imagine the sound.

By the way, Aunt Jolesch and her people were not the only ones to
commit transgressions against High German and its grammar.
When she said "at the couch" rather than using the correct form
"on the couch," she was using a variant that had become common
in many German dialects, particularly in Austria. Important au
thors such as Heimito von Doderer and his pupil Herbert Eisen-
reich retain it even in their printed texts. Indeed, Aunt Jolesch did
not say "in the country" either; instead she said "at the country."

"At the country one cannot spend the night," was one of the
phrases she had coined. "Country" signified roughly everything
that was not "city" and where, as a result of a backward culture and
standard of living, there were no acceptable accommodations to
spend the night. The concept "country" has to be complemented by
the notion "flat," because it did not refer to the predominantly
mountainous summer resort areas (more about those later); although the phrase "going to the country" was applied to them also,
it was used in a positive sense, juxtaposing a country characterized
by clean air and God's unfettered nature to the city.

This leads us to yet another of Aunt Jolesch's idiosyncrasies,
namely, her extreme reserve toward the "country" in either sense,
as well as all types of cities and towns regardless of their size and
renown, and toward changes of location in general. She even re-

sented the preparations prior to traveling because they were never finished in a timely fashion. "Departures are always precipitated," she said.

Moreover, as far as travels as such were concerned, she certainly had no use for them, although it was an almost indispensable matter of etiquette and upper-class living – similar to the custom of having the tailor and barber come "to the house" – to take trips as far and expensive as possible to distinguish oneself by having visited as many attractive cities as possible and to incite as much envy as possible by reporting about them in one's circle of acquaintances. For Aunt Jolesch none of this had the slightest appeal. She was not even in the habit of participating in conversations that involved savoring the exchange of experiences and comparisons. Only a single time did she intervene by making a concluding statement: "All cities are the same, only Venice is a little bit different."

Taken at face value, this statement calls to mind another of undocumented origin that was frequently cited in exile. Someone's aunt, uncle, or grandfather is usually configured as its originator. "I dislike a little bit being anywhere." But the similarity does not go beyond mere phonetics. If these two statements have anything in common at all, it is a certain lack of yearning for faraway places. It is not the decisive point. The decisive factor in favor of Aunt Jolesch is the profound skepticism vis-à-vis anything unfamiliar, the aversion to becoming enthused with foreign places and things just because they are foreign, the healthy trust in one's own perceptions and one's own judgment, which is not dazzled by any scenery or cliché. (In the English language this attitude is described by the both unique and untranslatable term "down-to-earth.")

I would like to ascribe to Aunt Jolesch a statement that unfortunately she cannot have made for reasons of chronology. Rather, it was made by old Mrs. Zwicker, who emigrated with her family to New York in 1938 and found a modest abode in Riverdale, far away from the city, on the second floor of a row house. There Mrs. Zwicker sat by the window for hours. She saw the vague, misty contours of the skyline in the far distance (which she may have taken for a Fata Morgana or something equally unreal), she saw nearby the sluggish and dirty Hudson River flow by, she saw the

garbage bins full to the brim and the stray cats, and she heard the
noise of playing children while she thought of times past.

A friend of the family, also an emigrant, came strolling by. "Well,
how do you like New York, Mrs. Zwicker?" he called up to her
window. And Mrs. Zwicker gave him an answer reverberating with
disgruntled surprise at his stupid question, "How am I supposed to
like the Balkans?"

Indeed, Aunt Jolesch could have said the very same thing. But at
that time she was no longer alive.

She died in 1932, peacefully and painlessly, cared for by doctors,
nursed by her family, at home in her bed – the way people used to
die at that time (and the way it was no longer granted to many of her
relatives who died soon thereafter).

Shortly before her demise her character and her wisdom revealed
themselves in one last statement. To this statement, in which she
relinquished the secret of her famous culinary skills, belongs an
entirely fitting background story.

Like all true cooks who practiced their art in the confines of their
homes – they will be discussed later – Aunt Jolesch's exclusive goal
was the enjoyment and comfort of those she served her immaculate
and incomparable dishes. Not she, but the others, were to savor
them. As for herself, she considered it enough to appease her hunger. Once, asked about her favorite dish, she did not know how to
answer. "But you must have established what you like to eat best,"
the person asking the question insisted.

No, she was not concerned about such things, Aunt Jolesch replied with equal insistence (actually she did not say "things," but
"foolish things." The exact term she used was *narrischkaten*).

The questioner did not give up and after some back and forth
specified the question in such a way that in his opinion it became
seemingly inescapable,

"Just imagine, Aunt – God forbid it should ever happen – but let
us assume: you are sitting in a restaurant knowing that you have
only half an hour to live. What do you order?"

"Something that is already prepared," Aunt Jolesch replied.

If the lovers of her culinary skills had had their way, she would
have had to prepare her very own *krautfleckerln* as her farewell din-

ner, that delicious pastry dish prepared with strips of dough cut
into small pieces and baked with minced cabbage that, depending
on the region, could tend either toward the sweet or the tart side. In
the Hungarian part of the empire it was sprinkled with powdered
sugar, in the Austrian part with pepper and salt. Krautfleckerln
were the most famous of Aunt Jolesch's masterful creations. As
soon as word got out that Aunt Jolesch planned on making Krautfleckerln for the coming Sunday – and without fail word did get out,
the rumor spread among the members of her entire clan in myste-
rious ways, no matter where they lived, as far as Brünn and Prague
and Vienna and Budapest and (perhaps they used African drums)
the most remote corners of the Puszta – Krautfleckerln lovers began to pour in from all directions. None of them ate or drank
anything during their journey, as they saved their hunger for the
Krautfleckerln and quenched their thirst with the water collecting
in their mouths in expectation of future delight. And each time it
was a new delight, an unprecedented delight.

For years they tried to extract from Aunt Jolesch the recipe for her
incomparable creation by using all sorts of ruses and tricks. In vain.
She did not relinquish it. And since over time she became quite
annoyed when pressured to do so, people eventually gave up.

And then, finally, Aunt Jolesch's end drew near, her clock had
run out, the family had gathered around her deathbed. Nothing but
the muttering of prayers and muffled sobs could be heard in the
oppressive silence. Aunt Jolesch lay motionless in her pillows, still
breathing.

Then her favorite niece, Louise, took courage and approached
her. Choked up, but urgently nonetheless, she uttered the following
words: "Aunt, since you cannot take the recipe to your grave, won't
you finally let us have it? Won't you finally tell us why your Krautfleckerln were always so good?"

Aunt Jolesch gathered her fading strength and lifted herself up a
little: "Because I never made enough."

She said it, smiled, and passed on.

With this anecdote I believe I have reported all I can possibly report
in honor of her memory.

However, I'll add yet another small postscript that will do no damage to her memory: Aunt Jolesch was not beautiful. Although kindness, warmth, and intelligence were expressed in her features too distinctly for her to appear ugly, she was certainly not beautiful. Generally speaking, aunts of her type were not beautiful. An uncle of my friend Robert Pick had taken for his wife someone so ugly that his nephew asked him one day straight out, "Tell me, Uncle, for what reason did you marry Aunt Mathilde?" The uncle reflected for a while, then he shrugged his shoulders and said apologetically, "Because she was there."

As far as Aunt Jolesch was concerned, it was by no means a matter of such excessive ugliness, and she herself never concerned herself with what was "beautiful" and what was "ugly." She subsumed such matters under the same concept of *narrischkeiten* – foolishness – as the question about her favorite dish. She was thoroughly convinced that such external matters did not have to be taken seriously, and whoever nonetheless did so risked her criticism, if not her contempt. When one of her nephews courted a woman and had nothing to say about the lady of his choice but that she was beautiful, Aunt Jolesch countered with the sarcastic reprimand, "She is beautiful? So what? You can cover beauty with one hand!"

No, she did not think highly of beauty, neither in women or in men. Let me end this chapter with a statement that shows Aunt Jolesch at the height of her ability to coin phrases, not only in terms of language: "When a man is more beautiful than a monkey, it is a luxury."

This leads us to an important digression concerning language theory.

Hans Weigel

Hans Weigel was born into an established Jewish family in Vienna in 1908. He had already started his career as a writer when he had to seek exile in Switzerland. His satirical utopian novel *Der grüne Stern* (1946, The Green Star) reflects his experiences of and insights into German and international anti-Semitism. In 1945 Weigel was one of the first Jewish intellectuals to return to Vienna, where he played a significant role in postwar literary life. He encouraged and sponsored young authors such as Ilse Aichinger, Ingeborg Bachmann, and Marlen Haushofer, whose works he published in his series *Junge Österreichische Autoren*, and he published his views in many literary journals. Unlike many other returnees, including Hilde Spiel and Friedrich Torberg, who remained skeptical of post-Shoah Austria, Weigel, without being blind to the residues of the past, fully embraced Austrian tradition and the culture of the Second Republic and advocated the continuation of the Austrian-German tradition, as shown in the views he expresses in *O Du Mein Österreich* (1956; O my Austria). Weigel was instrumental in articulating a myth- and history-based Austrian identity palatable to the citizens of the Second Republic, for example in *Flucht vor der Grösse* (1960; Flight from greatness), in which he celebrates Adalbert Stifter's modesty and restraint as the essence of the Austrian spirit, and in his study on the Austrian playwright and satirist Nestroy, *Johann Nestroy* (1972), whose keen irony he also associated with the Austrian character. Weigel did not write about the Holocaust, and he rarely addressed Jewish concerns. He opposed literary experiments and castigated German authors for compromising the ideals of art and language to which he adhered. Weigel's critical work on language, *Die Leiden der jungen Wörter: Ein Antiwörterbuch*

(1974; The sorrows of young words), shows him to be a linguistic purist adverse to neologisms. Indeed, the overpowering conservative influence of Weigel and other critics discouraged experimental authors from pursuing a literary career in Austria. Many of them left and published in West Germany. A performer, dramatist, satirist, and critic, Weigel lived until his death in 1991 with his companion, the prominent actress Elfriede Ott, in Maria Enzersdorf, close to Vienna. His plays include the tragedy *Barrabas und der fünfzigste Geburtstag* (1946; Barrabas and the fiftieth birthday), the comedy *Das wissen die Götter* (1947; Only the gods know), and the tragicomedy *Hölle oder Fegefeuer* (1948; Hell or purgatory). Like many Austrian Jewish writers of Weigel's generation, he had a tenuous relationship with Jewish culture. In *In memoriam* (1979), a volume dedicated to the memory of many notable twentieth-century Austrian writers, Weigel commemorates his contemporaries, including Arthur Schnitzler, Ingeborg Bachmann, Heimito von Doderer, Reinhard Federmann, and authors associated with Austria such as Paul Celan. At the same time, the selection made by the passionately Austrian Weigel, although including certain Jewish writers, reveals a deliberate avoidance of all too Jewish voices or a Jewish agenda.

Hans Weigel

The Draped Window

In order to be true to our convictions we must respect in you what you did not respect in others. We want to destroy your power without crippling your souls.
—ALBERT CAMUS, *Letters to a German Friend*

We must not be idle and wait for punishment to bear fruit. Instead, we must become actively involved in the attempt of allowing a Germany to unfold with which it is possible to coexist. Such a Germany can only be constructed together with the Germans.
—JEAN SCHLUMBERGER IN *Figaro*

When the great purge, undertaken by competent parties, is completed, we ought to be able to bury the hatred and allow the German intelligentsia to work together with us once again.
—WALTER ZÖLLNER IN *Neue Schweizer Rundschau*

The explicit purpose of the recent world war was the victory over extreme nationalism. It ended in the nationalists' total defeat, and now it is up to the victors as well as the defeated to draw the consequences from it and complete the victory intellectually in the same unrelenting and systematic fashion in which the enemy was overcome strategically.

We Austrians find ourselves in a peculiar, perhaps fortuitous and morally obligating, intermediary position between the victors and the conquered. We have the special duty to assess the task at hand appropriately. Indeed, we are entirely cognizant of this fact, and in many of our programmatic declarations we invoke, with justified pride, the supranational, cosmopolitan tradition that has been characteristic of our culture for a long time. We try to build bridges to the east and to the west, we open wide the windows of our damaged, somewhat weather-beaten house, whose foundation has, however, remained intact, the windows down on the ground floor, designed to provide us with a view of our neighbors, and those high above, pointing into vast space, toward freedom. Associations to promote mutual cultural interchanges are being established, communiqués are being exchanged, and the first messengers are already going back and forth. By and by the earth is becoming drier and gradually accessible. The great flood is over.

It is regrettable that our window to the south is not yet open all the way, that at this point one hears little about a cultural exchange with Italy, with which so much connects us and has to connect us. However, in the long run, establishing contact in this case will, and must be, a matter of course. Yet another window, however, remains closed, nailed shut, draped – not a ray of light penetrates to the inside and to the outside. Regardless of how unpopular the mere mention of it may still be today: sooner or later this window will have to be discussed.

I am talking about the window that shall allow us a free view of Germany. I am aware that in statements of this kind it is more elegant to avoid and circumvent the word "I." But I have to say it this time to preclude any misunderstandings. Being a "racially persecuted" person, who had to leave his native country and profession and many of whose relatives perished in Theresienstadt and Poland, I consider myself above the suspicion of camouflaging some sort of Nazi propaganda by taking such a position. However, precisely because I am not suspect, I have the urgent desire to say a word in support of the Germans. I am not a Christian. Yet, I have the most profound respect for the Christian religion and its great command, "Love your enemies!" After all, this war was as much about my life as about the Christian faith. Now the war has been ended by that peace on earth for which all people of good will wished in their hearts and minds, and now the life of all people has to begin anew, with each other, for each other.

The guilt of the Germans has caused us Austrians unspeakable suffering. I do not know if everyone of us will now be able to love these Germans. But this is not about those at whose hands we suffered. During those years, Austrians suffered also at the hands of Austrians, just as Germans suffered at the hands of Austrians. They are prosecuted according to German, Austrian, and newly created international laws. The Germans, however, who today occupy visible positions (and instead of focussing on politics, let us consider only cultural politics here), these Germans are our friends, our brothers. "The German brothers," this phrase used to carry somewhat contemptuous connotations in Austrian usage; but now the time has come for the term "German Brother" to gradually regain its literal meaning. Whosoever teaches, writes, and is artistically active in today's Germany has, exactly like the best of us, gone through an inferno of spiritual suffering and physical threat. Whosoever has been admitted as a German scholar or artist by the four occupying powers has legitimated himself as being ideologically above reproach on the basis of his process alone. A community of suffering has been formed in the concentration camps irrespective of the Passau–Freilassing demarcation line. In exile we Austrians associated with German émigrés as colleagues and comrades. Where can this community still be experienced today?

In occasional reports we hear about the revival of the arts in Berlin, Hamburg, and Munich and about the Heidelberg circle around the philosopher Jaspers and the journal *Die Wandlung*. We hear about plays by new, antifascist authors, about plans to establish publishing houses. We hear very little, but what we hear cannot but fill us with an ardent interest. Because sooner or later the time will have come when a rapprochement, an understanding, will be unavoidable. Should our publishers and German publishers – just to mention one obvious example – reprint the same works and market them exclusively in their own country at a time when the entire body of world literature in the German language requires renewed critical attention? Should theaters produce the same Anglo-Saxon, French, Russian, and classical plays over here and over there but not perform the new German authors here and the new Austrian authors in Germany? Merely from a practical point of view communication will have to be established, and Austria is certain to profit in this respect, since in the intellectual and artistic sector Austria has always been an exporting nation, a surplus nation. In normal times there were always more Austrian journalists and actors in Germany than there were German ones here in our parts. We would only damage ourselves by a consistent permanent isolation.

But not only economic factors are at stake. Nor is it only a matter of the Austrian spirit, so often evoked when there is talk of reconstruction. Under certain circumstances a good German professor teaching at an Austrian university is preferable to a mediocre Austrian one; for the only justifiable basis for the Austrian spirit is quality, intellectual achievement, cultural refinement, and universality, rather than a resident's card. Exemplary scholarly achievement in the spirit of the "Vienna School" is accomplished in the Austrian spirit even if its originator came to us from the outside, as was the case with many great minds of the past who found their way to us. Beyond all that it is a matter of the most lofty ideal, the future of the German-speaking cultural sphere. We belong to it, once and for all, neither revocation nor renunciation is an option. For that reason, in our country the odium of an insult should no longer be attached to the word "German," which after all encompasses the language of Goethe and Adalbert Stifter. National thinking has had its day. Those who still reject things German wholesale bear an embarrassing resemblance to those who objected to things "Jewish" regardless of the person involved. After all, there remains enough that is worth rejecting, even when geography is eliminated as a standard. The choice between Johannes Brahms and Gauleiter Eigruber will be an easy one to make even for the most radical patriot. German friends who work in our country are, as is generally known, supposed to receive Austrian citizenship. That is gratifying for them and for us. But also those who are and will remain Germans can be, must become, our friends.

A marriage, entered into under duress, has broken apart. The side effects were more than unpleasant. Is that a reason to communicate only through a lawyer and by registered letters? Is it not possible to establish a new, more distant, but honest human relationship? There is common property that must not be squandered or destroyed. If only for that reason it is necessary to come to terms with one another. Perhaps it is still too early to open the window, but at least let us take off the obscuring curtain and loosen the nails and boards. There will come a time when the new spirit will flow in and out of this window.

Hans Weigel

EXCERPT FROM
It Is Impossible To Speak about It Dispassionately

Is it possible that two thousand years after the Sermon on the Mount we know this Sermon on the Mount so well and nonetheless have turned out this way?

Are we allowed to pray in Christian churches although we know the Sermon on the Mount and nonetheless have turned out this way?

"What is your purpose for me, dear God?" a poor young girl asks in a work by Ödön von Horvath.

In the desert of Sinai you gave us the dear God, dear God, you made us wait for forty years in the desert, you let us stray, and then you led us to the Promised Land, to Jerusalem. And then, when you made us leave Jerusalem, we parted with the valediction: "Next year in Jerusalem!" And one year this next year had come, and we were back in Jerusalem. God allowed us to assert our Jerusalem in a courageous battle. God had blessed the people of money changers and merchants by fulfilling the words of the prophet. We were in Jerusalem. And we marched against our brothers and killed them with Molotov cocktails.

What is your purpose for us, dear God?

You gave us the dear God; what did you allow us to do with him?

The Ten Commandments – what a party program! What did you allow us to turn them into?

God gave us Michelangelo and Leonardo, Titian, Velázquez, and Rembrandt, Goya, Caspar David Friedrich, and van Gogh; he gave us Bach and Mozart and Haydn and Beethoven and Schubert, Lessing, and Goethe, Claudius and Stifter, Shakespeare and Molière, Kant, Spinoza, and Schopenhauer; God gave us Rossini and Verdi and Johann Strauss, Berg, Bartók, and Stravinsky – what have we done with them? What are we doing with them?

God gave us heaven and earth; he gave us light, inanimate and animate nature; God gave us the beauty of the earth and the power to rule over it; he taught us to read, write, and calculate, to plan, build, and construct. But he took from us the gift of ruling ourselves.

What is God's purpose for us?

⋆

It would be more than tactless, it would be completely and entirely awful, it would be godless, it is unthinkable not to state emphatically that they, too, were and are victims at the very moment when an attempt has been made to state and prove that they are and were not the only ones who were victims.

Moses chose and cursed them through his command that, in order not to perish, they be different, distinguish themselves, be recognizable by their clothes, food, hairstyle, and a decisive part of the male anatomy.

Without Moses they would have ceased to exist a long time ago. Are they chosen or cursed?

Johann Nestroy: "I always say that one would have an easier time if one had never been there in the first place."

Alfred Polgar: "Not being born at all is best. But who is that lucky? Less than one in a million."

But a long time before Moses, before the desert, before the golden calf, even before the patriarch Abraham, immediately after man's first step from Paradise into his world, already in the second generation the first victim died. However, it was not because of the knowledge of good and evil. After all, the evil guy killed the good guy. Abel was murdered. He was the first victim, and he was a Jewish victim. And he was killed by a Jewish murderer.

Did the dear God choose mankind or did he curse it by allowing it to strive for the knowledge of good and evil?

Paradise would have worked without the Ten Commandments and the Sermon on the Mount. But what would it have been and remained? A Paradise without Beethoven.

Indeed, there had to be suffering so that human beings would be comforted.

Human beings have been killed by human beings from the time of Cain to that of Anne Frank, but they were not the only ones.

And time and again at the end of a tragedy there is a Horatio who believes that now there will be an end to tragedy.

> *And let me speak to the yet unknowing world*
> *How these things came about. So shall you hear*
> *Of carnal, bloody and unnatural acts;*
> *Of accidental judgments, casual slaughters,*
> *Of deaths put on by cunning and forced cause;*
> *And, in this upshot, purposes mistook*
> *Fall'n on the inventors' heads: all this can I*
> *Truly deliver.*
> (Shakespeare, Hamlet)

Horatio always believes that now the worst is over, all one has to do is tell it to the still ignorant world, and Fortinbras, the new master, will introduce the new age; but Fortinbras will have to use diplomacy and form coalitions and pacts also; he, too, will have to make concessions.

Since the creation of the universe the last days of mankind have been prophesied, and the mere fact that it is a retroactive prophecy will prove a disclaimer of the prophecy.

We were also informed by Thornton Wilder in *The Skin of Our Teeth* and in *Wir sind noch einmal davongekommen* (We barely survived) that time and again mankind has just barely prevailed in its struggle for survival, and that it will do so again and again, after the ice age, after the deluge, after wars.

Cain may be triumphant, time and again, but he is not victorious.

To think at every turn that it is all over now is cheap and conventional. And yet I feel that at the present time we have reached a new phase, a new juncture on our road.

"Cain, where is your brother, Abel?"

Cain: "Abel, oh well, Abel – I completely forgot about him."

He did not kill him, he lets him die.

We have developed the sciences, but not the scientists.

We have invented all kinds of memory aids and immediately thereafter lost our memory.

We need a machine to determine how much is seven times eight.

We no longer know where the great earthquake took place a few weeks ago.

We like to donate money, as an Indulgence, so to speak, for Abessinia, for the Sahel region, we donate money for cancer relief and children's aid, and we never know exactly where the money really goes.

Once we donated money for the victims of a natural catastrophe in the Netherlands, and then the objects that were donated were allegedly kept lying around somewhere because the Dutch people did not want to accept German-speaking blankets and tents.

We donate money for southern Italy and have to pay the Mafia for protection so that the victims may profit as well.

Cain is a young doctor who does not give a damn about his patients from Friday noon until Monday morning.

Cain is a politician who does not want to resign when something goes wrong in his department, a Belgian politician, for example, who does not want to resign after a massacre in a football stadium for which he was partly responsible.

Cain receives commissions and briberies.

Cain is Israel. Abel is the civilian population of Lebanon.

Cain is everywhere. Abel is everywhere.

 ★

Whoever does not like or holds a grudge against a woman or a man who is Jewish, an Israelite, Israeli, a member of the Mosaic faith . . . what do I know? – the entire problem lies with these alternatives – may refer to me.

It is impossible that there be only likable, irreproachable people. There are also repugnant French, English, and Scandinavian people, repulsive Eskimos, Fuegians, Protestants, Catholics, Zen Buddhists. . . .

Having (justified) reservations against Fritz Kortner or Otto Klemperer did not make a person an anti-Semite. Fritz Kortner was a magnificent actor, a pretty terrible director, and quite a nasty person. Otto Klemperer was a rather good conductor and very mean-spirited. And as far as Ernst Deutsch was concerned, one simply had to like him, not because but rather despite or beyond him. Ernst Deutsch, Manfred Inger. Those grandiose new music interpreters with their "Jewish" names. I own the Mozart piano concertos by Daniel Barenboim; I cannot listen to them enough, but this would also be the case if his name were Klaus-Dieter Schlabrendorff. I used to love the violinist Fritz Kreisler more than anyone else; I considered him second only to the violinist Adolf Busch from Westphalia. I also like Yehudi Menuhin quite well, and Isaac Stern, David Oistrach, Schlomo Mintz, and Nathan Milstein. But in the eventuality of my memorial service I prefer the Viennese sound of the ensemble "Bella Musica," since for that purpose I would not want to consider the Alban Berg Quartet. I would not want to give myself the liberty of being dead so soon.

As for the violinist Bronislaw Huberman and the pianist Paul Weingarten, I found them awful.

My father had three sisters: Aunt Fanni, Aunt Karla, Aunt Regi. All three of them had to leave their places of residence because in Munich Chamberlain, Daladier, Mussolini, and Hitler gave the Czechoslovakian territories, the majority of whose inhabitants were German-speaking (among them many "Jews," who had been settled there for generations), to the Germans. Who was concerned about them at that time? Somehow they lived in what remained of Czechoslovakia. No one was concerned about them, not even the Red Cross, of which I am not very fond in general. (I would much rather be rescued by "Amnesty International" than by the Red Cross.)

Aunt Fanni, Aunt Karla, and Aunt Regi perished miserably. Their children were able to emigrate to the United States, to Chile, to Palestine. Only the oldest daughter of my Aunt Fanni, my cousin Emmi, and her husband did not manage to get away in time. Emmi and her husband died in a concentration camp. Their daughter Hanka survived. She works in Prague as a choreographer and gymnastics teacher. I met her recently. She has three fine daughters, and we like each other very much.

The older daughter of Aunt Regi, Mizzi, keeps the entire family together by means of a lively correspondence. She lives in Seattle and recently visited Europe, including us, in Maria Enzersdorf.

In Eisenstein, which is close to the German border, surrounded by the beautiful Bohemian forest, and where my grandparents lived, the owners of a little land and a grocery store, Mizzi had an exceedingly local friend her own age, Wiesner-Gretl. A nice girl, predestined to become the ideal "Sudeten German" prototype. She got married in Munich and lives now somewhere in Bavaria. After the end of the war Gretl got hold of Mizzi's address. Both were still – and once again – friends and started a correspondence.

When Mizzi recently came to central Europe for the first time, she also visited Wiesner-Gretl, and I obtained her address and telephone number. Since that time there has been an occasional exchange of letters and telephone calls between Mrs. Grete Dallmaier, née Wiesner, and me. What beautiful counterevidence in the face of terrible prejudices!

Incidentally, I hope that I do not need to convince you that the cruel death of my father's sisters and their children's and grandchildren's fate affected and continues to affect me deeply!

Worlds cannot express what I – and not I alone – lost. One can only repress it and gradually undertake the work of mourning. My task is far from being finished.

My beloved friend Hans Horwitz left the country in the midthirties because he had married a competent woman. His brother had likewise ended up in the United States. His mother stayed in Vienna. After the beginning of the war, when I was in Switzerland, she would write me, and I would forward her letters to America. And would send his letters on to Vienna. In the first few years there were always letters from Vienna. Then they ceased to arrive.

Hans Horwitz, a musical genius, pianist, composer (a student of Milhaud's), and cabaret artist eked out a living in California by providing shabby minor musical services. I saw him once over there in America and on the occasion of one of my birthdays arranged for him to receive financial support for a trip to Vienna from a number of local charitable institutions. A boat trip down the Danube River from Linz to Vienna was his greatest wish. I picked him up in Linz, and since we already happened to be there, the two of us gave a performance. The next day we traveled down the Danube to Vienna and gave an evening performance at the Austrian Society for Music, which was recorded by ORF (Austrian Broadcasting Service). He played and sang at my birthday celebration at the Palffy Palace. Then we gave an evening performance in Graz. From there we went to the Salzkammergut, the area around Salzburg. He remembered the days we had spent together at Lake Grundl in the early 1930s. He was overcome with homesickness and gratitude for the few days, but, of course, no one felt an obligation to make it possible for him to spend the last years of his life at the place from which he had been exiled. He was exceptionally gifted and would have, had he been given a chance, proven himself royally.

He was (is) not the only one. There are the musicians Ferdinand Pisen, who has made his home somewhere in France, Endre Singer, now a serious composer in the United States, Willi Spira, an excellent cartoonist and caricaturist . . . and Jimmy Berg, the in-house composer of the cabaret ABC. He had written a Viennese song shortly before his emigration – he also wrote lyrics – with the title "It's Closing Time." He had taken it along on a visit to Vienna and shown it to Gerhard Bronner, from whom Hans Moser heard it. Moser, already halfway in the beyond, taped it as his last song for a recording. Alongside the "Kellergasse" it is probably his most touching song.

Peter Hammerschlag had to die, Jura Soyfer had to die.

I would like to dedicate a plaque honoring all the people of that time, my relatives, friends, and colleagues. Each year I would like to observe one memorial Sunday dedicated to their memory; I think of them, and not only of them. Jura Soyfer is the only one after whom a street was named in Vienna; the others have fallen into oblivion, as would I, had I not searched for the road back all by myself.

Now that I have reached this point in my essay – New Year's is long past and has given way to the firmly established year nineteen hundred and eighty-six of the common era – now that I am writing these words, I have become aware once again of my disastrously paradoxical attitude:

I want to build monuments for the dead, but I do not want to place the living under protection as if they were historical monuments.

I mourn for my relatives and friends and colleagues. I appreciate Leonard Bernstein, but I do not want to be forced to appreciate Lorin Maazel.

It was horrible to die because of Hitler, but it was permitted to live under Hitler.

People who survived the dozen years in Germany and the seven years in our country, who had to participate in the war, actively or passively, have my immediate sympathy. They have been punished enough for the time being.

In Prague and Budapest I look at the people with kindness, even more so in Yugoslavia, and my glances, as it were, want to ask forgiveness for my having been a contemporary of Emperor Franz Joseph and of Berchtolf, his minister of foreign affairs, who got us into this mess and caused this unheard-of loss of human lives.

For a publishing house affiliated with the Austrian Social Democratic Party I once wrote a small booklet about Vienna, stating that in my opinion World War I erupted in Vienna. The person in charge of the company frowned.

When the NPD (National Democratic Party) had its successes in the Federal Republic of Germany, I wrote an article in the following vein: that these events were rather disturbing, but if in the spring of 1945 anyone had said that after so many years there would be only one relatively small German nationalist party, which was not even purely national socialist, I would have been considered a starry-eyed optimist; I wrote that it was understandable that certain voters sympathized with this party, for example, if they had suffered harm in the East or if, for example, they had to a permissible degree an affinity for the military, and so on and so forth. . . .

I sent this article to *Weltwoche*, a paper with which I was on rather good terms, adding: "If you print this article, you may distance yourselves in a preamble categorically from its content, even if this might imply an attack on my honor."

But, nonetheless, *Weltwoche* did not want to print the article. Fortunately, Hans Dichand subsequently published it in the *Kronenzeitung*. The title, incidentally, was, "Are Germans not allowed to be foolish?"

National Socialism did happen, it did so with all its implications and criminal aspects, and it severely affected many generations worldwide, including its adherents, male and female.

Of the things that happened nothing must be denied, nothing whitewashed!

They persecuted Jews, Gipsies, homosexuals; they persecuted prisoners of war, their own officers; they persecuted the churches –

all this, and not only this, has become notorious, and we neither want to nor are we allowed to forget it.

Where was there restitution for the gypsies?

We do not want to, we must not assign to the Jews the status of being the sole victims and label all Germans National Socialists.

★

World War III has already begun.

The second one was different from the way one would have imagined it after the first one.

The second one was not a war conducted with poison gas.

The third one is different from what one would have imagined after the second.

The third one is not an atomic war. Instead it makes the revival of the Middle Ages complete by taking us back to the migration of nations. It carries with it a maximum of lawlessness in a highly developed constitutional state.

Unlike World War II, World War III is not fought for the sake of democracy. Its symptom is that democracy has turned suicidal. Its symptom is that the fact that indecency, the acceptance of provisions and bribes, irregularities, nepotism, lack of objectivity, and corruption are no longer the exception but the rule.

Its characteristic gesture is shrugging one's shoulders.

World War III: the loss of imagination. The fading of the public sphere as a result of the unchecked proliferation of information.

World War III takes from millions of people the fundamental human right: the right to work.

World War III:

Critical thought capitulates to advertisement.

The critical establishment resigns itself to conducting staged battles about minor events and ignores the events that concern millions.

World War III reduces the adult citizen to the kindergarten level.

World War III:

The victory march of falsehood, not the great, heroic falsehood à la Machiavelli, but the ugly, small, unattractive, lousy, greasy everyday lie.

World War III is not fought by power blocs against one another, but in every country, every city, every village, every house.

World War III seals the demise of science because of its unstop-
pable development.

World War III has devalued the truth and destroyed our vigilance.

World War III has effected equality among poisons.

World War III: letters have been dethroned by numbers.

World War III: the collective guilt of all human beings.

There was no peace treaty after World War II. It was simply over.

Likewise, World War III will simply be over one day. And people
will wonder how it was possible for it to happen in the first place.

⋆

And now my essay is moving toward its conclusion.

During the course of its progression it took an independent turn,
it became more general than I had initially intended. When one
becomes involved in a book, one never knows ahead of time where
it will take one.

Now it has come to pass that the book after next has already
become my next one.

There are so many more books I would like to write. The one
mentioned before about peace and pacifism, for example, a book
about falsehood, a book on journalism. A book (or a long essay) on
Franz Molnár, on Ferdinand Raimund, on Karl Valentin. I almost
began a book on Molière. Yet my publisher wants a book on Jewish
and other jokes.

What's the use?

I am very happy that at least I finished this one, no matter how it
turned out in the end.

I hope I did not hurt anyone by what I wrote. In addition, I
wonder again and again if this book was necessary in these times of
hostility; but, after all, it is a book against hostility.

And, aren't you, Hans Weigel, afraid of being applauded by the
wrong party?

Yes, of course, but in closing I would like to reduce this fear by
saying:

I hate everything fascist, but I try to differentiate between "national socialist" and "fascist." And even the term "fascist" is all too
frequently misused. Bruno Kreisky used the term "fascistoid" in
connection with Israel.

I hate everything fascist, everything fascistoid, or nationalist, no matter who is involved. I hate all Jew haters who hate without provocation.

I am ashamed that in Upper Austria naming a street after Jägerstätter, a martyr of nonviolence, caused a controversy.

I am ashamed that a member of our predominantly socialist government honored a war criminal. I am outraged that in Germany naming a street after Anne Frank caused a controversy.

"There he goes again," my friends say with indulgence and my enemies with criticism. But I believe that this book had to be written. And there simply was no one else to write it.

Since the superdevil is not around any longer and only medium-sized or smaller devils are in charge of our world, everything this book deals with can be subsumed under the rubric of one of many terrible things. That's what I think.

The reason: Nothing in this world is perfect. And whoever wants perfection is naive. And if it is perfect, it is artificial, synthetic.

Recently I heard a perfect recording of Schumann's First Symphony by the Vienna Philharmonic Orchestra under the baton of Furtwängler. I had attended the original performance a long time ago. The recording was perfect: All interfering noises, the auditorium atmosphere, the applause, had been edited out. Everything had been made perfect, but it was naked, so to speak, it was inhuman. The Unfinished Symphony by Schumann.

Yesterday two young people came to see me. Married for seven years. "We are happy!" they beamed. But certainly their happiness did not consist of seven times 365 radiant days without a cloud in the sky. "C'est plein de disputes, le bonheur," Anouilh says in *Antigone*. Happiness is full of crises, it is not the absence of crises, but dealing with them.

So infinitely much is wrong on earth: children are tormented by their fellow students and their parents, women are wronged, not enough is being done to make the difficult life of the disabled easier. Colleagues, men and women, are nasty to one another, subordinates are treated badly, minorities are discriminated against, dissenters are harmed, promises are not kept, there is stealing, cheating, robbing, abusing, lying – one has to live with it, what else can one do?

This is also true for those whom I refer to as "Jews" in quotation marks. As for everyone who is wronged, I feel sorry for them also if they wronged; also and if.

    ★

I would like to be a Christian in order to know what it is like: Love your enemies. I am unable to do it. Not even my adversaries.

I would stand up for them when they are wronged; I would try to save them when they are in danger.

After I spoke out in a vehement attack against the Soviet-dominated film producer Rosenhügel, I was called by one of their local associates. She said that she had heard about the matter but did not know what I had said. Of course I sent her a carbon copy. I believe that this is the way it is done in England. It's called democracy. But that does not mean that I love the Russian film producer who disregarded our laws.

The Old Testament asks me to love my neighbor as myself. I do not wish that upon him. And being treated the same way as many other contemporaries treat themselves is nothing I want to impose on anyone.

I do not love "the Jews," because it is impossible to love either a people or a religious community. Neither do I love "the Austrians," at most I love Austria.

I do love some citizens of Israel.

I do not love Israel. And I do not love anti-Semites.

Anti-Semitism is too complicated an issue to leave to the anti-Semites.

    ★

Now, dear friend, the time has come for me to say farewell to you.

Do you feel that I have gradually begun to neglect you? I hope not! You were always there, a bridge between my text and its readers.

And now that everything has been said, I shall retroactively endow you with specific traits, you who up until now have been a more or less undefined, generalized, and deliberately colorless entity. What I have stated here is of course intended for everyone who wishes to take note of it.

But at this point I deliberately want to consider you to be one of the young people who live all around us today and who may regard the things that move me as very distant. They may hardly be able to understand them entirely. From your perspective Hitler is history, even more so Franz Joseph [Austrian emperor, 1830–1916]. From your perspective World War I is far away, without contours, as the wars in the Balkans were from mine when I was a young person myself.

I ask you, dear young friend, to take notice of some, of as many of the things I am about to tell you as possible.

Because of the date of my birth in 1908, and because my political awareness began to develop in 1914, and because I can remember the years 1912 and 1913 I am, as it were, identical with the century that is also still your century, that is, in other words, our shared century.

There is a growing interest in the era that was the time of my youth.

In Austria everything happens belatedly, at second instance. Thirty years ago Franz Schubert barely existed, Mozart was only taking on his true dimensions when I was already in control of my conscious mind. Nestroy made a gradual comeback fifty years after his death. Karl Kraus is just now experiencing a glorious revival. In the early fifties nobody paid attention to Schnitzler. And Austria itself had to pass through the horrible First Republic and through seven years of nonexistence in order to make a new start.

Since I began taking part in our Second Republic, I have always had friends younger than myself. Many of my young authors of the 1950s are now already in their sixties. But new talents are continually emerging.

You, my dear young friend, will face hardships; but do think of the long succession of all those who did face hardships and who nonetheless shaped your century, this terrible, awesome twentieth century.

Today, even more so than at the time of the First Republic, a multitude of important colleagues, men and women, still crowd around me, and I enjoy their trust and friendship.

You, my dear friend, may be the student of German language and literature in Innsbruck, the young teacher from the area around

Salzburg, the young lyric poet from Brigittenau – all of you versatile, diligent, and talented in your own special way.

You must realize how things were with us in order to be at the cutting edge of all that is and will be, my dear young friends.

MARIA ENZERSDORF, February 1986

The text was completed and handed to the publisher in February of 1986, in other words, prior to the beginning of the debate about Dr. Kurt Waldheim. Since that time it has not been expanded or updated in any way.

Simon Wiesenthal

Simon Wiesenthal was born in Buczacz, Ukraine, near Lvov, in 1908. His father died in World War I, and his mother fled with the family to Vienna. Later she returned to Buczacz and remarried. After his graduation from the Gymnasium in 1928 he tried to enroll in the Polytechnic Institute in Lvov, but was rejected because of quota restrictions on Jews. He studied at the Technical University of Prague and completed his degree as an architectural engineer in 1932. Until his arrest by the Nazis in 1941 he worked as an architect in Lvov. He survived the Nazi concentration camps at Plaszow, Groß-Rosen, Buchenwald, and Mauthausen, Upper Austria. After the liberation of the camps by the Allies, Wiesenthal worked for the War Crimes Commission, the U.S. Office of Strategic Services, and the Counterintelligence Corps until 1947. His documentary and literary writings include *KZ Mauthausen* (1946), *Großmufti-Großagent der Achse* (1947; *The great mufti, great agent of the Axis*), *Ich jagte Eichmann* (1961; *I hunted Eichmann*), *Doch die Mörder leben* (1967; *The Murderers among Us*), *Die Sonnenblume* (1970; *The Sunflower*), *Recht, nicht Rache* (1979; *Justice, not Vengeance*), *Krystyna: Die Tragödie des polnischen Widerstands* (1989; *Krystyna: The Tragedy of the Polish Resistance*). Wiesenthal's works address issues of world politics as they pertain to Jewish life, including the situation in the Middle East and in the Balkans. Wiesenthal has been the recipient of numerous international awards, including the Freedom Medals of the Netherlands and Luxembourg, Commendatore de la Republica Italiana Medal, the Congressional Medal of Honor, and the Jerusalem Medal.

Simon Wiesenthal

The Waldheim Case

At the beginning of 1986, when it was known that the conservative Austrian People's Party would put forward Dr. Kurt Waldheim, the former Secretary General of the United Nations, as its candidate in the presidential elections, two members of the Austrian resistance movement called on me. They wanted to know if I had anything on Waldheim. Both were members of the Social Democratic Party and I could not help asking them where they had stood in the Peter case. "I had a fat dossier against Peter, but you weren't interested." My visitors were at a loss for an answer, and as I was anyway unable to tell them anything about Waldheim they left my office empty-handed.

Shortly afterwards I received a letter from a former Auschwitz inmate, whom I had known for dozens of years and who was also a long-standing member of the Socialist Party. He asked me to support a historian, Dr. Georg Tidl, in an Austrian television documentary programme about the Wehrmacht general Panwitz and his Cossack division. I was astonished at the interest shown by Austrian television in this issue, but when the author of the letter also telephoned to ask for my help, I agreed.

A few days later Tidl himself was on the other end of the line. He too told me about the planned TV documentary, and when I again expressed surprise at the fact that, all of a sudden, television was interested in the Cossack division – which was moreover a pure fighting division – he came clean: "Waldheim is reputed to have been in that division. In February 1945 the smashed Cossack division had been amalgamated with an SS division – which meant that Waldheim had been a member of the SS.

"Have you actually researched into whether the people from the Cossack division had a chance of resisting incorporation in the SS?" I enquired.

But to him the matter was more simple: whether or not he had wanted to be one, Waldheim had been an SS man.

When I asked whether that was all he could produce against Waldheim, Tidl observed that he was still at the beginning of his work. I suggested he ring me when he was a little closer to the end.

Seven years earlier I had received an inquiry on Waldheim. That time friends from Israel had shown an interest in him. It had struck them that, as Secretary General of the United Nations, Waldheim had so emphatically sided with the Arabs and against Israel, that it was possible it might have been the result of a Nazi past. The question interested me too, and I phoned my friend Axel Springer in Berlin and asked him to make inquiries for me at the Documentation Center there as soon as possible (I myself would have had to accept an endless waiting period). Springer's answer came by return of post. Its contents, according to the observer's point of view, were either satisfactory or disappointing: Waldheim had not belonged to any Nazi organization. Attached to this negative report was the information from the "Wehrmacht information office" that Waldheim had repeatedly been in hospital and that he had served as a lieutenant with Army Group E in the Balkans.

After my telephone conversation with Dr. Tidl I fished out that Wehrmacht information again, to discover whether General Panwitz's Cossack division was mentioned in it. But there was no mention of it anywhere, let alone any incorporation in the SS. If Dr. Tidl had again phoned me I would have told him. But Tidl evidently was busy.

By mere chance I learned that the legal adviser of the World Jewish Congress, Eli Rosenbaum, had been visiting Vienna – allegedly even twice – without visiting me or even telephoning me. This surprised me because I knew the WJC people from the days when Nahum Goldmann was president and when the brothers Jacob and Nehemiah Robinson were actively helping to bring Nazi criminals to justice. When the two died, Dr. Karbach took over their department, and with him, too, I had been in continuous contact. Following Dr. Goldmann's departure I did not hear from the WJC for a long time, until it staged a congress in Vienna in 1985. I attended only on the first day, and for some time it was even doubtful if there would be a second day. The reason was that many delegates demanded that the meeting be cut short in protest against the Reder-Frischenschlager affair. The Austrian Minister of Defence, Dr. Friedhelm Frischenschlager, had welcomed SS Obersturmbann-führer Walter Reder, sentenced for mass murder in Italy and just released from detention at the fortress of Gaeta, by shaking his hand on his arrival in Austria and thereby causing a worldwide storm of indignation. Even in Austria criticism was loudly voiced and the Opposition demanded Frischenschlager's resignation. But the Liberal Party, to which he belonged, stood squarely behind him, and the Socialists, who together with the Liberals formed the government, did not wish to affront their coalition partner. With the party discipline typical of them, all Socialist deputies voted against the Austrian People's Party's motion of censure. Only with difficulty, and because members of the board of the Jewish community were begging the WJC, was the congress seen through.

I think it probable that some of the people who later played a part in the Waldheim affair may have been active then as intermediaries between the Socialists and the WJC. In February 1986 the news magazine profil published Kurt Waldheim's service book, from which it emerged that he had been in the Mounted Corps of the SA and in the Nazi Students' Association. The event had for some weeks been preceded by rumours about the alleged Nazi past of Kurt Waldheim. I knew from the publisher of profil that they had been receiving anonymous hints and photographs. Profil, however, did not regard the photos as providing any strong evidence. Finally journalists from that magazine learned that some old Socialists had wept on the shoulders of the Austrian People's Party friends about something quite awful being about to surface in the matter of Waldheim. There was a plan, they said, to make a big splash with Waldheim's Nazi past. These reports would be published not in an Austrian paper but abroad. The whole spectacle, the alarmed comrades are reported to have said, would run "like a production at the Burgtheater." This they didn't think right, even if it harmed their political opponents, the Austrian People's Party.

The editors of profil pursued this and similar rumours and eventually discovered that the New York Times was in possession of a voluminous Waldheim dossier which it would shortly start publishing. Furnished with this information, profil approached Dr. Waldheim and advised him to reveal his wartime past on his own accord. He would have to expect, however, that the editorial office would check his information most painstakingly. Waldheim agreed, even though – typically – he gave away nothing about his SA Mounted Corps membership nor about his service in the Balkans. With his approval a *profil* editor, Johannes Czernin, inspected Waldheim's army record, which until then had been under lock and key in the Austrian War Archives. To everyone's surprise the record contained the information on Waldheim's membership in the SA and in the Nazi Students' Association.

My friends Peter Michael Lingens published an exceedingly well-balanced commentary in *profil*. Membership in the student's association was harmless, he said; this was necessary even to obtain a room in a students' hostel. The SA, admittedly, while still illegal had been an unsavoury organization of rowdy brawlers, but anyone joining it after the *Anschluss* did not thereby manifest any deep ties with Nazism but probably just a certain opportunism. The charge against Waldheim was not so much that he had committed those youthful sins as that, rather irritatingly, he had in his memoirs portrayed himself almost as a victim of Nazism.

Waldheim objected: he had merely belonged to a riding club and didn't know it had been incorporated into the SA. He himself had never signed a membership form of the SA and therefore had not regarded himself as a member. (In point of fact no SA document with Waldheim's signature has been found.) He had likewise found himself in the students' association without his knowledge when all the members of his youth group were automatically enrolled.

The article in *profil* could well have triggered off a meaningful discussion of Waldheim's credibility – if the World Jewish Congress had not started up the machinery of its long-prepared campaign a few days later. While the *New York Times*, as predicted, carried its first report on Waldheim, the WJC proclaimed Waldheim a hard-line Nazi and a well-nigh convicted war criminal. The case developed a colossal media dynamism: the world's newspapers vied with each other in producing new incriminating Waldheim material, and the WJC added its comments.

For a long time what Waldheim offered in his defence scarcely made any impact internationally. People who hardly knew the dif-

ference between the SA and the SS found the question of whether a
riding club could, without knowledge of its members, be incorporated in the SA way above their heads. Even less did they realize that
the Mounted Corps in the Third Reich had become a catchment
bowl for opponents of the Nazis, who, for a variety of reasons, had
to be "members" somewhere and did not wish to be in the Nazi
party. In fact, Kurt Waldheim was a fairly good illustration of those
constraints: his father was a committed Christian Social Party man,
who immediately lost his post under the Nazis. In the regional
records of the Nazi party the family was listed as emphatically anti-
Nazi, and Kurt Waldheim himself had, immediately before the Anschluss, distributed leaflets calling for a "No" vote. Because of that
he had been beaten up by the Nazi hitmen. For anyone wishing to
complete his studies at the Konsularakademie against such pres-
sures, it was more than sensible to join the Nazi students or the SA
horsemen voluntarily, to avoid difficulties.

One may think it more heroic to accept such difficulties knowingly – but in view of conditions prevailing at the time one should
be careful not to condemn too severely the opportunism that was
inevitably spreading. University graduates, for instance, who were
unable to prove membership of at least a small Nazi club had
virtually no hope of finding a post in the civil service. That may have
been a matter of irrelevance for the sons of rich families – but it was
by no means irrelevant for Kurt Waldheim, who came from a modest background.

Nevertheless I believed from the very outset that the credibility of
the former UN Secretary General left something to be desired: a
person of his standing might be expected to speak on his own
initiative and fully about all he did at the time, instead of having
every detail painfully extracted from him. But this is still some way
from being a "hard-line Nazi," and even further from being a "war
criminal" (these terms were used by the WJC long before those
Yugoslav documents turned up which proved that Waldheim at
least knew about war crimes). It was along these lines that I answered all the telephone calls which came into my office – and they
numbered a dozen per hour. I said that we had made inquiries
earlier at the Documentation Center in Berlin and had been unable
to learn anything to Waldheim's discredit. He had not been a mem-

ber of a Nazi organization, because the National Socialist Students'
Association and the SA Mounted Corps were not, for the reasons
I've outlined above, subject to registration in Austria.

But it was of course possible that the WJC possessed evidence
which we did not know about. The Simon Wiesenthal Center in Los
Angeles therefore got in touch with the Secretary General of the
World Jewish Congress, Israel Singer, to find out what they had on
Waldheim. Singer stated explicitly that he had been promised
weighty material from people close to the Austrian government.
Now I understood why Eli Rosenbaum had come to Vienna: evidently to gather preliminary information. That I was not involved
may have been for two reasons: for one thing, the subject matter
of my telephone conversation with Dr. Tidl might have got about
and there might have been some anxiety that the laboriously constructed charges could collapse in the light of my precise acquaintance with the facts. (I have occasionally encountered this journalis-
tic phenomenon: journalists being reluctant to see a good story
spoilt by excessive detailed research.) But I also think it possible
that I may have been thought biased: in connection with my dispute
with Bruno Kreisky in the Friedrich Peter Affair a number of Austrian People's Party politicians – especially the then future President
of the Austrian National Bank, recently deceased, Stefan Koren –
had taken my side, which had given rise to the rumour that I was an
Austrian People's Party member. At any rate, I have frequently been
accused of failing to attack Waldheim for that reason.

The truth was simpler. I was not prepared to attack Kurt Waldheim as a Nazi or a war criminal because, from all I knew about him
and from all that emerged from the documents, he had been neither a Nazi nor a war criminal.

As for his credibility, I have always questioned that – except that
no one in Austria or in New York cared about it during the first few
months. The WJC – in spite of its grandiose name no more than a
small Jewish organization of inferior importance – used the Waldheim case to get itself into the headlines of the major American
papers, headlines at first readily made available to it. (It was only
gradually that newspaper editors discovered the real complexity of
the issue, and from that point onward began to differentiate between the accusations of the WJC and their own findings.)

But it was in Austria that the activities of the World Jewish Congress turned into disaster: on 9 March 1986 *profil* carried an interview with the Director of the WJC, Elan Steinberg, and its Secretary General, Israel Singer. In this interview the two WJC officers indulged in grotesque threats, not only against Waldheim but against all Austrians. If Waldheim were elected President, they said, every holder of an Austrian passport would feel the effects of it when he went abroad: he would find himself surrounded by a "cloud of mistrust." The result of the interview could have been predicted: even those Austrians who until then had regarded Waldheim as an incompetent opportunist began to defend him. And the numerous anti-Semites at last had grist for their mill: evidence at last of the "world-wide Jewish conspiracy." A lot of young people, especially for whom anti-Semitism no longer was an issue, were confused. Thus a young man phoned me to enquire why he should feel ashamed when travelling abroad, seeing that he wasn't going to vote for Waldheim and that there had not been a single Nazi in his family. "What, Herr Wiesenthal, do the Jews have against me?"

For the first time reference was again being made to "the Jews," instead of people saying: "Elan Steinberg of the World Jewish Congress" or "Israel Singer of the World Jewish Congress." In a population with a deep-rooted traditional anti-Semitism, a population which had undergone seven years of *Stürmer* indoctrination, the ideas of Nazism could not have died from one day to the next. The men of yesterday were only too ready to say: "Now you see how right we were – now you see what they are really like, the Jews." But even the fellow travellers were glad of a belated excuse: "There are some bad sides to the Jews, that's a fact all right." And the young people, who scarcely had any personal experience of Jews, were confused: "Could the Jews really be what some people say they are?"

It is true that all these reactions are ultimately anti-Semitic to various degrees (or at any rate reactions rooted in the anti-Semitic tradition), but this does not mean that officials of a Jewish organization have the right to trigger off such a reaction needlessly, to provoke it. Least of all is it the right of two young Jewish officials who live in the U.S.A., while we Austrian Jews are the ones to suffer the consequences. But we were not asked – even though, according to its statute, the WJC would have been obliged to consult with the local Jewish community or, at least, inform it of its intentions. The desperate efforts of Dr. Hacker, the recently deceased president of the Vienna Jewish community, to persuade Singer and Steinberg to retract their interview were unfortunately to no avail. Instead, there was an internal split: some young people who – thank God – had only known Nazism by hearsay, now felt obliged to be more merciless than the men and women who had spent years in the concentration camps of the Third Reich and supported Singer and Steinberg. Especially as this was an opportunity for getting rid of some older board members. But these young people, too, were functionaries: their views did not coincide with those of the members of the Jewish community who had to live day in and day out with a more or less pronounced Austrian anti-Semitism. A member of that community phoned Mr. Singer and complained to him.

"How many Jews are there living in Austria?" the WJC Secretary General enquired.

"Seven thousand."

"Well then," Mr. Singer suggested, "why don't you just emigrate?"

In a Canadian Jewish paper he grandly declared that "the cause" had made it necessary to accept the hardships the Austrian Jews would face.

Inappropriate as the reaction of the WJC was, so of course was the reaction of a number of Austrian institutions. The Austrian People's Party, which had made Kurt Waldheim its candidate, daily during its campaign aroused anti-Semitic sentiments which it then claimed it had "not wished to arouse." Its chairman Alois Mock missed no opportunity to pillory "certain circles" on the east coast for having fanned a campaign against Austria, and with this phrase once more helped the WJC to become "the Jews." The same line was taken, even more noisily, by the Secretary General of the Austrian People's Party, Dr. Michael Graff (who later had to resign because of a serious anti-Semitic impropriety); needless to say, Kurt Waldheim had no objection to this kind of election campaign.

The biggest gutter press daily in the country, Kronen-Zeitung, which had distinguished itself earlier with a highly controversial series about Jewry, was daily adding fuel to the flames, and the broadsheet press hardly lagged behind. Both kinds of papers were able to gauge the success of their reports by a series of anti-Semitic letters to the editor – not to mention the turns of phrase which once again became acceptable in tavern talk. I know of several cases of taxi drivers refusing to take Jewish passengers. In this respect the Waldheim affair, though not essentially designed to do so, in fact stirred up and made apparent what had long been regarded as dead: anti-Semitism has in no way been overcome in Austria.

This in turn gave rise to justified concern among the Jewish community in the U.S.A. It was suddenly recalled that Austria had made no kind of restitution to the victims of Nazism, on the grounds that Austria did not exist during the war. It was conveniently forgotten that, under the Kreuznach agreement, Austria after the war was only permitted to keep extensive German assets because she undertook to compensate victims of Nazism appropriately. People also remembered the curious role which Kreisky had played in all discussions on Israel. Waldheim, who had become U N Secretary General upon Kreisky's proposal, had in that post simply followed the policy which is propagated by the "Sun King" to this day: the prime objective of Austria's Middle East policy is not security or recognition for the state of Israel, but must instead be the establishment of a Palestinian state. His friendship with Gaddafi and Arafat did not make him especially popular in the U.S.A.

None of this did Austria's image in the U.S.A. any good. Behind the traditional sympathy for the land of the Vienna Boys' Choir and the Lipizzaner horses a good deal of criticism had been building up even before the Waldheim case. While Austria was no longer quite as popular as before, Waldheim was altogether one of the most unpopular figures in the U.S.A. The majority of Americans anyway regard the United Nations as an unnecessary and incompetent organization, and Waldheim as its most unnecessary and most incompetent Secretary General. Even people who realized that the majority in the U N consisted of Communist and Third World countries could not understand why Kurt Waldheim was quite so eager to join their side.

Least of all, of course, could the Jews understand it. They were aware that the resolution "Zionism is racism" was adopted in his era, and they also remembered his refusal, when visiting Yad Vashem, to cover his head, or his statement that the Israeli rescue operation in Entebbe was "a breach of international law." Kurt Waldheim was seen by the Jews – for understandable reasons – as an enemy, and now the World Jewish Congress saw a unique chance of painting this enemy brown and dressing him up in the uniform of a war criminal. The American public in general and the Jewish population in particular were only too happy to believe that image.

Waldheim himself reacted with the diplomatic finesse which had characterized him as UN Secretary General. When it was pointed out that he had served in the Balkans with a unit involved in extensive war crimes, he stated that he had "only done his duty." This assured him of the approval of the so-called war generation within Austria, which had been using this phrase for decades to run away from all responsibilities. That it might also be possible to say that it would have been difficult to avoid military service does not seem to have occurred to many members of that generation, any more than it did to Waldheim. One of my pleasanter experiences, however, within that unpleasant affair was the fact that many young Austrians found Waldheim's formula particularly repellent and contrasted it with a different categorical imperative: if there was such a thing as duty, then it was their duty to resist.

No one, however, demanded such heroism from Waldheim. It would have been entirely sufficient for him to find clear words to describe his wartime past. As a man who knew so much – owing to his position on the staff Waldheim was one of the best-informed officers – he should have stood up as a witness to that period and informed the young generation about the bestialities of the Nazi regime. Instead, Waldheim missed no opportunity to sweep the Nazis' predatory war in the Balkans on to the same pile as partisan resistance, and the shooting of hostages by the German Wehrmacht with the excesses of the partisan struggle. Instead of making a statement, belated though it would be, he had to be confronted with a document each time before his memory would stir. Thus he told an interviewer from profil that he had known nothing about illegal reprisals in the fight against partisans, only to declare three days later, faced with a flood of documents bearing his signature, that surely the fact that hostages were shot was generally known.

Shortly afterwards he claimed that he had only learned from the newspapers about the deportations of Jews from Salonika. When thereupon I declared that by this remark Kurt Waldheim had forfeited all credibility, he telephoned me and the following dialogue developed:

"Herr Dr. Waldheim, the Jewish community in Salonika was one of the largest and most ancient in the world and your headquarters was less than five miles from Salonika. It is impossible that you didn't notice anything about the deportation of the Jews."

"Believe me, I knew nothing about it."

"The deportations went on for six weeks. Some two thousand Jews were deported every other day; the military trains which brought down equipment for the Wehrmacht, that is for your people, took away the Jews on their return run."

"I had nothing to do with it."

"Surely you were often at the officers' club: did no transport officer ever mention these things?"

"No, never."

"The ss at the time had no provisions for the Jews, so the Wehrmacht made available for each Jew one loaf of bread and twelve olives. Every supply officer knew about this. Did none of them ever talk to you either?"

"No."

"You would go into Salonika time and again. The Jews made up almost one-third of the population there. Did you never notice anything? Jewish shops being locked up, groups of people being escorted through the streets, an air of despair?"

"No. I didn't notice anything."

I could only reply what the commission of historians likewise made clear in its report: "I cannot believe you."

By his public attitude towards the deportation of the Salonika Jews, if for no other reason, Kurt Waldheim made himself unacceptable to me as a Federal President. But the wjc was still trying to brand him a war criminal. Their basis was the well-known list of the Yugoslav War Crimes Commission, according to which Kurt Waldheim was wanted for murder. When I first learned of that list I sent a telegram to the Yugoslav Premier Milka Planinc, requesting her to publish all the documents on Waldheim which existed in Yugoslavia.

She replied the same day – she happened to be in Vienna – only to say that Yugoslavia did not interfere in the internal affairs of Austria. I didn't let matters rest there but flew to the U.S.A. to persuade UN Secretary General Pérez de Cuéllar, to ask the Yugoslavs officially to publish their evidence. To this day this has not occurred.

Nevertheless, a fairly clear picture emerges from the available documents. The charges against Waldheim go back to a German officer who was himself guilty of the massacre of which he accused Waldheim (and who was also executed for it). A second incriminating testimony came from a soldier whose widow was interviewed by profil: she stated that her husband had confessed to her that the accusation was false. It had been a general principle during interrogations to attribute responsibility to someone who was already safely abroad. In point of fact, Waldheim never hid after the war but became the secretary to the Minister of Foreign Affairs, Karl Gruber, a meritorious resistance fighter. The Yugoslavs themselves never requested Waldheim's extradition, evidently because they realized that their file was insecurely documented. Presumably it was in existence only because it was thought possible to use it for blackmail. Meanwhile a carefully researched book has appeared on the subject: The Missing Years by Professor Robert Herzstein. Certainly the proposition that Waldheim was a war criminal can in no way be maintained on the basis of the material at present available to us. The accusations of the World Jewish Congress were rash. As I once put it to a WJC official: "I am in the habit of researching first and making accusations later. You made an accusation first and only then started researching."

The undifferentiated manner in which Kurt Waldheim was attacked has undone years of educational work in Austria: in a vast number of lectures, interviews and personal conversations I, and other people, had tried to show that a distinction had to be made between the indifferent, the fellow travellers and fanatical Nazis; that just any Wehrmacht officer could not be equated with a member of a murder brigade; that although Hitler's war was a criminal war, it must nevertheless be distinguished from war crimes, and that war crimes have to be distinguished from crimes merely committed during the war. The "Waldheim case" once more blurred all these distinctions.

What I find frightening is that only in the Eichmann case did I witness a similar measure of media interest in Nazi crimes. Yet one man had been one of the worst criminals in world history, and the other had not even been a Nazi. One had been responsible for the murder of millions of Jews, while the other had only been clumsy enough to deny his knowledge of the deportation of the Salonika Jews. Rarely have I witnessed such a confusion of values and words. Thus the wjc held a conference in Geneva in April 1986 under the chairmanship of Israel Singer, at which a certain Kalman Sultanik, vice-president of that organization, made a speech. In it he said literally: "Waldheim, who sent the Jews to the gas chambers, is being supported and defended by the prominent Jew Simon Wiesenthal." When, at that, the representative from Austria, Paul Gross (now president of the Jewish community), asked to speak, Israel Singer decided to close the discussion.

Even in my own office I had experience of how the Waldheim case could induce a seemingly sensible, seemingly decent, person to commit an incomprehensible action. One of my staff, Mrs. Silvana Konieczny-Origlia, took a copy of a private letter to me, believing that she could thereby prove Waldheim to be a war criminal who was being protected by me. The letter was from Professor Fleming, later to become a member of the commission of historians, and it contained a number of documents concerning British prisoners of war, with the note that I was the only person who did not possess them. Careful researches, however, disclosed that these documents had been discussed in *Der Spiegel* two weeks earlier and that Greville Janner, MP, and old friend of mine, had already addressed a question about them to the British Foreign Office. But my employee knew nothing about this at the time, and passed the letter on (naturally without my knowledge) to the Italian journal *Epoca*, which thereupon made it into a big story against me. The Italian journalist Fiamma Nierenstein accused me of having suppressed the evidence in order to help Waldheim; other papers took up the accusation, and on French television Serge Klarsfeld had a real go at me. A week later *Epoca* carried an article which Elan Steinberg had written against me. My friend Paul Gross telephoned the wjc to speak to Steinberg, but he was not available. From talking to his secretary it emerged that the wjc director had written that article

considerably earlier. If it had not taken so long to translate it
into Italian it would presumably have appeared alongside Mrs.
Konieczny-Origlia's "revelations."

There is a cynical explanation for all these phenomena: the World
Jewish Council and a few other people had got their teeth into the
business and were not prepared, under any circumstances, to admit
their mistakes and reduce the charges against Waldheim to a reasonable level. They were, in a sense, urged on by their own success
to make their announcements true: somewhere a document had to
turn up that would unmask Waldheim as a war criminal – otherwise
his accusers would be exposed as slanderers. It was undoubtedly
that kind of thinking that played a part in the continuation of the
Waldheim case.

But there is also another, more charitable, explanation: young
Jews who could not comprehend that their parents did not resist
more (and whose knowledge of the period is too slight for them to
know how difficult such resistance would have been) were now,
half a century too late, performing something they saw as resistance. In the absence of a more suitable figure they magnified Kurt
Waldheim into the symbol of the persecutor and were now going all
out for him, by proxy, as it were, for their parents. Added to this is
the fact that many American Jews have something akin to a sense of
guilt in their subconscious anyway, for not having done enough for
the persecuted Jews of Europe during the war. The Waldheim case
offered them an opportunity to take a demonstrative stance. Disin-
formation from some American television services and newspapers
was a further factor. And the rest was provided by anti-Semitic
incidents in Austria. The Americans therefore concluded that wjc
had been correct with its charges against Waldheim and Austria.
The Austrian anti-Semites saw themselves justified in their anti-
Semitic actions by the attitude of the wjc and the reaction of the
Americans. Thus the vicious circle continued.

I had hoped to cut that Gordian knot by proposing, on the very
day of Waldheim's election, 8 June 1986, that a commission of
historians be set up to determine, to the best of their knowledge
and conscience, the truth and nothing but the truth. On 8 February
1988 the commission of historians arrived at the result I had expected: Waldheim had known about what he denied knowing. He

had been in "consultative proximity" to war crimes, but he had not been personally involved in any way.

I thought that Waldheim would use this opportunity to resign without loss of face, for the sake of Austria: one cannot remain Federal President when one has been publicly proved to lack credibility – and it is the duty of every Federal President to serve his country. Waldheim's resignation would have done a service to Austria's international reputation. Yet Kurt Waldheim decided differently: he is willing to live in conflict with the truth. That induced me, on 9 February 1988 on Austrian television, to call on him to resign. Simultaneously I appealed to the intellectual elite of the country to draw their conclusions with regard to Waldheim. Not because he was a Nazi or a war criminal, but because he had shown himself unworthy of his office and of his responsibility.

A committee was formed which took up my appeal, and thousands of people, including the leading cultural figures and intellectuals in Austria, rallied every week in the Stephansplatz, the square around St. Stephen's Cathedral, to demand Waldheim's resignation. Opinion polls revealed that the percentage of those in favour of Waldheim's continuation in office had declined to less than forty. At this point the President of the WJC, Edgar Bronfman, went to Brussels to protest against Austria's admission to the EEC (European Economic Community). Since then the Waldheim supporters have again topped 50 percent and are increasing in number with every further statement made by the World Jewish Council on Austria.

Hilde Spiel

Hilde Spiel was born in Vienna in 1911 as the daughter of the scientist Hugo Spiel and his wife Marie, née Gutfeld. Her family was of Jewish origin, but fully assimilated. Both of her parents were baptized. Spiel was Roman Catholic by religion but not all of her immediate family members were. She grew up in an integrated cosmopolitan society, whose loss she mourned deeply. In 1936 she received a Doctor of Philosophy degree from the University of Vienna. The same year she married the writer Peter de Mendelssohn, with whom she moved to England, where the couple and their two children lived during the Nazi years. After 1945 Spiel made frequent visits to Vienna and in 1963 took up residence there. She is the author of several novels and numerous essays. Her novels include *Kati auf der Brücke* (1933; Kati on the bridge), *Sommer am Wolfgangsee* (1961; Summer on Lake Wolfgang), and *Lisas Zimmer* (1965; *The Darkened Room*). Spiel also wrote a biography of Sir Laurence Olivier. A cultural historian, she authored a biography of the German Jewish salonnière Fanny von Arnstein, entitled *Fanny von Arnstein, oder Die Emanzipation: Ein Frauenleben an der Zeitwende, 1758–1818* (1962; *Fanny von Arnstein: A Daughter of the Enlightenment, 1758–1818*). In 1933 Spiel was awarded the Julius Reich Prize. Only a few years later her books were outlawed under National Socialism. For her exceptional contribution to postwar Austrian and German culture Spiel was awarded an honorary professorship by the president of the Austrian Republic, and she received the Cross of Merit, First Class, from the Federal Republic of Germany. For her literary works she was honored with the Salzburg Critics Prize, the Austrian Cross for Arts and Literature, and the prize of the city of Vienna. After returning to Austria, Spiel wrote for the *New Statesman* and *Die Welt*. In 1971 she married her second husband, Hans Flesch Edler von Brunningen. Spiel died in Vienna in 1990. Although she was not blind to post-Shoah Austrian anti-Semitism and the widespread resentment against returning exiles, her love for Austria prevailed. It is documented in such essays as "Verliebt in Döbling: Die Dörfer unter dem Himmel" (1965; In love with Döbling: The villages under heaven).

Hilde Spiel

I Love Living in Austria

As far as I am concerned, none of this is a matter of distance, calculation, or cold judgment. The task at hand is to report about the most burning and private concerns – after all, what could be more burning than a wound not yet healed, what more private than the feeling of security, of belonging, of being at home, or the occasional lack of these.

In 1936 I went into exile because the Austrian right-wing Christian government made me nauseous, because I felt a constant pressure in my stomach, a slight buzzing in the solar plexus, and a continuous dizziness in my brain. That was not my world: peasantlike vainglory coupled with willingness to form pacts on all fronts, to pass the devil on the right, to sell out democracy rather than perishing with it. There was no freedom left, only a slovenly lack of freedom with many loopholes still open, none of which I wanted to take advantage of. I had the good fortune of having received my doctorate degree before membership in the Patriotic Front became a prerequisite for it. Not even my love for the streets in Vienna's suburbs, for the Tyrolian mountains, for the Salzburg meadows in summertime counterbalanced my disgust at the rooster feathers adorning the hats. Even Hans Habe, the friend of my youth, had taken to wearing them. I no longer wanted to see the boldly angular, and at the same time calflike, stormtrooper face and took off for London in October of the very year when the Hitler-Schuschnigg treaty was signed.

The events caught up with me. My native country, which could still be visited for the time being, was pulled out from under my feet. But I had not lived through the infernal April and the blissful merger of the almost-Nazis with the Third Reich, and I had not witnessed the horror of many an illegal Nazi Party member when their erstwhile, delusionary idealism crumbled in the face of the filthy reality into which their idea of the Third Reich had been transformed. I had no personal experience of the heinous humiliations at the hands of ruffians and street punks, of being completely at the mercy of wolves – *homo homini lupus* – of being pushed into the snake pit. But it sufficed to observe all that from a distance, knowing that my own parents were thrown into the cesspool. It sufficed to know that my delicate mother was uprooted and cast out, in spite of her passionate love for her country, her ancestral ties to Döbling, and her graceful walks through the Inner City, to know that my brave father was stripped of his courage and his pride, of his scientist's trust in reason, logic, and order.

The chasm had burst open, the ties had been cut. Torn from one's heart was everything once associated with the terms childhood, youth, religion, propriety, goodwill, intimacy with one's friends and neighbors. Enveloped by foreignness as if by a protective coat, one covered one's eyes to see no more of the atrocities committed by the dehumanized beings whose language one shared. Over and done with were the awakening into life, the first rhymes and songs, laburnum, hazelnut bushes, grapevines on the Nußberg, the "do go and have your ringlets combed." Then came the autumn of 1938 when the people of London were fitted for gas masks, then came the war and the winter and the blitz and the miracle weapons, and my own children sang: "Baa baa black sheep have you any wool," and they played on the beautiful, frequently watered and mowed lawn, while only a few kilometers away a V2 thundered through the sound barrier and blasted down on other English children.

How could all of that be possibly erased from the conscious mind even after the loathsome wizardry had been swallowed by the earth? "Am I an animal," Hofmannsthal's Elektra asks, "that I could forget?" Of course, I had not been split in two like my friend Garda on Thornton Road, a German countess married to a man from a great Jewish family from Berlin, who had followed him into exile. During every air raid she would think that her brother was sitting up there in his Messerschmidt airplane and let bombs rain down on her house. I had no siblings; my only uncle had fallen in Spain, my closest relatives were safe in England, my grandmother, a Christian by religion and a romantic, had disappeared in Theresienstadt. At the first possible occasion, in January 1946, I traveled to Vienna and was faced with a heart-rending reality, a degree of misery, disappointment, remorse, introspection, and ultimately relief that the aberration was over like Titania's dream, in spite of the starvation and the pressure imposed by the occupying forces. At any rate, it was enough to extinguish any desire for revenge on my part before it could arise and to fill me with compassion.

But should everything that had been valid for decades be rescinded? Could I transplant a family that had never been at home in Austria? To uproot children – the example of Garda a few years later was terrible enough. She and her husband, unflaggingly German, had taken their son and their daughter from the English schools to postwar Western Germany. The son complied – but ultimately he returned to Great Britain when he was grown up. The daughter, at a critical age, could not cope with her parents' changed point of view and the inexplicable transformation of the enemies into fellow citizens. She cried until she was sent to Switzerland to attend a boarding school. There, still perturbed about the break with her London childhood, she hanged herself from her bedpost. Who would risk having one's own child succumb to such a profound anguish of the soul, to such perplexity of the mind?

I lived in England until 1963. One evening many of my very close friends – some of them had stayed in Austria, some had returned – were having an informal gathering at the Viennese cellar bar "Linde." They were devoted to me like brothers and sisters, and they resolved that there had to be an end to exile. Should I really return? Only one of them, not a former exile, shook his head. He did not want to exclude the possibility that at some point I might come to harm again. He did not dare to vouch for his fellow citizens, because for seven years he had experienced them at an unspeakable moral low and in ambiguous, embarrassing, and distressing situations. I returned – under which circumstances, by giving up which relationships, and with which hesitations and second thoughts is irrelevant in this context. I came and regretted it only three times, in each instance for a brief moment. I knew very well that these incidents were mere obscurations, unable to cancel my decision, and that this decision had been correct despite everything.

Two instances involved superficial insults directed against me
by – I wonder why? – individuals in fine arts, one of them a painter.
After drinking his fill of wine, he began a diatribe against the returned exiles who usurped from those who had never left the country – and as a result had suffered much greater harm at the hands of
the Nazis – the support of those in power and grabbed the more
lucrative posts and honorary appointments. Although I was not one
of them, having waited almost two decades before I returned and
made my living abroad, I was deeply offended, because the attacker
had used as his example my noble friend, Franz Theodor Csokor.
The other incident involved a museum director, who, like the other
individual, was completely drunk. Under the guise of sympathy,
emphasizing his former willingness to oppose the Nazis, he did not
refrain from making anti-Semitic remarks. And, finally, in 1972, I
was faced with an intrigue so abominable and far reaching – it
involved betrayal by contemporaries of mine, some of whom had
been my friends – that I was distraught for a long time and yearned
for the integrity, the fairness, and the goodwill of the English people as if for a protective roof that I had abandoned all too carelessly
while the thunderstorm was still raging outside.

It passed. I love living in Austria, in Döbling, in my house by
the creek. I am in harmony with the city, the landscape, the music,
the literature, but not always and not under all circumstances with
the people. But who needs people, when one can breathe the air of a
gazebo in Heiligenstadt, listen to the touch of the strings at the
Vienna Philharmonic, socialize with Karl Bühl, with Genia Hofrei-
ter, with Editha Pastré, with the First Lieutenant Silverstolpe? They
continue to be closer to me, much closer, than the etched glass
panes of the London pubs that I love so much and the swishing of
the Thames where it is termed Isis under the oars of the students at
Oxford. They are even closer to me than Mrs. Ramsay in Virginia
Woolfe's most beautiful book, *To the Lighthouse.* They are closer to
me, because one cannot forever remove oneself from one's origin,
and that is the reason why I am at home here again and without
regret.

Hilde Spiel

Aura and Origin

In certain moments, during an evening at the Salzburg Mozarteum or at the Vienna Concert House, in the foyer, I sense it again and very closely: the breath, the fragrance, the aura of my childhood. During the war years and for a while still thereafter, before the hectic shapes of expressionism began to leave their marks also on everyday life, the architecture, the furnishings, the ladies' dresses, their jewelry, their lamps and vases were of a soothing simplicity reminiscent of the Biedermeier era. The voluptuous blossoms of the art nouveau had fallen. Modest wreaths and garlands decorating the walls remained; occasionally, as in the decor above the entrance door of the Café Bazar, they surrounded pudgy putti embracing one another, as they do in the ceramics of Wally Wieselthier.

Just as Otto Wagner had overcome historicism in his era by embracing Biedermeier harmonies, there was no trace left of the often monstrously gaudy decor à la Klimt in the Vienna Workshops (Wiener Werkstätten), whose utensils, prints, fabrics, china, and book covers continued to determine the taste of the time. In those two musical establishments, which to this day remain untouched by either art deco or functionalism or the Empire style of the Third Reich, the glass chandeliers of my young years are still hanging, and black or golden letters in the curved italic letters of my childhood books indicate the buffets and rest rooms. There, and only there, I feel as if transported back to the atmosphere and way of life of the late Francis-Josephinian era that came to an end with the shots fired in Sarajevo.

The armoires, beds, consoles, sewing tables, and chairs in my parents' bedroom were blond. The sizable clothes cabinets, restored to me in labyrinthine fashion after my return, stand in my basement in the Cottagegasse. Decorated with plain, fluted rails and brass fittings, they are rather austere and very spacious. The long dresses and suits that my mother wore until the early 1920s did not brush against the bottom of the armoire. There was enough room for her cambric undergarments replete with ribbons in the linen closet. I often sat bent over my homework at the little sewing table, while she took her afternoon nap. She considered the scraping of my pen a pleasant accompaniment for her slumber.

The remaining furnishings in our garden apartment in Heiligenstadt, where everything at all possible was painted or lacquered white, likewise showed the influence of Josef Hoffmann, whose designs served even third-rate manufacturers as a model at that time. I remember the dark stain of my father's desk, the easy chairs with flowery patterns. My mother's evening gown, her pointed gold-beetle shoes, tried to recapture a painting of which prints hung in many middle-class houses: a lady in an iridescent, green dress, listening to music with dreamlike abandon. I do not recall the painter.

My mother's maiden name was Marie Gutfeld. She came from a family that was paradigmatic of the development of an educated social stratum of Jewish background and of the latter's already accomplished passage into Vienna society. One of her ancestors, the earliest one of whom I have knowledge, was an educated man who had worked his way up to being the head of his community in the small town of Nikolsburg at the age of thirty-five. Soon thereafter he became the chief rabbi of Moravia. Markus Benedict had been born in 1753 in the Hungarian district of Somogy. He had studied at the feet of great scholars of the Talmud, first in Nikolsburg, then in Fürth, and finally in Prague before he began his ascent in the religious hierarchy.

I learned from a historical study that later in life he devoted himself to Hebrew grammar, to the major philosophical works of Moses Maimonides in particular, and the writings of Moses Mendelssohn. This "intellectual hero," as the historian Hugo Gold calls him, "did not disdain secular education despite his rigorous observance in all religious matters. He had very modern views and contrary to other prominent Talmudists of his time, he did not consider speaking and writing correct German forbidden. Characteristic of his commendable liberalism is the fact that in his draft of a curricu-

lum for candidates aspiring to the office of rabbi he submitted to
the government a proposal according to which the students would
not only undergo strict rabbinical training but those older than
eighteen would also have to be privately tutored in all high-school
subjects, including Latin and German, and take a public test in
order to study philosophy." It is also mentioned that "numerous
miracles, even supernatural powers were ascribed to him" and that
he was "worshiped like a saint" already in his lifetime.

Markus Benedict died in 1829 in the resort town of Karlsbad,
where he went every summer to take the waters. His son Jakob, who
was born six years before the turn of the century, moved to Vienna.
He seems to have settled there in the era preceding the revolution of
1848. One of his grandsons, my great-uncle Gustav Singer, a court
counselor, a head physician, and the director of the Vienna Rudolf
Hospital, was able to provide me with several additional pieces of
information about this Jakob, especially about his father, the il-
lustrious ancestor: "He was a trusted advisor of the greatly blessed
late Emperor Franz. An inscription in Hebrew letters on a rock
plateau in Karlsbad vis-à-vis Pupp commemorates his services.
Emperor Franz would meet him in Karlsbad on the promenade,
squeeze his hand, and take a short stroll with him. The relic was in
all likelihood destroyed by the Nazis. But I remember that when I
was with Archduke Eugen in Karlsbad for the first time I directed
his attention to this inscription. . . . I believe that for the sake of my
ancestors I advanced to some kind of chamberlain right then."

In the midst of World War II, in January 1941, I began writing a
novel about the final decades of the last century and asked my great-
uncle for family memoirs. His reply came from the country hotel
Selsdon Park. The former castle had become a luxurious resort for
the gentry, who hoped to escape the bomb attacks on English cities
in the rolling hills of the county of Surrey. "His Eminence," as my
father called him, the former personal physician of said Archduke
Eugen, but also of the sinister prelate Seipel, the long-time chancellor of the first Austrian Republic, lived in exile with the same ele-
gance and dignity that he had possessed as a luminary of the Vienna
medical school. Having converted many years ago and married a
Christian woman, he discussed his forefathers, whose faith and
way of life he had forsworn, with considerable pride in his letter.

"Grandfather Kopel B. was a respected Viennese citizen, who founded a large silk business. He was primarily a scholar of Scripture and famous for his succinct and insightful statements, a man of exemplary conduct who strictly upheld the highest business ethics and standards. Aside from the auspicious times he owed the success of his house in particular to the diligence and cooperation of his wife Luise (Deborah). In her youth she had been a very beautiful, exceptionally intelligent and energetic woman, who spent her life between office desk and childbed. In spite of her many children she managed the administrative part of the business, hired and supervised the employees, and undertook business trips." For a woman to be so actively involved, my great-uncle wrote, "was highly uncommon at that time – the middle of the last century."

"Nonetheless," he added, "this woman, who spoke High German, was very educated and well-read and had a circle of friends, especially among politicians; she was a brilliant housewife (her cuisine was exquisite and famous) and provided her many children with a modern education. She engaged excellent tutors, French and later English governesses, and paid a great deal of attention to physical education. All of her children were excellent in gymnastics, ice skating, swimming, and dancing; my own mother was a renowned swimmer and jumper. They lived in a huge, old patrician house (located in Wieden, in the Pressgasse), and the spirit pervading that house was one of traditional Viennese lightheartedness. . . . With my grandfather I associate the memory of a magnificent clock collection and a drawer filled with beautiful golden tobacco boxes. My grandmother took snuff also and had a valuable lace collection. Overall, the family gave an impression of cosy, idyllic dignity."

As for that swimmer and jumper, my great-grandmother, I still knew her. She was one of the nine daughters to whom Luise Deborah had given birth. Their names – Netti, Kathi, Fanny, Fevi, Tini, Gini, Rosy, Pauly, Eugenie – have been preserved, those of their six brothers and of the five siblings of the altogether twenty who died in early childhood have not. Fanny, whose married name was Singer, lived in Döbling when she was a widow, the preferred district of the relatives on my mother's side. In her old age she lived in Baden by Vienna at the Hotel Elisabeth. My mother took me there on the Baden tram for family reunions. It was a peaceful trip, even during wartime, but the drunken men made it less safe on the way back. In the well-equipped hotel room the matron, a small bonnet on her head, held court. She was surrounded by her descendents and had coffee and pastry served. The joker among them was Leo, an attorney. He inspired her again and again to a rejuvenating laughter. Prior to her death she neither had a presentiment that two of her sons, Gustav and Leo, would climb the ladder of success and become court counselors and authorities in their field, nor that they would – at least until Hitler's invasion – be completely absorbed into the Christian faith.

She had married her daughters off in good time, thereby delaying a similar absorption into the larger society for a generation. Irene married a man in Budapest and moved there. Melanie, my mother's mother, was not married to the coal baron Gutmann, as initially contemplated, but had to settle for a man without fortune by the name of Adolf Gutfeld. The union ended in disaster. After the wedding night at the Grand Hotel she ran away. She was sent back to him by her parents, and she resigned herself. Occasionally she cheated on him, for example, with the captain of the side-wheeler *Franz Josef I* on Lake Wolfgang. She separated from him as soon as the children, Marie and Felix, had come of age. A romantic at heart, she loved pink and light blue ribbons, played Schumann and Chopin on the piano, and protected all those art nouveau knick-knacks we detested and advised her to throw away. Left without means, she subsisted on the support grudgingly granted her by "His Eminence" and some small earnings of her own. Throughout her sad life she nonetheless often displayed a good sense of humor.

My mother left the house early. Felix, after a long time as a prisoner of war in Russia, much longer than the end of the war, finally completed his doctorate in law. Yet, he was unable to find a position as a junior attorney and continued living in a small room in the apartment where he had grown up. He read, wrote, and brooded, then he turned to Socialism and went on a search for truth, worldly, religious, and cosmic. "Since my seventeenth year," he confessed to his friend Otto prior to an unsuccessful suicide attempt in 1925, "I have constantly and untiringly been preoccupied with attempts to construct my own view of the world." He immersed himself in many problems, some of a rhetorical nature, "by

studying eagerly and in depth Jesaias Deutero, Demosthenes, and
Cicero, as well as the speeches of Bossuet, Bourdaloue, and Mira-
beau, Pitt, Burke, Macaulay, Brougham, and Lassalle, among others, and allowing them to make an impact on me." In the Russian
camp he authored a "Treatise about the Nature of Rhetoric, on the
Theatric, on the Tragic, Romanticism, and Decadence." He wanted
to design a philosophically based theory of art for which he intended the term "phenomenological aesthetic."

It was a coincidence that his twenty-four-page essay addressed to
a friend whom I did not know was not lost. It is a heart-wrenching
document showing unused talent, unproductive profundity of
thought, high-flown and never realized ideas. All the lectures he
presented while still in Russia after he had been drawn into the
rapids of the revolution – 1919 in Irkutsk-Ratarejnaja, and later in
Omsk and Moscow – and a later one in Vienna on the topic "Spar-
tacus or Gracchus? Revolutionary Mass Movements in Ancient
Rome" given at an executive meeting of the Communist faction
Döbling in approximately 1923, all, he says, "bombed." All these
and his poetry translations "from Greek, Latin, French, English,
Hungarian, and Middle High German originals" are gone, perished
in the maelstrom of the 1920s, the hunger years.

A quiet, pale man, he visited us occasionally for half an hour, as
long as his transit ticket for the tram allowed him. He presented me
with a poetry volume, perhaps one by Villon, stroked my cheek, and
was already leaving. In October 1935 the right-wing Catholic government imprisoned him for six weeks at the detention camp
Wöllersdorf. By the end of the following year – I was already in
England – he disappeared forever. He had confided to someone that
he had to "seek God in Spain." He was killed as a medical orderly in
the Spanish civil war on 20 February 1937 at the Jamara, a river
near Madrid.

My mother, a beautiful girl of dark complexion, remained un-
affected by such turmoil of the soul and the times. From her ancestors she had inherited a cheerful disposition, good taste, musical
talent, and a certain dreamy nonchalance that occasionally, but not
in her case, is coupled with or precedes contemplative introspection. Contrary to her brother, she was easygoing as long as fate did
not harm her. She was deeply attached to Vienna and longed for her

city on every trip, every vacation. She had a delicate nose, a delicate mouth. Her friends called her Mizzi; this name, reminiscent of Schnitzler, fit her mentality. My father called her Mimi, as I later did as well.

When she met my father, she conformed to his propensities without opposition. His propensities included: natural science, alpine tourism, music, especially Wagner and Schubert, and his "Couleur" friends, the members of a liberal fraternity. Although she merely respected his knowledge and his personally enriching pursuits in chemistry and technology without taking part in them, and although she did not join him climbing the Dachstein but only climbed the more moderate alpine mountain tops with him, she did follow him up to the fourth gallery of the Imperial Opera and to the evenings of the Suevia [university fraternity] whenever ladies were admitted.

One has to imagine my father to be an athletic man of average height and a courageous face with two deep cuts on his chin, dating back to youthful fraternity duels. He was capable of unspeakably tender emotions toward human beings, animals, and music, but also of outbursts of rage and real violence, for example, when a woman was in need of protection against a ruffian. Prior to my birth he had fought a pistol duel. On his honeymoon he almost drowned in a turbulence in the Danube River in front of my mother's eyes. On his Alpine mountain tours he always strayed from the marked path and saved himself from taking serious falls through daredevil maneuvers. A fraternity student whom later the uniform of an Imperial and Royal reserve officer would fit like a glove; at the same time an intellectual, a researcher, and an inventor who spent days and nights experimenting and evaluating, recording the results in his meticulous small handwriting; a man driven by the thirst for knowledge but at the same time a man of action, no less aware of his physical than his intellectual potential. His "fraternity cuts," which at first sight gave him the appearance of a fire-eater, later saved him from undeserved shame.

But he too was exposed to the shame of his descent when certain Viennese began to be distinguished from other Viennese. To be sure, it cannot be easily explained how a man like him had descended from his particular ancestors – among other things, too little is known about them. He and his sister Leonie were definitely not related to a certain Georg Heinrich Gerhard Spiel who in 1819 published a Patriotic Archive of the Kingdom of Hanover. Neither were they related to the families of the few persons in his native city who carry this name today, among them advertising consultants and police officers, but also doctors and eminent psychologists.

Three photographs from the estate of Aunt Lonny – pronounced "Loni" – yield little information. One of them, taken in Vienna in 1897, shows an elegant gentleman with a blond or whitish moustache, dressed in city furs and a top hat: my great-grandfather Spiel when he was sixty-three years of age. In a second photo, taken at Lake Hallstatt in September 1916, one sees his son, my grandfather Jacques, next to his wife Laura and his daughter Lonny in a long dirndl dress, posing before the background of a little village. Two months before his death his roundish face with the dark moustache appears relaxed. In his hands he holds the butt of a Virginia cigar; the plaid cap in conjunction with the city suit emphasize the sojourn in the country.

That's all. Where did they come from, these Spiels, what was their bourgeois existence based on? I don't know. Grandfather Jacques imported lace and other accessories from Paris and traveled there frequently, that much could be ascertained. That may be origin of the French form of his first name, which is given in his baptismal certificate as "Jakob." Presumably this branch of the family too had resided in Vienna for quite some time. My grandmother Laura is the only one who came from the east, even if it is impossible to establish exactly from where. My father, who was not happy to admit this fact, nonetheless told us occasionally that at the estate of his grandfather on his mother's side he had traveled in coaches and ridden horses when he was a little boy. Apparently they had been well-to-do, living on their own country estate. When I read the memoirs of Salka Viertel, in which she describes her childhood as the daughter of a major landowner in Wychylowka in Galicia, I was reminded of my father's scattered memories, which he hesitated to share.

The family in eastern Europe was named Birnbaum. The name sounds better when one substitutes its Sephardic form, Pereira. Could it be that in the distant past their wanderings had taken them there from Portugal? Clearly, all this lies at the bottom of forgotten memory. A third photograph, yellowed by age, conjures up my grandmother's brother, Heinrich, about whom only three facts are known: he was a doctor, he was homosexual, and he took his own life. In the picture he looks cheerful. He sits in a coffee house, reading the paper. He too does not show the characteristics that people of his background supposedly possess: he could be a department head in the ministry of traffic who is reading a report about the opening of a new railroad line in the Crown Province of Croatia.

No one in my family with whom I had any personal acquaintance was noticeably religious. As a child I did not know that the faith of my forefathers had not been the same as mine. My father had become a Catholic, perhaps when he was a student. My mother, whose two uncles had already converted, followed suit without any fuss. They had a church wedding only a few months before I was born – I cannot deny it. "His Eminence," being the head of my mother's clan, opposed the marriage of his twenty-year-old niece to a doctor of chemistry and technical science who had just recently completed his degree and, moreover, seemed to have seduced her. When this became obvious, the wedding took place.

I grew up with the other children in the Heiligenstadt elementary school, accustomed to the sequence of Christian holidays; I went to the Nativity display, took First Communion, attended the May services and the Corpus Christi processions. But there was one thing I did not understand. When I took a walk in the Inner City with my grandmother Laura, it seemed to bother her that I made the sign of the cross in front of each of the many churches. If that was necessary, she asked me once. Yes, of course, why not? After that she rested her case.

Jean Améry

Jean Améry (Hans Maier; Jewish name Chaim
Wiener; pseudonyms Johannes or Hanns Mayer,
Peter Frühwirth) was born in Vienna in 1912 to an
assimilated Austrian-Jewish father and a Gentile Austrian mother. He grew up in the Catholic tradition in
the famous imperial summer resort of Bad Ischl in
rural Austria. After his father's death in World War I,
his mother became an innkeeper. Améry financed his
studies of philosophy and literature at the University
of Vienna by doing odd jobs. The passing of the 1935
Nuremberg Laws marked the beginning of Améry's
lifelong intellectual struggle with his Jewishness and
anti-Semitism. His treatises on the issues of violence, torture, and human rights are informed by his
concentration-camp experiences at Gurs, Auschwitz,
Buchenwald, and Bergen-Belsen, where he was
incarcerated as a political prisoner and eventually
identified as a Jew. After the liberation Améry's major
topics were the Shoah, its legacy in German-
speaking countries, and leftist anti-Semitism. Améry's critical approach is influenced by existentialism.
Améry moved back to Belgium, his country of exile,
and he and his wife, Maria, lived in Brussels. In 1978,
six months after a lecture tour in Germany, Jean Améry, who had on different occasions written about
suicide as an act of free choice, took his own life in a
Salzburg hotel room. Améry wrote philosophical
treatises and essays, many of them translated into
English, including *Jenseits von Schuld und Sühne* (1980;
At the Mind's Limits), *Der integrale Humanismus* (1985),
Radical Humanism (1984), *Preface to the Future: Culture in
a Consumer Society* (1964); fiction, *Lefeu oder der Abbruch*
(1974), and an autobiographical work, *Unmeisterliche
Wanderjahre* (1985; Apprenticeship and travels unlike
Wilhelm Meister).

Jean Améry

Antisemitism on the Left –
The Respectable Antisemitism

This essay was originally delivered as an address ("Respectable Antisemitism") on March 7, 1976, in Hamburg, at the opening session of Brotherhood Week, an interfaith event sponsored annually since 1951 by the Gesellschaft für Christlich-Jüdische Zusammenarbeit (Society for Christian-Jewish Cooperation).

It is not a happy moment at which I appear before you to offer my thoughts on the Jewish Problem. It evidently exists once again and, indeed, on an international scale. It's "Brotherhood Week." But where are the brothers? If I were cynical enough, I would quote the American mathematician and chansonnier Tom Lehrer, who already years ago on the occasion of the American "Brotherhood Week" sang: "And the Catholics hate the Protestants and the Protestants hate the Catholics and the Moslems hate the Hindus – and everybody hates the Jews."

   Of course, we are still far from a general hatred of the Jews as an ethnic group and religious community; fortunately so, even if we are perhaps not so far from it as optimists assume. Only one thing is already certain: there is a general uneasiness regarding the Jews. One is beginning to feel disturbing reservations, especially among people who only ten years ago tried one's patience with their philosemitic pretenses. Antisemitism has a collective infrastructure that is historically and psychologically deeply imbedded. If it is again becoming a reality today, three decades after the discovery of what was done by the Nazis, then this has to do not only with time, which silently and steadily erodes ethical indignation, but also, indeed probably first and foremost, with the situation in the Near

East. It is very dismaying that before our incredulous eyes young people, and particularly those who in the broadest sense of the term regard themselves as socialists, are reviving the age-old phenomenon we had believed was long since dead. We know it from the debate now in progress within the Second International, which traditionally has been well disposed toward the Jews and pro-Israel. The young socialists, to whom the Palestinians now appear as the freedom fighters and the Israelis as the imperialist opponents, are insisting that the Second International disassociate itself from Israel. For the Third International the question doesn't arise anyway. For it, Israel is an imperialist, cancerous growth and the Jews in general are accomplices of the permanent capitalist conspiracy. The *Führer*, the USSR, commanded and one obeyed.

To be sure, there will be objections that Israel has nothing to do with the Jewish Problem in the broader sense. *One is not antisemitic, but anti-Israel.* It is easy to reply to this objection, all too easy. At this point, please permit me to quote the Germanist Hans Mayer, a man of thorough Marxist schooling. This author writes in his noteworthy book *Aussenseiter* (*Outsiders*):

Whoever attacks Zionism, but by no means wishes to say anything against the Jews, is fooling himself or others. The State of Israel is a Jewish state. Whoever wants to destroy it, openly or through policies that can effect nothing else but such destruction, is practicing the Jew-hatred of yesterday and time immemorial. How clearly this can be observed in the interplay of foreign and domestic politics is shown by the internal policies of the currently anti-Zionist countries. Internally, they will regard their Jewish citizens as virtual "Zionists" and treat them accordingly.

To what extent anti-Zionism makes use of the traditional antisemitic or anti-Jewish phantasms became clear to me recently while I was reading the French newspaper *Le Monde*, which I do daily. Its special correspondent for the Near East, Michel Tatu, cited a photo volume published by the Egyptian government on the second anniversary of the October War; its text says literally: "In no army of the world are Jews desired . . . because for them money is always more important than principles. . . . Usurers are not fighters." Don't laugh at the fact that his is the voice of a country that in October 1973 was saved *in extremis* by America's pressure on Israel. Rather listen further. The journalist adds that this is a relatively moderate attack, that in the "more hawkish" Arab countries, Syria, Iraq, Algeria, one hears a still quite different tone. There is not need to insist that this sort of thing has nothing in common with – unfortunately "normal" – territorial conflicts between sovereign states such as, for example, the conflict between Algeria and Morocco. It is unadulterated Streicher. It is the most scandalous and, besides, the most stupid antisemitism. But in stating this, we must unfortunately take note of the fact that what is both base and stupid has triumphed more than once in the course of world history, and that there is no relying in the least on Professor Georg Wilhelm Friedrich Hegel.

It is with this outrageous and stupid antisemitism, to the extent that it passes itself off merely as anti-Zionism, that young people are joining forces. Not just a few Nazi offspring of incorrigible parents or grandparents – but alleged socialists. And no one is opposing them with the necessary vigor. On the contrary, the bourgeoisie, whether German, French, or Belgian, breathes a sigh of relief that for once it can march along in the same step with the young generation, which it otherwise regards as a nuisance and whose antiauthoritarian outbursts get on its nerves. Entirely aside from its traditional, dormant antisemitism, this bourgeoisie has its special interests too, which now coincide most exactly and in a comforting way with the thoughtless antisemitism of the young, who often have yet to see a Jew face to face. These bourgeois are interested in business deals: in oil and other things. One must make haste in order to "get in on a good deal," as they put it. *Les affaires sont les affaires.*

Those multinational corporations that in all Western democracies are ready to accede to the Arab boycott demands for the sake of business know this very well. And they are happy at the thought that they, too, for a change, are moving in the direction of the objective spirit – providing that they have ever heard of it. In this way, antisemitism is becoming what it has not been and could not be since the discovery of the Nazi horrors: respectable.

One must concede, to be sure, that antisemitism as such would perhaps not have gained this respectability if there were really not a very deep tie and, if you will excuse the worn-out word, *existential* bond between every Jew and the State of Israel. I say "every Jew," and immediately draw a line; for naturally there are a few self-hating Jews on call everywhere who are prepared to deny this solidarity, which applies to them, too, for the sake of some ideological phantasm or for reasons of both an illusory and a suicidal "objectivity."

Aside from these special cases, who are more to be pitied than censured, the Jews feel bound to the fortunes and misfortunes of Israel, whether they are religious Jews or not, whether they adhere to Zionism or reject it, whether they are newly arrived in their host countries or deeply rooted there. I gladly offer my own person as a not entirely untypical example. I never belonged to the Jewish religious community; I was raised as a Catholic; I have no relatives at all in Israel and soon I will see the country for the first time in my life; I stem from an old Vorarlberg family; my cultural homeland once was Germany; today it is France; for the last thirty-eight years I have been living in Belgium. And yet to the extent that I am interested at all in the national existence and independence of a community, it is Israel.

All this, of course, has nothing to do with any sort of abstruse myths of blood and race. It is very simply that the existence of a Jewish state has taught all the Jews of the world to walk with their head high once more – a Jewish state whose inhabitants are not only merchants but also farmers, not only intellectuals but also professional soldiers, and not those "usurers" that the new Egypt is blathering about, despite all the empirical evidence, but rather, in their majority, craftsmen, industrial and agricultural proletarians. Some Jews had thought that in the socialist societies they would be able to walk upright as a matter of course. The Soviet Union and its vassal countries have done everything imaginable to cure them of their Marxism-Leninism. For there is no more evident example than the fate of Leopold Trepper, the leader of the spy network "The Red Orchestra," who had been truly a totally convinced Marxist, and who in the end, driven from his Polish homeland, found refuge in Israel.

When I speak of refuge, I am employing still another key word. For more is at stake for the Jews than just to walk upright. Israel is not only the country in which the Jew no longer permits his enemy to stamp him with a self-image, as Sartre understood it; it is also the virtual shelter for all of the insulted and injured Jews of the earth. Think only of the Jews in the Soviet Union and other Eastern bloc countries, for whom an exit visa to Israel is the last hope of leading a life in dignity and decency. I expressly say: Israel is a *virtual hope*. If these Soviet Jews were to attain full, and no longer insultingly restricted, Soviet citizenship, probably only a small percentage of them would want to emigrate to Israel – just as today there are but few American Jews who are pressing into that Mediterranean country described by Thomas Mann as "dusty and stony." But the virtuality is what counts. If ever somewhere in the world a grim fool should turn up whose *idée fixe* it might be to expel the Jews, the possibility of finding the shelter in Israel that, in Hitler's time – thanks to British Mandate policies – was granted to relatively few Jews, binds every Jew to the fate of this tiny polity in the Near East.

I'd like to see them just once in the face of threat from a new Hitler – Messrs. Maxime Rodinson, Ernest Mandel, Eric Rouleau – all of them Jewish by birth, ideologically alienated, anti-Israel Jews! In lamentable fashion they would haunt the waiting rooms of Israeli consulates in order to secure the piece of paper that would save them, and they wouldn't give a damn about Marx's antisemitic aberrations, which at the moment are still sacred texts to them.

So much for what I have called the existential tie of all Jews to the State of Israel, and this has nothing, absolutely nothing, to do with nationalistic or religious mysticism, which is always only mystification. I am talking about very real, political, social, and psychological facts. And already I hear the objections, and the questions: "And the Arabs? And their state? And their national dignity?" They are raised justifiably and demand an answer.

I am no specialist on Middle East questions and no better versed in the history of Zionism than any newspaper reader. But my scant knowledge suffices completely for making a few observations that must be just as obvious to common sense as to those experts who are not ideologically twisted. The Palestinians, who did not exist as a nation when the first Zionist immigrants set foot on the soil of present-day Israel, but who in our time are in the phase of becoming a nation, have a right to a state of their own. The Arabs who inhabited Israeli territory within its borders prior to the Six Day War have a right not to be treated as second-class citizens. I have already said on another occasion that in this entire conflict *right opposes right.*

It must be borne in mind, however, that the rights of the Palestinians – those who are now living within the area that became the State of Israel in 1948 and those who were driven from their homesteads by the wars (for which their fellow Arabs, after all, were not so entirely without blame) – the rights of these Palestinian Arabs in principle can be satisfied without insuperable difficulties. What is expected of the one group? That they be loyal citizens of Israel. What is demanded of the others? That once and for all they clearly acknowledge the fact of the Jewish national state. The rest is of a purely technical nature and can therefore be overcome with some intelligence and good will.

And finally, what is expected of a public opinion that, from the far right to the far left, is ready to condemn Israel in the name of national identities and the right to peoples' self-determination? Nothing more than the recognition of the obvious fact that the much-maligned Zionism is also a national liberation movement, that the Jews, too, the most martyred, most tragic people in the world, have right to their national identity – insofar as they are searching for one and have not already assimilated religiously and ethnically to their host peoples. For that is certainly also a solution, but one that always requires two groups of participants: the ones who are assimilating and the ones who are prepared for their absorption.

All this is terribly banal. But it is nonetheless true since, after all – contrary to a distorted tenet of Adorno's holding that the banal cannot be true – it is always true, for otherwise it could not have become a banality. I repeat: in the Near East conflict *one right opposes another.* And I add: *danger, however, does not oppose danger of the same order.* The fact is that the Arab nations – from the Saudi Arabian despot who is spreading the *Protocols of the Elders of Zion* to the religiously possessed Qaddafi down to the "moderate," pro-Western Sadat and the self-styled Marxist Habash – are all determined to wipe out the State of Israel, as a Herr Göring once wanted to wipe out the cities of England. And it is another incontrovertible fact that in the whole world there is no one who will sound the alarm before a new genocide is set into motion. Really no one? Of course, that isn't entirely true. There are, for example, such personalities as Jean-Paul Sartre and Simone de Beauvoir, known everywhere to be lackeys of imperialism, who protested against the shameless UN and UNESCO decisions. These two and a handful of others. But they have no power. Wherever there is power – from the White House in Washington to the Palais d'Elysée, to Downing Street, or the Kremlin (where they have long ago suppressed the fact that it was mainly Jews who stamped the Motherland of the World's Workers out of the ground of old Russia) – there is the readiness, paraphrasing the matter more or less diplomatically, to defend the "right of the Arabs," which can be quantified in Petrodollars, and to sell the right of the Jews, which is the eternal nonright of the poor, for a few pieces of silver.

This kind of *Realpolitik* – in French one says "La réalpolitik" when speaking of vile opportunism – seeps, uncheckably and constantly, into the lifeblood of what is called public opinion, which, as we know from sociological studies, consists of nothing but opinions about opinions. And we can regard as characteristic of this change in public opinion (not too long ago still favorable to Israel) the behavior of the Christian religious bodies, and especially that of the Vatican. In February 1976, during an Islamic-Christian colloquium – convening, of all places, in Qaddafi's Tripoli – Vatican representatives, first with hesitation but in the end submissively, signed a general condemnation of Israel in which Zionism was once again stigmatized as racism. And in a special reference to Jerusalem it stated: "The Islamic character of Jerusalem is a fact. . . . Judaizing of the city is as much to be avoided as the division and internationalization of the Holy City." One thought one was dreaming: the nightmare of a joint Crescent-and-Cross crusade against Jewry! Surely, the Vatican later disassociated itself from this document that its representatives had, so inconceivably, countersigned. It went even beyond that: at a meeting between Catholic and Jewish theologians in Jerusalem, Rome assumed a position of an almost pro-Israel character.

Nonetheless, the Tripoli colloquium did not vanish from the collective consciousness. Nor does the Vatican's later pro-Israel position disavow what a Moslem participant in Tripoli had assured Western journalists in a private conversation: "The Vatican is isolated," the man had said; "it desperately needs the good will of the Moslem world with it vast population and power."

It actually is the fascination with power that produced this change in the political climate. Nobody wants to swim against the tide, something that everyone knows is quite strenuous. Only few dare to stand by what yesterday was self-evident but now suddenly causes displeasure. Only a while ago it was natural to support the Israelis' right to their sovereignty; and now one suddenly catches oneself feeling that such a declaration has become a real test of courage and that, perhaps, it will become an offense tomorrow. From the political officeholder to the cautious journalist down to the man holding forth on politics on the street corner – everyone looks about expectantly, as though wanting to ask: What and how much is actually permitted again? Whoever has some insight and a bit of flair for recognizing the fluctuations of the forever fluctuating, will be inclined to assure these impatient people that, in fact, a good deal is not only permitted but called for. Wiseacres speak with relief of breaking a taboo, and have no inkling of the dark powers to which they are lending their voices.

The point is, however (and now I return to the subject that I have taken on here), that all this – I mean: the self-alienation of the Left, the interests of international high finance and of the political powers, the maliciousness of the rulers, and the effusive exaltation of the subjected and dispossessed – all this has its effects on the world, in which, today as yesterday, the Jew will be burned. Such is the will of "sound popular instinct" in Harlem (New York), at the regular beer round in some Fürth or another, in the Café de Commerce in Dijon, or in some tiny town in Kent – and, naturally, all the more in every Arab bazaar.

Permit me now to open a parenthesis. In the familiar argumentation of the friends of the Arab cause it is routinely pointed out that in the world of Islam, in contrast to the Christian world, the Jews had always lived together with the Arabs peacefully and by mutual consent. That this was by no means so has been proven most irrefutably in an excellently documented book by Albert Memmi, a Tunisian Jew living in France, a man, moreover, who had always supported the Arabs when they were under French domination in North Africa.

Antisemitism or anti-Judaism was always a matter of course for the Moslems. In the territory of Islamic rule the Jews were and always remained second-class citizens, and where they worked their way up, as in Moorish Spain, their situation was always precarious. In the most favorable instances they were tolerated, but they were never accepted. That has not changed. While it is possible in Israel for a politician who is a Communist and, at the same time, an Arab nationalist to become the mayor of a city, the few Jews who still live in Syria or Iraq or even in supposedly modern Tunisia (where they may be no less indigenous than their Arab oppressors) eke out their existence amidst constant humiliation and threat. The Christian world is as little concerned with their fate as with that of the Soviet Jews, for whom not only the road of total assimilation is blocked but also the flight to a land that even under the most difficult economic conditions must appear to them as the "Promised" one.

Existentialist-positivist and stubborn atheist that I am, it doesn't occur to me to convert the Jewish fate into a metaphysical phenomenon. In my eyes the Jews are as little a chosen people as an accursed one. They are nothing but the chance result of historical constellations that were unfavorable to them for two thousand years. Two millennia: that is a very tiny span of time in the unrecordable history of the human species. I can well imagine that a man of the stamp of a Lévi-Strauss, who is occupied with prehistoric societies and their structural myths, smiles gently and a bit scornfully at what are for him such microtemporal courses of events. This member of the Académie Française would cease smiling only if there were a rude knock at his door and a harsh voice, no matter in what language, commanded him, the Jew, to open immediately and come along. To lull himself into a false sense of security would be quite wrong. As we all know, a man of a still greater stature – Henri Bergson – was forced to wear the Yellow Star of David before a kind death saved him from the very worst.

No, the Jews and their historical existence are not a metaphysical phenomenon. They are, as I just said, more the victims of chance than of necessity – and also of that *indolence of the heart*, which in the Middle Ages plunged the peasant and in the heyday of capitalism the proletarian into unspeakable misery. Indolence of the heart: I choose to employ this old-fashioned formula. For it summarizes the factual situation better than the most sophisticated sociopsychological studies. The older ones among you may still have witnessed how, in the Third Reich, due to indolence of heart people quickly grew accustomed to their Jewish neighbor being fetched at night and deported.

Today everyone can observe how indolent hearts accommodate themselves when the world everywhere, be it the capitalist or the socialist one, is isolating the Israelis and the Jews who are one with them and thereby abandoning them to the catastrophe that is already hovering over their heads like a storm cloud.

In no time, the Near East question will become a new Jewish question. And we know from history how such a question is answered. The disassociation from Israel and with it from every individual Jew, as cautious as it is clear, hardly surprises the expert on indolent hearts. The millions of Jewish burnt offerings – oh, perhaps they were really "only" five million or even four, and not six million – have been paid off. And now let these eternal troublemakers be quiet; people have other worries; crisis, inflation, unemployment, energy problems. The wretch was led to his fall; suffering will overtake him and, like once Pontius Pilate did, the world will wash its hands of him.

Antisemitism, in the guise of anti-Zionism, has become respectable. I won't elaborate on its roots here. Everyone knows them; enough research has been done on the subject. I will merely state what many newspaper articles, especially in France, have made clear to me. With an indolent heart, people act as if they know nothing of the existential tie of Diaspora Jews to Israel. Obtusely, they do not want to recognize that this union of despair is not whimsical folly, but that it merely expresses the plain fact that burnt child, the Jew, knows in the depth of his heart where, and where alone, is the aid station willing to tend his burns.

The respectable antisemite has an enviably clear conscience, a spirit as calm as the sea. He also feels in agreement with historical developments, and this is conducive to his moral tranquility. If, occasionally, he awakens from his apathetic drowsing, he asks the ritual questions: Is Israel not an expansionist state, an imperialist outpost? Has not Israel itself caused the trouble that is besetting it from all sides with the "immobility" of its policies? Does not the very idea of Zionism bear in it the original sin of colonialism, so that every Jew who avows solidarity with this land becomes personally guilty? It hardly pays to discuss such questions. After all, Israel's expansion was the result of the bellicose Arab fanaticism that already in 1948 promised the Jews nothing more than to "throw them into the sea." Jewish colonialism was not a colonialism of conquest. The word itself, both etymologically and politically, derives from the Latin *colonus* – farmer. Israel's "immobility" can be explained when we consider the situation of someone who is standing with his back to the wall. This person is not immobile, but a priori immobilized.

All this does not mean that I am unaware of the errors of Israeli policies. But I know, still deeper and more precisely, that Israel's errors are in ridiculous disproportion to the indifference of the others who are motivated entirely by *Realpolitik*, the Russians and the English, the French and the Germans, and tomorrow very likely the Americans – not to speak of the Arabs, who become incomprehensible when at the great feast of their nationhood (which I heartily grant them), they seem compelled to present the Jews as a burnt offering. Human sacrifices without end.

But one is used to such sacrifices, especially when Jews are concerned. The sacrifice of the Jews is in the best tradition, a sanctified custom. One cannot prevail against it. What good then is Brotherhood Week, for which we have gathered here? I admit my pessimism. But since I am not only a born pessimist but by temperament an enlightener, and since, in addition, my home has been situated rather far to the left on the political map my whole life long, I don't wish to shrink from directing a few words to my friends from the leftist camp. The Right would hardly respond to me anyhow. For even where it makes out to be genuinely pro-Israel, it inspires me with skepticism.

Certainly, there is more than one righteous, conservative man – perhaps he is even a former National Socialist – who is earnest about his friendship for the Jews and the State of Israel; and his motivation may have nothing to do with personal relief from guilt but rather with an insight into the facts. This must be expressly stated. Yet, as a mouthpiece of the social class that the Right represents and of the tradition that it upholds and the political heritage that it transmits, it cannot possibly attain that unbiased, humane attitude toward the Jews, which is the only acceptable one. It would be entirely wrong to grant an advance in trust to those circles that a few decades ago were financing Hitler. For them Israel and the Jewish fate are only a welcome argument against everything that dares to question the existing social order. For the Right, let us not forget, stands for order.

But the Jews, and also the Israeli Jews, yes, especially they, are an element of creative disorder. Jews were present wherever fossilized structures were broken up: in Germany, starting with the "Young Germany" movement to the treatises of the Frankfurt School; in France, as members of the Popular Front, later as disciples of Sartre, and later still as structuralists; in the United States they are at the center of the liberal movements. And, concerning the Middle East, it was, without a doubt, the Jewish settlers in Palestine, with their attempt to create a democratic socialist society, who awoke the Arab nations from their centuries-long, deep feudal slumber. I ask the Left to consider all this; for although it may have been led astray it is by nature generous. The progeny of Heine and Börne, of Marx and Rosa Luxemburg, of Erich Mühsam and Gustav Landauer cannot, dare not be the ones to spread this respectable antisemitism. For this rabid anti-Zionism will inevitably lead to antisemitism, and for every Jew, no matter where he lives and what political persuasion he adheres to, it is a mortal threat.

I am not exaggerating. With just a bit of imagination everyone can picture what would happen if Israel were destroyed. The surviving Israelis, having once more become mythic Wandering Jews, would flee from the site of the prophet Mohammed and pour out into the world. And again the world would behave as it did after 1933, when such underpopulated countries as Canada and Australia shut their doors to the Jews as though they were bearing germs of pestilence. Again Jews would be forced to earn their living by dubious and illicit work, through obscure financial transactions. For they would not even be acceptable as "guest workers," in times of crisis less than ever before. Once more the public would be concerned with the very old "Jewish Question" – which, if we believe Sartre, never was that but rather always a question of antisemites.

No United Nations refugee committee then would be able to invest the Jews with normal civil rights. Anti-Zionism would be dead, all right. But crude antisemitism, aroused from the deepest layers of the collective unconscious and revitalized, would once again create a myth as a result of a historical chance constellation, the myth of the Wandering Jew, of Shylock.

All this however, would have a twofold result, of which we must urgently be forewarned even now, for time is running out: this twofold result is the total damnation of a human community and also the self-destruction process of what yesterday was still the Left. At this very moment, the process is in motion. We are already witnessing how political groups that regard themselves as "leftist" don't waste a word when a despot and paranoid in Uganda commits abominable murders; how they do not protest when the absolute ruler of Libya enacts laws under which adulterous women are stoned; how they are discreetly silent when in Algeria not a single one of the Revolution's great *chefs historiques* any longer appears on the scene. Ben Bella? He merely exchanged the prisons of the French fascist officer for those of the "socialist" Boumedienne. The Left holds its tongue. And to the degree that it talks, its vocabulary is distorted in the truest sense of the word. Stubbornly it terms "progressive" the tyrannic regimes of Syria and Iraq, where occasionally Communists, too, are thrown into jail.

Yet Israel – certainly no model state, but surely a polity that permits opposition, including antinational opposition – is in leftist mythology a "reactionary" land. All this is even worse than those uncanny dialectics that can be used to justify all and everything. It is political hocus-pocus. It is the total confusion of concepts, the definitive loss of moral-political standards.

I believe in all seriousness that the Left must redefine itself within the context of the problem of Israel – that is, the Jewish Problem. Does the Left still stand up for humanist values? Yes or no? Does it still believe that the concept of democracy embraces universal suffrage, freedom of speech, and the right of assembly – the *droits de l'homme*, which since the French Revolution, after all, have not exactly been unknown? Does the Left still regard nationalism, as it always has, as a political error born of obstinacy? Or, rather, does it find nationalism acceptable wherever, under the sign of tyranny, it is directed against Jews – and unjust as soon as the Jews, for their part and under unbearable pressure, fall reactively into its trap?

Finally: is the Left prepared to acknowledge that even if so-called *formal* democracy cannot attain realization as long as economic democracy does not complement it, that *formal* democracy still must have absolute priority, since economic democracy can be built only on its foundation. Now to the last question: Is the concept of justice still binding for the Left? Justice has been its *raison d'être* as long as it has existed; if the Left sacrifices this concept as a barter for the fetish of revolution, it will destroy itself.

This brings us back to the question of Israel and the Jews. The creation of the State of Israel was an act of justice, as Gromyko, too, clearly proclaimed at the time in the name of the Soviet Union. No one can deny, and I, too, cannot conceal it here that, in carrying out just rehabilitation, injustices toward Arabs have occurred. Nonetheless, the injustice done to the Palestinian Arabs can be redressed without creating a global conflict over the issue. Even today they are not actually homeless, but they possess two states: Jordan, where they constitute the majority of the population, and Lebanon, where in alliance with Syria they are imposing their will. Certainly, it ought to be required that Israel and the Jews of the world contribute their share to the restoration of the full rights of the Palestinian Arabs. But if the Jewish state were destroyed, which is the aim, admitted or not, of all Arab politics from the right to the far left, from the King of Saudi Arabia to George Habash, an *irreversible injustice* would occur. A fleeting glance at history suffices for us to perceive this, if we are at all prepared for objective analyses. Here, precisely at this point, a Left returning to its true self would take up its great task – if it were able to rid itself of a vocabulary to which it is compulsively clinging, and able to rid itself of a few political myths. Were it to withdraw from the Arabs its blind support and mechanical yes-vote, the Left could help solve the problem of Israel, as well as the Jewish Problem.

We can be sure that the great majority of Israeli Jews, who are under such terrible pressure, are willing to seek reconciliation. And we can be sure of the understanding of the Jews outside Israel. The powerful and rich Arab nations need harbor no fears. In a pacified Near East region, the dreamers of a Greater Israel would disappear of their own, just as would the Diaspora Jewry – which is plagued by constant anxiety and thus reacts aggressively. The Left would then have to demand that the Jews be given a double freedom: the freedom to assimilate in their host countries under the aegis of the Enlightenment, and the freedom to emigrate to an Israel that even within the pre-1967 borders would have enough room to receive a flow of immigrants that most likely would not be particularly large.

It seems crucial to me that the Left – which might possibly help to determine the future spirit and image of the Western world – stop pursuing this systematic anti-Zionism, which, for the Jews, and also in historical-objective terms, bears the repulsive features of traditional antisemitism.

Only a few, almost shamefully trivial insights are needed in order to comprehend this. All the young socialists, communists, Maoists, and Trotskyists have to do is imagine those in power telling them: "It isn't you we are combating, it is World Bolshevism. We have nothing against your stand on the Left. However: you are forbidden to be teachers; you are barred from the civil service; your public gatherings will be outlawed; if you continue to form parties you will be overstepping the law." With a minimum of imagination, you need only place yourselves in the situation, and you will understand that with their anti-Zionist emotional fervor these leftists awaken aggressive Zionist reactions on the one hand and, on the other, those antisemitic feelings that have been dragged along through the history of the Occident and the Orient for two millennia and are latently as present today as they ever were. The Left, and with a gesture of sharp rejection, must refuse to allow this antisemitism, now shabbily disguised as anti-Zionism, to become respectable again.

In contrast to a traditionally obstinate Right, the Left has no title to the aforementioned indolence of the heart. It has no title to self-mystification or to an absurd mythology of revolution, no title to that eccentric German idealism that Thomas Mann once characterized by saying, "If it did not sound so presumptuous, one would have to say that the Nazis committed their crimes out of unworldly idealism." If the Left properly understands itself, it knows that it is a child of the Enlightenment, of the Encyclopedists, the great French Revolution, the intellectual and poetic influence of Lessing, Heine, Börne, Moses Mendelssohn, Feuerbach. It is up to the Left, today more than ever, to concur energetically with Jean-Paul Sartre, who said in an interview in the days of the October War: I know only that in this conflict 3 million people are up against 100 million. In Israel every Jew must be trembling for his life, even if he is the bravest, and with him all of the Jews in every country of the earth. – Perhaps, though, only someone who was a witness to the murderous frenzy of the Third Reich knows and comprehends this.

The person who is speaking to you here *was* a witness. He himself was touched and squeezed, as in the fairy tale of Hänsel and Gretel, not to see whether he was fat enough but, rather, if he was lean enough to be slaughtered. I appeal to your feelings, to the world's feelings, but above all, certainly, to your intelligence, when I stress: antisemitism, even if it calls itself anti-Zionism, is not respectable. On the contrary, it is the indelible stain that mars the honor of civilized humanity.

Please do not regard this appeal as an address to you personally. I know, in any case, that those of you who have gathered here to open Brotherhood Week, no matter where you stand politically, are of sincere good will. Otherwise you would not have come. But since my words have a certain chance of reaching beyond our narrow circle of men and women who are in basic agreement with one another, I chose them as you have heard them. The problem of age-old antisemitism, appearing in the cloak of respectability and fashionable chic, goes far beyond anything that Christian-Jewish cooperation can solve. It is a matter for the world and its history. And wherever and whenever we, who are in agreement, have the possibility, even in the most modest way, to intervene with our word in the historical proceedings that are once again being conducted against the Jews, we are obliged to make ourselves heard: morally, politically, and with the emotion that befits a good cause.

2. The Interwar Generation

Elisabeth Freundlich

Elisabeth Freundlich was born in Vienna in 1916 as
the daughter of Jacques Freundlich and Olga
Freundlich-Lanzer. Freundlich's formative experiences were the post-Habsburg era with its social and
intellectual changes and assimilated Austrian
middle-class Jewish life in Vienna, including anti-
Semitism, which her family did not discuss. Freundlich studied German and Romance languages, history of art, and theater at the University of Vienna. As
a student she experienced the rise of National Socialism. Political tribulations and exile are important factors in both Freundlich's biography and her writings.
In 1938 she went into exile in France, and later in the
United States. She worked odd jobs until she secured
a position at the Metropolitan Museum of Art and
thereafter a lecturership of German at Princeton University. During those years she was also active as a
journalist. In 1950 she returned to Vienna, where she
wrote for various papers as well as for radio and television. From 1953 to 1978 she was a cultural correspondent for Der Ausschnitt, a Berlin newspaper.
Freundlich was married to the author and critic
Günther Anders, who wrote critical essays, including
Wir Eichmannssöhne (1964; We the sons of Eichmann).
Since 1978 she has devoted herself to her own works,
all of which show a keen interest in the point of view
of assimilated Jewish women and in Jewish post-
Emancipation history. The latter informs her documentary, autobiographical, and literary works. Elisabeth Freundlich's publications include Der eherne
Reiter (1960; The iron horseman), Sie wussten, was sie
wollten: Lebensbilder bedeutender Frauen aus drei Jahrhun-
derten (1981; They knew what they wanted: Biographical sketches of important women from three centuries), Die Ermordung einer Stadt namens Stanislau: NS
Vernichtungspolitik in Polen, 1939–1945 (1986; The

murder of a town named Stanislau: Nazi politics of extermination in Poland, 1939–45), *Finstere Zeiten* (1986; Dark times), *Die fahrenden Jahre* (1992; The travelling years), and the autobiographical novel *Der Seelenvogel* (1986; The soul bird), which, according to the author's statement, reflects the author's own family background and history. The novel is intended as a monument to the history and destruction of Austrian Jews.

Elisabeth Freundlich

EXCERPT FROM

The Soul Bird

Dedicated to the memory of my parents, Jacques Freundlich and Olga Freundlich-Lanzer, without whose partly cheerful, partly sad family memories this book could not have been written.

Cousin Marie, Uncle Eduard, Grandmama Rosalie, for my own life none of them seemed all that significant; of Grandmama Johanna I have only a vague conception: the way she sat under the nut tree after a life full of work. It seems to me that I have never again visited Grandmama Rosalie's grave after her funeral. And it did not impress me in the least that Uncle Eduard has no grave at all, that he, one of the first men missing in action during World War I, lies interred somewhere in Russian soil. All I remember is how unpleasant and irksome it was to me that my mother, my cheerful playmate, was not available to me and that every day we went to see Uncle Eduard's wife. There I had to sit quietly, and we had to wait together with the other family members until my aunt came to after one her deep fainting spells. They overcame her in regular intervals since the news had arrived. Because she was Jewish like all of us and mourned completely and without restraint, so dreadfully as only Jews do.

It is an ancient human yearning that the dead be buried in native soil, that they rest close to their relatives. In native soil! When the grandparents selected their burial place in the small cemetery overlooking all of Vienna, they considered it their native soil, where they would be able to rest.

Cousin Marie, Uncle Eduard, Grandmama Rosalie, they ought to have a grave, a family tomb, so that they would not be completely forgotten. It worries me, it haunts me that I am unable to do them this last service of love, that I cannot bury them together in a common tomb.

Paulus Diaconus writes that the Lombards erected a long pole on their family grave sites. On top of it sat a carved bird that turned in the direction of the countries where the relatives had died and where they had been interred; it was the bird that called their souls back so that they would find rest and peace in the family tomb. "Perticae id est, trabes erectae ut sciri possit in quam partem qui defunctus fuerat quiesceret," Paulus Diaconus says.

Oh, if only I could erect for them such a bird as my last service of love. But where?

At the tomb of the grandparents? It was destroyed and defaced long ago. And even if it still existed, too much has happened for it to be still a home to you.

There is a tenet among the Jews, namely, that whoever dies in foreign countries will have to meander restlessly through subterranean caverns all the way to the Promised Land to find peace. In the Promised Land? Is it there that I am supposed to erect the Soul Bird for you? You never considered it a promise.

Therefore all I can do is to plant the Soul Bird between these white sheets of paper; to try to wrench all of your lives from oblivion and to try to capture them in these sheets so that you may find peace and my soul also become more serene. May I have the strength to pull you into these sheets of paper as a means of giving you life once again to prevent you from being merely a handful of the six million who – since there are fifty million to be mourned altogether – will soon be forgotten.

My Soul Bird stands. The direction in which it looks has been determined. It almost seems to me as if you had been waiting for just that: I sense your figures approaching.

Surround me, help me. For if I am able to fill the still blank pages of this book with your lives – although I may not have succeeded in transferring your bodies to their native soil and bury them there as is my duty as the last descendent of my family – I feel that I will have rescued you and everyone like you from being forgotten until the day when we shall have reached the Promised Land, until we shall have created a world where everyone, no matter in which country, will be allowed to live and die in peace.

Regarding Grandfather Heinrich, all I remember are the style of his beard and his peculiar clothes, which I have only seen in old Viennese etchings since then: the plaid pants, the short, sand-colored overcoat, and the top hat, a kind of broad-brimmed, cylindrical hat similar to the one mentioned in certain of Nestroy's couplets. Grandfather Heinrich had served in the military for twelve years because he had been too poor to buy his way out. Strange Italian, Croatian, Serbian, and Czech words must have been part of his vocabulary. Occasionally they caused me to prick up my ears when Grandmama Rosalie or one of the aunts used them and, asked about the origin of the words, could say nothing but that they had been in use in Grandfather's days. The mixture of languages in the monarchy seems to have been a matter of course to him who had taken part in the campaign in Lombardy in 1859, far more ingrained than Jewish words and customs, at which he marveled in other branches of the family as if they were something very exotic. An orphan, he had grown up in a Bohemian village. The community had him trained as a locksmith, and prior to the time when his prosperous relatives suddenly remembered him, long after his proletarian Grand Tour through the monarchy, he had known hardly any Jews. He let his pious wife carry on, but having seen so many peoples, so many nations, life had made him a free spirit and a skeptic.

When I was a child, I loved to sit in Uncle Adolf's study. And I owe my love of plants to my Sunday afternoon walks with him in the palm house of Schönbrunn castle, where there were not only palm trees but the most remarkable exotic plants. How would Uncle Adolf have envied me had he known that at one time I would see them grow in the wild; in the course of my flight, which lasted several years, having slipped somehow through the network of immigration laws, I suddenly found myself in tropical countries where I saw many of the fairy-tale creations from the palm house again.

Uncle Adolf did not even dream of wishing to see his favorite plants growing in the wild, not even in his wildest dreams. Nonetheless he must have dreamed often and painfully of being an administrator of one of the state-owned gardens and greenhouses or of standing behind a lectern, imparting to an attentively listening audience his passion for his research. Who knows if the shy, timid man would have succeeded in doing so? Since to this day I get into the old festive mood when entering a greenhouse, I am inclined to believe that he would have been able to teach students to share his passion for his research. Instead he became a small-time journalist for a wretched paper, wrote gossip columns about different people and the court, and later society news. And if he was sometimes greeted respectfully, it was by people trying to climb the social ladder who hoped that in the column "At the Concordia Ball One Noticed among Others" they or their daughters would be distinguished by an epithet, rather than merely being lumped together with the "others."

Only when I was an adult did it become clear to me that his odd lifestyle between books on plant physiology, herbariums, microscopes, and photographs carrying spirited dedications of actors and commissioners who had been favorably mentioned by him, was a result of anti-Semitism that, in turn, bred more anti-Semitism.

My father dismissed this uncle with the adjective "corrupt" and "journaille" and let him feel precisely how much he despised his being "a hireling of the ruling class." He was so obvious about it that Uncle Adolf acted toward him with the same insecurity and exaggerated submission as with the director of the Schönbrunn greenhouses or the university professor whom "he had the audacity to ask humbly to glance through his modest observations upon occasion, whenever his busy schedule allowed."

That the term "journaille" did not in the least apply to Uncle Adolf I understood immediately after finding out the meaning of the word, which I did with great difficulty, and I considered my father unfair. But for a very long time I did not understand that the column "Society Notes" served the purpose of making a living, because an academic career, even the most insignificant position in the park administration, was off limits to him because he was a Jew, a fact that nobody had openly explained to me. One was not ashamed of being Jewish, one acknowledged it, and strangely enough the members of my family who had a strong Czech-Bohemian farmers' background that might have raised doubts about their descent stressed it frequently. Yet, it seemed almost as if people were ashamed of the other Jews who stood in their way.

Thus I never received a direct response to my exclamations: "Why aren't you my teacher?" when I, already a high school student, proudly reported during our Sunday afternoon walks that I had taken our teacher by surprise because of factual knowledge I owed to him. His distress because of this never-attained goal and the shame about those who denied him something that in all fairness should not have been allowed to be denied was probably so profound that I can only remember answers such as, "Oh well, I do have a profession, after all, I am a journalist." Yet, he was unable to suppress a satisfied smirk in response to his only student's adoring admiration.

Only when I was almost an adult did it become apparent to me that the "Society Notes" were purely commercial. My father dismissed Uncle's profession as a character defect; to me it remained a total mystery what connection there might exist between a money-making venture and an avocation, because both the society news and plant physiology appeared to me as such. To this day this connection has not become apparent to me.

When I was a child, it seemed to me as if my family wanted to compensate for the professional money lending practiced by former, unknown generations – the only profession they were allowed to practice – by simply not using the words "money" or "income." The ancestors I know about were book dealers at the most, if they were at all involved in trade. I do not remember ever receiving the following answers: "We are too poor to afford that," or: "To be able to afford that Father has to start earning more money" in response to any wish I expressed during my childhood. Neither do I remember that any child in our closer or larger circle of relatives was denied a wish for monetary reasons. The most unlikely pretexts were used to avoid having to say that this or that was outside of one's financial means. By contrast, I often heard my Christian classmates say without the slightest inhibition that there was not enough money for this or that purpose.

Oh, Uncle Adolf, you who were already so ashamed of your compatriots for not making you a professor – indeed, they *were* your compatriots, you had no others; traditional Jews wearing a caftan, even the most learned ones, already filled you with the same horror, the same revulsion they did the Christians, whose prejudices you had absorbed because you had been educated in the same school – how great must have been your shame when they arrested you to deport you to Poland.

During the days of the coup I saw you briefly one last time, but you were completely calm and composed. You had so many Christian friends. "Who knows," you said with a smile, "the fact that they never allowed me to become a professor may have its benefits after all. They have a guilty conscience, they will not permit me to be taken outdoors to scrub the streets."

For the first time in all those years you stated openly that they had barred you from your life's true pleasure. But at this point it was too late to keep it a secret any longer.

Uncle Adolf, soon you would have reason to be horribly ashamed of your compatriots – whom else could you have referred to by that term? And I am firmly convinced that even at that point you tried to compensate by being compliant in those things for which there was no compensating through respectful behavior. In all likelihood the Nazi mob considered your old-fashioned courtesy, your bows as the Jew's amusing fear of death. But I know that you were not afraid of death: One is not preoccupied one's entire long life with the becoming and perishing of nature without becoming a wise person, and that's what you were, Uncle Adolf, although your job was to write: "Among those present one noticed the charming spouse of . . . in a delightful little Surah dress."

Although it probably happened differently, I see you clearly before my eyes, Uncle Adolf, offering the Gestapo men who came to arrest you for deportation to Poland a seat while you collected your things. I *see* you very clearly holding the door for them and, bowing time and again, wanting to let them pass. And the last thing I *know* is how they, kicking and bellowing, propelled you down the stairs. How profoundly ashamed you must have been then, you who were ashamed of them all your life. I know that your amusing deference was designed to cover up for what happened to you and the others. Just as a husband wants to compensate for his wife's intolerable lack of tact by being particularly polite, fearfully trying to cover up for her to prevent her from being disgraced.

Far, far back it is getting brighter; one has to go very far back in time to call forth an image that is unblemished by hideous memories.

It is getting brighter and brighter; the sunlight is almost blinding. There is a beautiful sandy beach, and my cousin Gemma runs away from me. I run after her. All she wears are tiny white swim shorts, and her bushy blond mane swings up and down as she runs. "*Mia lionella*," the aunt says proudly. It is funny to have such a little sister all of a sudden, but one has to be damned careful not to let her slip through one's hands and escape.

The hot sand burns under my soles. That instant she takes a turn and disappears behind one of the beach chairs. When I think I have caught her, I fall flat on my face in the soft sand, and there is a giggle on the other side. Finally, I have caught her, and for a moment we lie on the ground, exhausted, and enjoy the silence. The beach chairs are positioned in three rows; between the rows there is a path that provides a little shade; we are now sitting there and paint with our toes figures in the sand, which right here is not so unbearably hot.

We hear children's laughter and the muted chattering of voices from afar. A subtle ringing pierces the sound of the rushing surf. Gemma points her finger in the direction; she knows much earlier than I do what it means.

"*Gelati*," she says and hugs me, before she stumbles forward. She has made me breathless and annoyed, because I take my task of not letting her out of my sight very seriously. Now she wants to placate me with a *gelato*. Now I can also distinctly hear the ringing of the bell and the calls, "*Gelati, gelati!*"

I run forward, back into the dazzling sunlight, and there stands the *gelati* man, white, wearing a white, peaked cap. He is surrounded by children. Gemma talks at him. Tiny, she stands in front of him, pointing toward our cabana; then we trot alongside him all the way up to the entrance, and, really, Aunt Romana steps out and buys each one of us a *gelato*, although she has her bad day today. The sirocco blows, which for her means migraine.

Later in Vienna I say precociously, "Soon everything will be fine again when the bora comes," when someone feels sick and goes to bed, and I cannot understand in the least why I am chided for saying such "nonsense." For I love the relatives in Trieste, and when Aunt Romana says that a person's well-being depends on the bora, it is probably correct.

I also like Uncle Riccardo, although he is incredibly noisy and gestures with his hands. I know that Grandmama would certainly have reprimanded him, "You are not in a Jewish school," she would have said. Uncle Riccardo is very funny, very noisy, only sometimes when I ask him something he all of a sudden acts as if he did not understand me. But immediately thereafter he'll say, "*Scusi, scusi, mia piccola nipote,*" and once again be very friendly. Only once he was furious. He entered the playroom when we sang, "May God keep our emperor, our emperor, our country" (the national anthem of Imperial Austria). I was very proud of how well Gemma had learned it from me.

At that point he yelled loudly, "*Basta, basta, una assurdita,*" and glared at me in anger, so that I was a little afraid of him. Afterward Aunt Romana talked to him, very fast and in Italian – for the most part they spoke German when I was around with only a few Italian phrases mixed in. The next day Gemma stayed in the cabana with her mother, and my uncle took me with him and showed me the sardine factory located not far from Grado, where fish were piled into huge barrels by women who had cleaned them earlier at long tables.

After a month had passed, we returned to Trieste; I was already reading to Gemma from her Italian children's books; she in turn understood Grimm's fairy tales, but she liked "Pinocchio" best.

We drove to Barcola to go swimming or took the cable car to Opčina, "Opicina," Uncle would correct me. "Leave it to Zlatka to say Opčina." Zlatka was the cook, who spoke yet another language that I did not understand at all when she talked to the delivery men or the maidservant next door.

Every night there were many visitors, and those who came were also noisy and gestured, and every night they seemed to discuss the same topic: "*Una università, dà,*" they said. "*Nostra giovinezza deve studiare a casa, in italiano,*" and then they all yelled "hurrah" and "bravo" and hugged and kissed each other; the men kissed each other, which I had never seen at home.

Meanwhile Gemma, the little lioness, had become my satellite, and I enslaved her thoroughly: "Do this, do that," I went on all day long, and she obeyed me with passionate devotion. "Don't talk so much with your hands!" I reprimanded her one day. "There is no need for anyone to know immediately that you are a Jewess."

Gemma was willing to do everything I demanded and buried her hands in her thick mane in shame – ashamed about having provoked my dissatisfaction.

But among the uncles and aunts my remark earned me an extraordinary peal of laughter, "Romana, *carissima*, that's the best joke," Uncle Riccardo hollered again and again, doubling over with laughter.

Aunt Romana believed she owed me an explanation, "*Carina*," she said, "there is no anti-Semitism in these parts. We want to be Italians because Italy signifies freedom, do you understand, freedom for all."

Uncle Riccardo cut her short, "Let the child be," he said, "this is something she really cannot understand."

I had often heard that one should not talk with one's hands because it is Jewish. But at this point I had no notion of anti-Semitism and freedom.

Another time we took the cable car to Opčina or Opicina, as I had meanwhile learned to pronounce it. The area had been afforested here, and the wood were the pride of the city; with enormous effort the soil for each individual tree had been transported here. Everyone in Trieste considered it a miracle that vegetation flourished here and we could rest in a shady forest, and while Uncle Riccardo tried to explain to me how this afforestation had been accomplished, we consumed the sandwiches we had taken along. Dark blue and sparkling the ocean lay beneath us; minutely small, the streetcars moved toward the beach of Barcola; the castle of Miramare gleamed in the very far distance. To this day I continue to remember this place as one of the most beautiful in the world.

"Who knows," my uncle said, comfortably stretching in the shade, "if we will be able to loll about here in the near future. Those damned Slovenians, before the elections they always burn down this magnificent forest, again and again. A gangster rabble!" Such statements hit with a bang, and I carried them with me, oftentimes for years, until one day I would pull them out and present them.

All those discussions did not interest me in the least. I was interested in the cable car, the steamboat trip to Capodistria, and the castle Miramare, which looked like a castle out of the Arabian Nights.

"Poor Emperor Max," I mused when we promenaded in the park

of Miramare, and I thought of a picture in a gilt-edged tome that I was occasionally allowed to leaf through at Grandmama's: *Execution of the Emperor Max by Juarez's Troops.*

"Would you like it if someone you do not know at all, about whom you have never heard, were to come and say he is your emperor and from now on you are his tributary?"

The term "tributary" pleased me inordinately. "I like to be a tributary," I said in earnest.

"Oh well, you little monkey, what a fool I have for a niece," my uncle laughed in comic despair, took my ear, for which he pretended to search underneath my hair for quite a while, and pulled me up a little. "Had he stayed here in his capacity as Grand Duke Max, he'd reside at Miramare to this day," he said and acted as if he had an exact insight into what went on in the world.

"The Indians murdered Emperor Max," I said, insisting on my wisdom. My uncle gave up on his attempts to shake my firm opinions any further.

The conversation at Miramare regarding the actual and possible course of world history was to be my last conversation with Uncle Riccardo before I returned to Vienna the next day; the vacation was over.

I was entrusted to the care of the conductor, my breakfast basket was filled with good things, my knapsack leaned in the corner of the compartment. It contained more edibles and a large thermos bottle. Around my neck I carried a papier-mâché sign with my name and address. A fierce battle had been fought about it; Aunt Romana had cut a huge sign, and Uncle Riccardo had spent an entire evening painting my name and address in colossal letters, first tracing them with a pencil, then filling them in with watercolor. Only my consistently escalating wailing, in which the little lioness had dutifully joined me, had caused the piece of cardboard to become smaller and smaller until it was the size of a business card and Uncle Riccardo's beautiful tracing with a calligraphy pen proved unnecessary. And finally I had even obtained permission to carry the small piece of cardboard *underneath* my dress. I would only pull it out in case of a most pressing emergency. I was seven years old, I knew how to read and write and thought it unnecessary to make such a fuss because of a twelve-hour train ride.

I stood by the window, next to the conductor. He lifted me up so that I could give those outside my hand once again. Gemma too was held up, and we kissed each other. Her blond tresses produced a pleasant tickle on my neck.

"You'll come back next year," my aunt comforted me. "Perhaps your parents will come too, and then all of us will go to the Lido together. In Venice there are gondolas, not only barges like at Molo San Carlo, and we shall travel on them through the entire city."

"And the gondolier sings, you know," said my uncle, to make the last minutes go by more quickly. "Do you know how?" And he began to sing: "*Funiculi, funicula, iambo, iambo.*" And the aunt and the little lioness joined in, and I sang too. Of course I knew "*Funiculi, funicula,*" of course I would travel with the gondolier through the waterways of Venice.

A jolt, the train pulled out of the station. The conductor held me up. Uncle Riccardo carried Gemma on his arm; they walked along for a few steps. We waved.

"*A rivederla, piccola. Respetti a genitori.*"

"*A rivederla, Aunt Romana. A rivederle, Uncle Riccardo. A rivederla,* little lioness, see you in a year's time!"

It was the year 1913, and it was the last summer of peace of the Austro-Hungarian monarchy.

We sat around the big dining room table, Mommy, Grandmama, and the aunts, stuffing cigarettes. That is, the adults were stuffing, and I was allowed to cut off the uneven tobacco strings with blunt paper scissors and then put the cigarettes into boxes. That was a fine job, I would have liked to do it all day. That there were so many people around was enjoyable as well, because my mother had stopped to really play with me, and in the evening, when the relatives had left, being alone with her was a little sad. Indeed, we needed many cigarettes, there could never be enough: for Uncle Eduard, who served with the Fourth Home Guard Regiment, for Father, who was a member of the Second Mounted Artillery Division – I could pronounce all that fluently and without faltering – and for Uncle Riccardo, who served in the Thirty-sixth Infantry Regiment at Kragujevac, a name that I managed to pronounce fluently and without faltering as well.

The cigarette stuffing in the family circle held a particular charm for me for yet other reasons: "Have the child recite something for us," one of the aunts would occasionally say. Then I put down my scissors, wiped my hands against my blue calico apron, positioned myself on the raised step leading to the alcove of our dining room as if it were a podium, and started out with: "The Heroic Girl of Rawaruska," ending with "Hail, my nation, you have triumphed." I stopped involuntarily because my mother made a face as if she had a toothache, shook her head, and said: "Well, that will do for today." And, turning toward the family – and I distinctly sensed a reprimand in her voice: "I really cannot stand to listen to that."

So I stood on the podium, tiny, with a pageboy haircut that had the appearance of a doll's ill-fitting wig, as I noticed with dissatisfaction when I eagerly peered into the mirror on the wall. Then I proceeded with an inexhaustible program in a reverberating voice that could be heard everywhere whatever bloodthirsty eulogies and hymns in praise of the House of Habsburg we had learned in school at that time – and resented my mother for stifling my talent.

Stuffing cigarettes did not remain such a cosy family festivity for long. Uncle Eduard's wife soon stopped coming, the Fourth Home Guard Regiment had been wiped out at the Lubkow pass, but Grandmama did not know it yet and continued stuffing.

Later we plucked lint; that was even nicer than arranging cigarettes, but in between one had to wash one's hands.

One midsummer day, when plucking lint had already become a routine, Grandmama sighed, "Oh, this Cesare Battisti. He met the end he deserved. Betraying his native country in such a way."

Never before had I heard that name, but it sounded pleasant to my ears because it reminded me of Trieste.

My mother raised her eyebrows and kept silent, but I felt distinctly that she disapproved of Grandmama's words.

"I just hope that Riccardo will not let himself be dragged into some kind of stupidity, he is so hotheaded," Grandmama sighed.

"Uncle Riccardo doesn't do stupid things," I suddenly heard myself say. "He is for Italy because he is for freedom. Italy means freedom, also for the Jews. There is no anti-Semitism in Italy." It was out, the word which to know I was so proud, it came without faltering.

Where had I picked all that up? My mother turned red as fire, Grandmama clasped her hands. "I wonder where the child has picked up that nonsense," she screamed. "What do you know about Jews and Christians? Whoever protects the fatherland, whoever protects the emperor, he matters, he is an Austrian, regardless of whether he is a Jew or a Christian."

"But Aunt Romana says," I yelled and pointed with wild gestures into the direction where I believed Trieste to be located, and then I made a few more helpless gestures without uttering a word, and the gestures were supposed to substitute for the things that were going awry in my head and that I did not know how to put into words. "*Università*," I cried, excited and desperate, "they have no *università*."

"Don't talk with your hands, that's Jewish," Grandmama chided me.

"In that case it would still be better for you to recite poems," my mother said, shaking her head, and I jumped at the opportunity. I was immediately back on the step, trumpeting "The Heroic Girl from Ruwaruska" through the room.

Ultimately I began to understand the reason for Grandmama's worries from the allusions and the unsuspecting answers of my aunts, with whom I pretended that I had all the information anyhow because Uncle Riccardo had told me. People did not like to discuss this dark aspect of Uncle Riccardo's past, but neither were they inclined on the other hand to forget the old story. Now I found out that when he was a student at the Gymnasium he had pierced the eyes of a portrait of Emperor Franz Joseph that was hanging opposite the crucifix on the classroom wall. Allegedly he himself had characterized the incident as a wild fit brought on by his hatred of tyrants. Subsequently he had been barred from all the Gymnasiums in the monarchy.

"Just imagine," Aunt Leonie said, and her abhorrence at this possibility could still be read on her face, "imagine that he would not have been able to get his high-school diploma and would have gone to war as an enlisted man. The harassment to which they would have subjected him: a Jew in the military, and an enlisted man to boot. Things are bad enough as they are."

And then I was informed that Aunt Anna had to request an

audience with the emperor, and what horrendous turmoil this had
entailed for the entire family when she arrived by train from Trieste
and was in fact finally received by the emperor at the Hofburg. As a
result of having taken his exams he was now a lieutenant and was
stationed with the Thirty-sixth Infantry Regiment in the woodlands
of the Carpathian Mountains.

All of a sudden I no longer considered Grandmama's worries so
unfounded, and in the course of the war years I understood more
and more the things that gave cause for concern as far as Riccardo
was concerned.

Uncle Riccardo, like my father, returned unharmed, but we who
lived in Vienna did not see him because naturally he wanted to go as
fast as possible to his now liberated Italian Trieste. Yet the beautiful
new port installations lay all too soon dead, and Trieste did not
exactly experience the ascent that Riccardo and his wildly gesturing
friends from Trent had imagined. But Uncle Riccardo became
something like a celebrity over there, and one could read about him
frequently in the papers.

Even after the end of the war I did not make it to Trieste, not to
speak of Venice, because my father considered the man who was at
the helm over there someone whom one had better avoid as much
as possible.

Not so Uncle Riccardo. Enthusiastic reports arrived concerning
the rise of the country and that finally the trains were on time; and
Uncle Riccardo was supposedly among those who rode on one of
the overcrowded trains all the way up to the city limits during the
Black Shirts' march on Rome.

The little lioness married at a very young age someone about
whom one could also read in the papers. The young couple moved
to Rome, and my uncle and aunt followed them soon. They moved
away from their beloved Trieste, which basically had become a dead
city, and the university for which they had clamored until they were
hoarse when I was a child was established there only much later.

At times I have thought of the forest in Opčina, which had taken
so much hard labor to plant, wondering if it had been allowed to
grow now, if the Slovenians, that gangster rabble, as my uncle had

called them, had found different methods to claim their rights now that they were suppressed by a different nation.

Uncle Riccardo came to Vienna one single time, approximately twenty years after my vacation in Trieste. It was in the spring of 1934, my father had been imprisoned on remand since 12 February, and Riccardo showed up. He was wearing a black shirt, a *commendatore*'s cross on his chest, and a beard à la Balbo, which was still fashionable in Italy, although the aviator Balbo had already fallen from grace.

That February in a sudden single blow our house was stripped of the solid stability I had taken for granted since childhood. It was only at that moment that I had to become an adult. All of a sudden, I had to negotiate with the authorities, to secretly relay vital messages from my father to foreign countries, and I had to make every effort to ensure that certain measures would be taken by the prison administration. I had to meet my mother's irrepressible outbursts with composure – in short: I had been pushed out into the world and had to prove myself in it.

Paul Celan

Paul Celan, one of the most prominent German-speaking poets of the post-Shoah era, was born as Paul Antschel in Czernovitz, Romania, in 1920. The multicultural, multilingual environment in which he grew up is reflected in his works, which combine concepts and ideas from many different epochs and traditions. Most notably, Celan integrated into his poetry motifs from Greek and Latin antiquity, from the Bible and the Talmud, European classics, and German literature of all periods, as well as French symbolism and surrealism, which experienced a renaissance in postwar Vienna, where Celan began his career as a poet. During World War II Celan was arrested and sent to a forced-labor camp. His liberation was followed by a brief stay in Vienna. Then Celan moved to Paris, where he worked as a teacher and translator. He was in contact with the most notable authors of his time, including Claire and Yvan Goll, Nelly Sachs, Ingeborg Bachmann, and Ilse Aichinger. As was the case with Nelly Sachs, Erich Fried, and Elias Canetti, Celan's literary language remained German. After 1951, the year of his first appearance before Gruppe 47, the most prominent literary forum of the postwar era, where he made his debut in West Germany alongside Ilse Aichinger, Celan published with Suhrkamp Verlag, one of the major West German publishers. "Death Fugue," which appeared in *Mohn und Gedächtnis* (1952) after it had been rejected in Austria because of its subject matter, the atrocities of the Holocaust, is his most explicit poem about the Shoah. In his later works he avoided descriptive passages that allowed his German audience easy access to the subjects that concerned him the most: the Shoah, the paradox of writing poetry in the language of the perpetrators, the inability to articulate Jewish concerns in a language in which Christian anti-

Jewish patterns were embedded, and at the same time his fascination with the language of Goethe, Hölderlin, and Rilke. Celan, whose parents had been murdered by the Nazis, suffered from depression and paranoia. His difficulties relating to post-Shoah reality are manifest in his later hermetic and inaccessible poems. In 1970 Paul Celan committed suicide in Paris. Celan received numerous literary prizes and awards for his poetry, including the prestigious Büchner Prize (1960). Recently, the Celan Prize was established in his honor. Celan's publications include *Der Sand aus den Urnen* (1948; The sand from the Urns), *Mohn und Gedächtnis* (1952; Poppy and memory), *Von Schwelle zu Schwelle* (1955; From threshold to threshold), *Sprachgitter* (1959; *Speech-Grille*), *Die Niemandsrose* (1963; The rose of no one), *Atemwende* (1967; Breathturn), *Fadensonnen* (1968; Strange attractors), *Lichtzwang* (1970; Lightforce), and *Schneepart: Letzte Gedichte* (1971; Snow part). The following two very different translations of Celan's most acclaimed poem by first-rate translators reveal some of the complexities of the original text and the difficulties involved in translating it.

Paul Celan

Death Fugue Translated by Michael Hamburger

Black milk of daybreak we drink it at sundown
we drink it at noon in the morning we drink it at night
we drink and we drink it
we dig a grave in the breezes there one lies unconfined
A man lives in the house he plays with the serpents he writes
he writes when dusk falls to Germany your golden hair
                                       Margarete
he writes it and steps out of doors and the stars are flashing
                            he whistles his pack out
he whistles his Jews out in earth has them dig for a grave
he commands us strike up for the dance

Black milk of daybreak we drink you at night
we drink in the morning at noon we drink you at sundown
we drink and we drink you
A man lives in the house he plays with the serpents he writes
he writes when dusk falls to Germany your golden hair
                                       Margarete
your ashen hair Shulamith we dig a grave in the breezes
                          there one lies unconfined.

He calls out jab deeper into the earth you lot you others sing
                                now and play
he grabs at the iron in his belt he waves it his eyes are blue
jab deeper you lot with your spades you others play on for
                               the dance

Black milk of daybreak we drink you at night
we drink you at noon in the morning we drink you at
                                                    sundown
we drink you and we drink you
a man lives in the house your golden hair Margarete
your ashen hair Shulamith he plays with the serpents

He calls out more sweetly play death is a master from
                                        Germany
he calls out more darkly now stroke your strings then as
                                    smoke you will rise into air
then a grave you will have in the clouds there one lies
                                            unconfined

Black milk of daybreak we drink you at night
we drink you at noon death is a master from Germany
we drink you at sundown and in the morning we drink and
                                            we drink you
death is a master from Germany his eyes are blue
he strikes you with leaden bullets his aim is true
a man lives in the house your golden hair Margarete
he sets his pack on to us he grants us a grave in the air
he plays with the serpents and daydreams death is a master
                                        from Germany

your golden hair Margarete
your ashen hair Shulamith

Paul Celan

Deathfugue Translated by John Felstiner

Black milk of daybreak we drink it at evening
we drink it at midday and morning we drink it at night
we drink and we drink
we shovel a grave in the air there you won't lie too cramped
A man lives in the house he plays with his vipers he writes
he writes when it grows dark to Deutschland your golden hair
    Margareta
he writes it and steps out of doors and the stars are all sparkling
    he whistles his hounds to come close
he whistles his Jews into rows has them shovel a grave in the ground
he commands us play up for the dance

Black milk of daybreak we drink you at night
we drink you at morning and midday we drink you at evening
we drink and we drink
A man lives in the house he plays with his vipers he writes
he writes when it grows dark to Deutschland your golden hair
    Margareta
Your ashen hair Shulamith we shovel a grave in the air there you won't
    lie too cramped

He shouts jab this earth deeper you lot there you others sing up and
    play
he grabs for the rod in his belt he swings it his eyes are so blue
jab your spades deeper you lot there you others play on for the dancing

Black milk of daybreak we drink you at night
we drink you at midday and morning we drink you at evening
we drink and we drink
a man lives in the house your goldenes Haar Margareta
your aschenes Haar Shulamith he plays with his vipers

He shouts play death more sweetly this Death is a master from
    Deutschland
he shouts scrape your strings darker you'll rise then as smoke to the sky
you'll have a grave then in the clouds there you won't lie too cramped

Black milk of daybreak we drink you at night
we drink you at midday Death is a master aus Deutschland
we drink you at evening and morning we drink and we drink
this Death is ein Meister aus Deutschland his eye is blue
he shoots you with shot made of lead shoots you level and true
a man lives in the house your goldenes Haar Margarete
he looses his hounds on us grants us a grave in the air
he plays with his vipers and daydreams der Tod ist ein Meister
    aus Deutschland

dein goldenes Haar Margarete
dein aschenes Haar Sulamith

Ilse Aichinger

Ilse Aichinger was born in Vienna in 1921 and grew up there and in Linz. Her mother was Berta Aichinger, née Kremer, a physician of Jewish background, and her father, Ludwig Aichinger, was a non-Jewish teacher. Aichinger was raised as a Catholic. After the Nazi invasion of Austria in 1938 she was able to finish her high-school education. Thereafter, however, instead of attending university as she had planned, she had to perform forced labor. After the liberation she enrolled in medical school at the University of Vienna, but gave up her studies in 1948 for the sake of a career as a writer. Aichinger's first novel, Die größere Hoffnung (1948; Herod's Children), had a mixed reception because it dealt with the persecution of Austrian Jews and the Holocaust, topics that were considered controversial by the non-Jewish public. Nonetheless, the book did establish her as a major author in post–World War II Austrian literature. Her next publications, including Rede unter dem Galgen (1951; Speech under the Gallows) deal in a more indirect manner with problems of postwar society. In the course of her career Aichinger moved increasingly toward more experimental and opaque forms of writing, reflecting partly the author's affinity for the Austrian tradition of language criticism informed by Wittgenstein, partly the predicament of a post-Shoah writer who faces the destruction of her culture and the loss of her intellectual home. Only in her most recent publications has Aichinger begun to write about her childhood experiences, the Nazi occupation, and the process of memory and mourning, most notably in Kleist, Moos, Fasane (1987; Kleist, moss, and pheasants). Aichinger was married to the German poet Günter Eich. Until Eich's death in 1972 the couple traveled extensively and lived in different southern German towns. After her mother's death in

1983 Aichinger moved to Frankfurt and, in 1988, to Vienna, where she now lives. She received prestigious literary awards, including the prize of the Group 47 (1952), the Austrian State Prize for the Encouragement of Literature (1952), the literature prize of the city of Bremen (1957), the Trakl Prize (1979), the Petrarca Prize of the city of Munich (1979), and the Franz Kafka Prize (1983).

Ilse Aichinger

A Summons to Mistrust

A printing error? Are your eyes getting weaker? No! You have read entirely correctly – although you may find this headline irresponsible, although . . . you find no words. Is it not precisely mistrust that is the worst and most incurable disease of this probing, injured world shaken by labor pain? Is it not the explosive charge that blows the bridges between nations up into the air, this terrible mistrust, is it not the cruel hand that scatters the goods of this world into the ocean, that overshadows mankind's gaze and, encroaching on it, obscures it? Is it necessary to call forth once again the cause of all torments and to lure it from its den? Have we not looked past each other long enough, have we not whispered instead of talking, have we not crept instead of walking? Have we not avoided one another long enough, paralyzed by fear? And where are we today? Do we not sneer at every authority, every agency, every measure we failed to take, every word we failed to speak? We are filled with mistrust toward God, toward the black marketeer with whom we do business, toward the future, toward nuclear research, and toward the growing grass. And what now? No, it is no error, it says clearly and distinctly: a summons to mistrust! In other words, a summons to poison ourselves? A summons to annihilation?

Calm down, poor, pale citizen of the twentieth century! Do not cry! You shall merely be immunized. You are supposed to receive a serum so that you will be all the more resistant next time around! To the smallest possible degree you shall experience the disease to prevent it from repeating itself on the largest scale. You must understand me correctly. You are supposed to experience the disease yourself! You are not supposed to mistrust your brother, not America, not Russia, and not God. *It is yourself you have to mistrust.* Well? Do you comprehend that? We must mistrust ourselves: the clarity of our intentions, the profundity of our thoughts, the goodness of our actions! We must mistrust our own truthfulness! Is it not again resonant with lies? Our own voice! Is it not void of love, like glass? Our own love! Is it not corrupted by selfishness? Our own honor! Is it not brittle with arrogance?

Didn't you say that you would have preferred living in the past century? It was a very elegant and rational century. Whoever had a full stomach and a white shirt had trust in himself. One praised its reason, its kindness, its humanity. And one put up a thousand safety measures to protect oneself against those who were dirty, ragged, and starved. But no one took safety measures against one's own self. Through the generations the monster thus grew without being watched or observed. We experienced it! We suffered it around us, on us, and perhaps even within us. And yet we are once again ready to become self-assured and patronizing and to flirt with our virtues. Barely have we learned to look up when we have already relearned how to despise and to negate. Barely have we learned to say a stammering "I" when we have already tried once again to emphasize it. Barely have we dared to once again say "you" when we have already misused it! And once again we calm down. But we are not supposed to calm down!

Let us trust in the divinity of everybody whom we encounter, and let us mistrust the snake in our hearts! Let us become mistrustful toward ourselves in order to be more trustworthy!

Ilse Aichinger

Rahel's Clothes

What if I no longer told the story about the ragpickers in Kensington to anyone? And also not the one about Rahel's clothes in the closets that were no closets but passages to the other side of the street, actually connecting staircases, although, according to my judgment, no one came through any more? Not only because of Rahel's clothes. If I did not relate anything any more at all and only complied with questions at the most and then only apparently? "Do you know perhaps why Rahel did not take her clothes when she moved away?" I could defend myself, if I were discreet enough, with long speeches. About the quality of Rahel's clothes, about the possibilities of using closets as connecting staircases or connecting staircases as closets. And perhaps about the necessity of some good locks, bolts, and other additional securities. Until the other person would take his leave, breathless, without the slightest answer to his question, securing his hat against another sudden blast of wind and thinking: I will never ask that one again. One could also in reply to such a question briefly shake one's head, but that would already be more gossipy, more explainable as an allusion. It would have something of secret mongering about it, which the discreet person avoids. That's how one recognizes him, if one has enough desire to recognize him. And this abrupt shaking of one's head would entail the next question: "Or do you have a presentiment why Rahel does not have her stuff forwarded? After seventeen years?" Without hesitation I could reply to this question in the negative, had I not already succeeded in avoiding it. Because I have no presentiment why. I know it. And since one usually no longer has a presentiment about things that one knows for a fact and even chases after knowledge about certain things only in order lose the presentiment one has about them, I would be justified. Once, although I already knew, I had a suspicion as to why Rahel does not have her stuff forwarded. It was terrible. One of the dangerous exceptions to an old, useful law that one rather avoids. It was twelve years ago, to be sure. Today I have no more presentiment. I tell the truth. Then the other person, hesitantly: "Seventeen years. If one considers it a bit, a time span in which a daughter could not only have been born to oneself, but could also have grown up already." "Really?" I could interject, being perplexed at this point, for it would not have occurred to me to reflect upon something of this nature. Such reflections belong to the presentiments that the questioner who knows nothing still has. Should the conversation, however, take such a turn, it would be better to change the subject quickly, for now I would run the risk of burdening the questioning person with my knowledge and of distracting the rest of his presentiments. Exactly at the point when I might consider my discretion to be the most disputable, I would run this risk. Now I should turn the discussion to daughters and sons in general, or, even better, point out the bus that perhaps stops a couple of meters in front of us, and, after a hasty handshake and a subdued, regretful remark, throw myself into it in order to ride benumbed and weak into a neighborhood totally unknown to me, while the other one would remain behind in surprise, wondering what I might be looking for at this time with the help of this bus line, let's say, number one hundred forty-seven. But Rahel's secret would be kept, the shadow of her fate would have approached mine in the same small degree in which I would have succeeded in denying my knowledge.

And on this occasion I could, if I left the bus at the third-to-last station, discover Peggy's grave only a few meters behind the rows of graves of the reverend sisters in one of the small south-western cloister cemeteries, and I could translate to myself the epitaph on it as incorrectly or correctly as I wanted to, since my English is better, but not much better, than my Spanish. Untranslatable, because absolutely accessible to my knowledge, would only be what could be read in figures on the fading marker, which is that Peggy had been born in the sign of Pisces and had died at the age of seven, just barely in the sign of Leo. And also the dates, which could prove to me that all our years are equally far in the past, in case I should have forgotten this afternoon that Peggy's seven years had been past for some time longer than the seven, thirty-five, and ninety-five years of many other people. Already those of her neighbor, whose name I would probably forget and who, one winter day, did the same at the age of fifteen as Peggy did – represented themselves to me as a little less long gone than those of Peggy, using this kind of calculation. And so forth. It cannot have been a happy year for the convent, those dying children, dying sisters, many from faraway places. I could imagine Peggy, how she ran across one of the long hallways and saw a window swinging to-and-fro and how she burst into laughter about the beginning of her dying. I could imagine that, that is how far it goes with me. And besides that only in the case of the bus line one hundred and forty-seven. There are other cases and other lines.

Thus, at the moment when our conversation about Rahel would take a dangerous turn, a taxi could be approaching quickly. I could begin to yell and wave; again the short handshake, the subdued, regretful remark, and, immediately after that, the impatient question of the cab driver about the destination. From where would I take the necessary split-second, and yet composed, answer? Perhaps right then the address of my half-Danish cousin would come to mind, perhaps I would be lucky and she would not be home, I would catch the taxi at the point of turning, and, this time, I would indicate to the driver the neighborhood of the convent – without thinking the slightest thing about Peggy. Really, I had never been there, I would think with surprise, and that as an afterthought. And I would again wind up at Peggy's grave. But since my taxi would have been faster than the bus, I would have more time to devote to the inscription, to ponder possibilities of translation, so much time that I would lose track of it, that the increasing nightfall would cause me to leave the small cemetery, to see the lights flare up in the different tracts of the convent, to cross the street, and to reach the keeper's lodge, perhaps to slip quite skillfully through the garden gate past a group of loudly talking former pupils who would be coming from a reunion. Here, after asking the keeper's permission to call a cab, and after her polite invitation to wait with her in the warmth since it was rather windy outside, and also after having learned that these days it was no longer a reunion of former pupils, "old pupils," she might perhaps say, but that of sisters from all over the world, who unfortunately wore the most varying habits, I could shift the conversation to Peggy, in whose day the same habit for sisters of the same order had been as little questioned as the daily prayer for a good death. "Surprisingly courageous," I could ask, why would it be "surprisingly courageous," and I would find out in the process that it is not surprisingly, but exceedingly, beyond all means, to the highest degree. My careless dealings with foreign languages would once again have caused me embarrassment, but not a great embarrassment, since the keeper would certainly add smilingly that one could not say "surprisingly courageous" when speaking about dying in this house, but rather "surprisingly fearful" – one could not, however, write that on a tombstone. And, after a while, and somewhat more softly, that it also hardly happened at all. "Hardly at all, hardly at all," that would keep ringing in my ear if I was lucky and my cab would arrive at this moment, that is, if I did not learn any more about Peggy, whose name was actually Margaret, just like that of other Peggys, that she was born in Gloucestershire and had come to this house already at the age of four and a half because of the transfer of her father to some remote part of India. So that the thought could not occur to me while riding home in the cab that the daily prayer for a good death had to have become as self-understood to Peggy as the pattern of the stone tiles, almost a daily prayer for the daily death; so that my presentiment about Peggy would remain undestroyed, definitely and exactly defined by "hardly at all, hardly at all," rounded off and made untransgressable forever, here in the cab on my way home, just as at the equally certain and uncertain moment of my own last trial. If one wants to call it that. I know many who want to call it that. But I? Do I want to call it that? Do I know myself? This question is unreasonable. Where have I ended up? The lights of the inner city already become clear: familiar neon signs, Eliza, Eliza, the boutique in the corner where I bought myself a cap years ago, not yet recognizable for my eyes but for my, albeit slight, rationality: the nearness of the destination. Now, quickly, quickly, all my questions once more. Who triggered them, who was it, Rahel, Peggy, the keeper? Too late. There is no time left now to look for strange culprits. Only the questions and their sequence now. How did it start out? With the place – equally certain and uncertain – of my last trial. If one wants to call it that. I know many who want to call it that. But I? There. But I? The question is as dangerous as it is unavoidable. It is not my fault. And further. Does it not remind me of the gestures of certain plaster statues, frozen stiff at the moment of giving the blessing? This question could be avoided, but it is less dangerous, it is exchangeable, too. The next one: Do I want to call it that? This one would also still be possible, but not as precipitated, as crude as before. And if I were softer, if I asked more gently? Would I then come across my last question less thoughtlessly? Do I know myself? Myself – myself – myself – myself? This one echoes, is not correct; this one excludes almost nothing. I believe I behaved like someone who set out to learn to fear in order to escape fear. I did not stick to the advice that is rightfully given to those who are wandering in darkness as it says, I believe: More fear, more fear, enough fear, jump! "Wandering," that made me laugh already at the age of seven. Therefore once again. My driver is already slowing down, the merchant of herbs, where I buy my mallow tea, is in sight from the other direction. Now quickly. Quickly and warily, I still have it in my ear: The equally certain and uncertain moment of my last trial. If one wants to call it that. I know many who want to call it that. But I? Does it not remind me of the gestures of certain plaster statues, frozen stiff at the moment of giving the blessing? And do I want to call it that? Do I know myself? Guessed it? Guessed wrong, away from the one who lies. That is the one who is not it. Try to trivialize me into sleep. How is the last question stated? Is it named after us who will only be named as soon as we get into the womb and who have yet been named immediately afterward, as soon as our ashes drift across the abandoned vineyards? And who could swear that Solomon was not named Solomon, David not David? No, not after us, so similar and so wrong. We have to do better. But how? How is the last question stated? My driver switches on the light in the car, reads his meter, will soon name the price. How is the last question stated? How is it stated? Yes, that's how it is stated. My car stops.

Ilse Aichinger

My Father

He sat on the bench
when I arrived.
The snow rose from the path.
He asked me about Laudon's grave,
but I did not know.

Erich Fried

Erich Fried was born in Vienna in 1921 as the son of
Hugo Fried, a contractor and a hypnotist, and his
wife, Nellie, née Stein, a fashion designer. Fried's social conscience was awakened when he witnessed the
police brutality during the burning of the Vienna
Palace of Justice in 1927, an event that was a turning
point in the intellectual development of many Austrian Jews. Fried's father died of the aftereffects of a
Gestapo interrogation in 1938. Soon thereafter, at
age seventeen, he escaped with his mother to London, where he became involved in refugee organizations. At that time he began to publish his first
poems. In 1942 Fried's grandmother Malvine Stein
was killed in Auschwitz. After his Austrian high-
school education was disrupted because of the Nazi
takeover, Fried worked in London as a chemist,
librarian, and glass-factory worker, but his main interests were literary and political, as is obvious already from his first collections of poetry, *Deutschland*
(1944), and *Österreich* (1945). These works, including
the poetry in *Reich der Steine* (1963; Realm of stones)
were devoted to the memory of pre-Nazi culture, of
Nazi atrocities, and to the memory of the victims of
the Shoah. In the postwar years Fried became associated with the West German Gruppe 47. Fried, a Socialist and a prolific and controversial poet, playwright, and prose writer, set forth unconventional
viewpoints regarding the relationships between Jews
and Germans, former perpetrators and victims, in his
novel *Ein Soldat und ein Mädchen* (1960; A soldier and a
girl). Here and elsewhere, his position is pacifist and
conciliatory, opposed to retribution and militance.
Painfully aware of the central European legacy of
anti-Semitism, Austrofascism, and Nazism, Fried
took on the role of a spokesman for the downtrod-
den, regardless from which nation. In the opera li-

bretto *Arden muss sterben* (1967; *Arden Must Die*), which recasts an Elizabethan play for a modern audience, he subtly points to the complicity with the killers and the hypocrisy on which the new German states were based, hinting at the still present proto-Fascist tendencies in post-Shoah Germany. Fried was also an outspoken critic of the war in Vietnam, as shown in his collection of poems *Und Vietnam und . . .* (1966; *And Vietnam and . . .*). He was often criticized for his compassion for the Palestinians, his anti-Zionism in the anthology *Höre, Israel!* (1974; Schema Israel), and the understanding he demonstrated for the Palestinian cause. As he does in his poetry, Fried exposes and satirizes commonplace Western logic and thought patterns in his short prose texts *Kinder und Narren* (1965; *Children and Fools*), *Fast alles Mögliche* (1975; Almost all that's possible), and *Das Unmaß aller Dinge* (1982; The excess of all things). Fried is also known for his translations of Dylan Thomas, William Shakespeare, Graham Greene, and Aristophanes. He was awarded the Schiller Gedächtnispreis (1967), the International Publishers' Prize (1977), the literature prize of the city of Vienna (1980), and the literature prize of the city of Bremen. Erich Fried was married several times, to Maria Marburg, Nan Spence, and Katherine Boswell. He died in England in 1988.

Erich Fried

To Austria

It would be unkind not to speak about your guilt
that bends you to the ground and threatens to crush you.
And this very guilt of yours becomes entirely my own
like your mountains and your misery.
One day you shall not just point your finger at me:
Punish the evil neighbor who compelled me!
It is you who must confess to your guilt
and name your own name in court.

It fills me with fear to return to you,
to atone with you, I who never struck a blow.
I will defend myself against false penitents,
and you will be smooth with deceit again and again!
Probably I might teach you this or that,
and learn as well. . . . But am I strong enough?
Yet, the train takes me on a homebound course.
You are my risk – and I must take my chance with you.

Erich Fried

My Girlfriends

Slowly in three to four weeks
or suddenly over night
my girls turn into
my aunts and elderly cousins

I seem them anxiously
chewing their false teeth
and with arthritic fingers
wipe their spat-at faces

They arrive at Theresienstadt
with suitcases and bundles
They fall out of the window
still groping for their glasses

When they stretch in my bed
they are trying to stand to attention
in order to be spared
when the sick are picked out

I see them discoloured blue
when I kiss them in the morning
stacked in sixes
– the shit and vomited bile

washed off with garden hoses –
ready for transfer
from the gas chamber
to the incinerators

Erich Fried

Is Anti-Zionism
Anti-Semitism?

Zionists
with a wrong left-wing consciousness
Zionists
with a wrong right-wing consciousness

Anti-Semites
with a wrong right-wing consciousness
anti-Semites
with a wrong left-wing consciousness
and anti-Semites
with a wrong Zionist consciousness

No consciousness
that can justify
anti-Semitism
or Zionism.

After the inconceivable murders committed by the Nazis, who put millions of Jews to death, among them half my family, it is correct and to be welcomed that in Germany anti-Semitism is despised not only officially but also by the large majority of the population. Precisely for that reason I find it so horrible when in one case the accusation of anti-Semitism is misapplied and when it is raised in another where anti-Semitism is not involved at all.

Very recently Gerhard Zwerenz and Rainer Werner Fassbinder were attacked in the Federal Republic of Germany in a grossly irresponsible manner for being so-called leftist anti-Semites be-

cause they address a specific situation in Frankfurt am Main, where
a small and highly unusual group of Jewish real-estate speculators,
brothel owners, and criminals has formed. Zwerenz uses them as
subject matter for his novel *Die Erde ist unbewohnbar wie der Mond*, and
Fassbinder in his dramatization of Zwerenz's book, which was to
serve as the basis for a film. To be sure, neither Zwerenz nor Fassbinder are anti-Semites. The reasons why this small clique, which,
by the way, is most atypical of the Jews living inside and outside of
Germany, could establish itself at all is today a fairly well-known
fact. After the war so-called Displaced Persons Camps for Jews and
other concentration camp survivors who had no reason to feel any
moral obligation toward the defeated Germans had been established in the U.S. occupation zone. The American-Jewish support
committee JOINT decided to pay the support for these people
predominantly in form of cigarettes. Five hundred cigarettes per
week were not a small amount of money prior to the currency
reform, but many of the younger Jews from the survivor camps
wanted to leave for Palestine and sold their ration cards for a cheap
price to the "camp capitalists." With his fifty to sixty "toiten kurtn"
(dead cards) such a camp capitalist was able to obtain fifty to sixty
times five hundred cigarettes in addition to large quantities of food.
Thus these uprooted people ended up on the black market and
became involved in crooked restitution dealings almost as a matter
of course. They acquired ruins, had them superficially restored, and
found that amusement sites for American soldiers were more prof-
itable than housing for the homeless.

So much about the historical background for Zwerenz's and
Fassbinder's topics. But the unfair phrase of "leftist anti-Semitism"
is much older than the attacks against these two authors. Primarily
it was derived from Zionist propaganda, but not all Zionists have
engaged in this type of propaganda or even have knowledge of it.

The tendency to characterize anti-Zionism as covert anti-
Semitism has multiple roots. To begin with, Zionists have always
claimed to have a monopoly on the right of representing all Jews. At
the Second Zionist Congress held in Basel in 1898, Max Nordau,
Theodor Herzl's chief ideologist and the founder of modern political Zionism, already stated the following: "For this reason it is inappropriate to speak of a Zionist 'Party' within Judaism. We reject this

term with scorn and disdain. The Zionists are no party: they represent the essence of the Jewish culture. Their number, their current number, is irrelevant. The seed of the most imposing linden tree is but a minute element, but it is the concentration and sum total of the tree's vitality, the goal of all its efforts as a living organism. . . . Everything in Jewish culture that has any vitality, everything endowed with masculine dignity and the desire to develop is Zionist."

The claim of being the only ones who could legitimately represent all Jews later caused Zionists to label Jews *not* in support of Zionism as "human dust" or even as Jewish anti-Semites. They proceeded not entirely unlike German right-wing radicals and later the Nazis who considered Germans opposed to their dreams of world domination and racism vagabonds without a fatherland or traitors to the fatherland. I still remember how after Israel's so-called Six-Day War in 1967 I wrote in favor of the Palestinians and against an especially cruel measure taken by Israeli officers. At that time I was attacked by several persons who knew me: "How can you, a Jew, say anything against Israel? Have you never heard of the voice of the blood?" "Yes," I responded. "Indeed, I heard about it just once, from Hitler, and once is enough for me."

Of course many Zionists were inclined to suspect every opponent of Zionism of being an anti-Semite, particularly since many Jews had turned to Zionism only as a result of being persecuted as Jews. And one has to admit that in *individual* cases there exists indeed a combination of anti-Semitism and anti-Zionism, for example in certain right-wing extremist cliques in the Federal Republic of Germany, in the so-called initiative Widerstand (Resistance), and in certain papers as well. The same is true for the campaigns during the Stalin era "against Zionists and rootless cosmopolitans" that in Czechoslovakia, as a result of the so-called Slansky trial, led to the execution of Otto Sling, whom I knew personally. Other similar campaigns, whether in Poland or in Stalin's Soviet Union, were in actuality not at all free from anti-Semitic ingredients. Sling, who by the way has long been rehabilitated by the Czech Communists, was a Jew; he was never a Zionist, but a Communist and had fought in Spain against Franco. Just to mention in passing something that is unfortunately frequently forgotten these days: leftist Zionists too fought in Spain against Franco.

Finally, as far as the resolution of the United Nations of 10 November 1957 is concerned, which states that "Zionism is a form of racism and racist discrimination," all I can say, and I do not say it lightly, is: I believe that this is unfortunately correct. There is much evidence for this fact, beginning with the actual inequality between Jews and Arab Palestinians, even if the latter are legally Israeli citizens. The claim that Zionism is not really racist is frequently supported by the odd reference to the fact that in Israel, as far as jobs, housing, and civil rights are concerned, not only the Arabs are being disadvantaged but also the so-called black Jews, in other words, the dark-skinned Jews from the various Arab countries, although they are Israeli citizens. Arabs, on the other hand, assert that the discrimination against black Jews is in fact proof of racism, since these Middle Eastern people are actually Arabs of Jewish faith. It must be pointed out that in recent years the strongest anti-Zionist movement among Israelis, the so-called Black Panthers, has formed precisely among these black Jews.

Professor Israel Shahak, a chemist at Jerusalem University, a survivor of the Warsaw ghetto and the concentration camp Belsen, went to Israel after the war as a religious Zionist. However, he considered the discrimination against the Palestinians on the part of Israeli Zionists so appalling that he turned away from Zionism and today, as the president of the Israeli Society for Civil and Human Rights, fights against the discrimination of non-Jewish Palestinians. One example Shahak mentions to illustrate this discrimination are the "emergency statutes" that the British had imposed on Palestine during their mandate. At that time the Jewish settlers, who were affected by the statutes as much as the Arabs, declared these emergency statutes inhumane. Yet, after the foundation of the state of Israel they simply took over these emergency statutes, except that nowadays they are applied exclusively to Arabs, including all Arabs holding Israeli citizenship, but not to Jews. Whoever is not a descendent of a Jewish grandmother is at a disadvantage. The discrimination concerns both marriage and property laws, including leases. After all, the primary owner of the land is, as already planned by Theodor Herzl, the Jewish National Fund. It issues cheap real-estate leases to collective settlements in particular, the so-called kibbutzim, under the condition that the land may only be leased to Jews and that only persons of Jewish blood may work on this land.[1] Shahak was correct in stating – and he made the same statement during his lecture tour in the Federal Republic of Germany: "One just would have to imagine a similar law in Germany, decreeing that only persons of German blood have the right to lease land and cultivate it. In that case there would be no lengthy discussions by the international forum whether or not this constitutes racism."

As stated earlier, I completely agree with Israel Shahak's assessment that unfortunately Zionism is indeed racist, not only with regard to its programs and laws, but also in view of the effects these laws have. Shahak recorded in a comprehensive statistical publication that in 1948 there were 475 Arab villages on Israeli territory; but two years ago there were only 90; the remaining 385 villages had been destroyed by the Israelis. To be sure, we also agreed during our discussions of the matters I present to you today that among the governments who voted in favor of the United Nations resolution against the racism of the Zionists there are some that are even more racist than the Zionists, for example, the truly quite generally anti-Jewish government of Saudi Arabia, which, however, because of its wealth in oil alone is treated very politely by the same papers that spread the nonsense about "leftist anti-Semitism." Or Idi Amin, the dictator of Uganda, who not only makes disgusting anti-Semitic remarks but in addition treated his Indian majority in such as way that one cannot but call it the worst kind of racism. In Egypt and Jordan the government likewise repeatedly made *general* anti-Jewish statements and issued genuine calls for genocide during the Six-Day War in 1967. One must not forget that Hussein's Bedouins, when they slaughtered close to twenty thousand Palestinians in 1972, did so with the rationale that the Palestine Liberation Organization consisted, in effect, of Jew lovers; after all they allegedly did not oppose Jews but only Zionism. They claimed that they married Jewish girls and were altogether unbelieving leftists rather than true sons of Islam.

This notwithstanding, the state of Israel is involved in negotiations with Sadat's Egypt and Hussein's Jordan but refuses obstinately to negotiate with the Palestine Liberation Organization, even though the latter has declared again and again through its speaker

Yasser Arafat that it was not against the Jews but for the equal coexistence of Jews and Arabs in a free Palestine. Israel's rejection has of course political reasons. Already Theodor Herzl wrote in his fundamental book, *The Jewish State*: "For Europe we would represent a piece of the bulwark against Asia in that part of the world. We would serve as an outpost of culture against barbarism." Today Israel seeks to secure itself by serving as an outpost for the United States and against the movements that transform Asia and Africa. Not all Zionists want that, but even highly regarded opponents of these politics such as Nahum Goldmann, who for many years tried to disentangle Israel from the Cold War strategy, were unable to assert themselves. So were the leftist Zionists in Israel who tried to end the discrimination against the Arabs. Yet, we must not forget that even *within* Zionism there are such countermovements. All of the Jews in Israel who today oppose Zionism were at one point "leftist Zionists." Later, to be sure, they found their socialist ideals to be incompatible with Zionism. And of course one must not act as if all Zionists were nothing but fanatic racists, and all anti-Zionists inherent humanitarians. Besides, even among the Zionists who continue to approve of the acts of so-called racial retribution following Palestinian guerilla activity, there are many who already have serious doubts. But they consider deterrence the only way out of the impasse. Many of them experience pangs of conscience sooner or later. And among the Jews in Israel who are involved in fighting Zionism because it is racist are, aside from the Middle Eastern "black Jews," for the most part kibbutzniks or sons of kibbutzniks who studied at universities and later encountered this conflict of conscience. Many of them remember Martin Buber's erstwhile warning (1929, in "Battle for Israel"): "Jews and Arabs living *side by side* will cause them to live *against one another*. For the sake of the future they must live *together*." I want to, I must hope that this living together will overcome and outlast the taboos of Zionism.

But to return to the ominous term "leftist anti-Semitism" in the Federal Republic of Germany: Based on my experience, I am convinced that in reality this phenomenon does not exist. Certainly, members of leftist groups will occasionally say something like: "Once again, the 'Jews' dropped napalm on a Palestinian refugee camp," the same way they said during the napalm war in Vietnam:

"the Americans." Yet they were never anti-American, they merely opposed the American way of waging war and were happy about every American student who protested against it. By the same token, they are *not* anti-Semites!

The first time I encountered the reproach that the Left was anti-Semitic was in a journal for Jewish university students entitled *Shofar*, after the biblical Jewish battle horn. Published in Vienna, it was also distributed in the Federal Republic. This journal contained a page with cartoons of the most diverse types of anti-Zionists. It showed, for example, a German student looking like a disheveled lunatic with a caption that read: "Pipi, the unreflected pseudorevolutionary, who became Ivan's tool and hides his latent atavistic anti-Semitism under the guise of anti-Zionism." The cartoons and texts were strongly reminiscent of the journal *Der Stürmer* of the Hitler era. Arabs were represented in a disgusting fashion, similar to the way Jews had been depicted in the *Stürmer*, and former concentration camp prisoners appeared as well, slandered as anti-Semites. Furthermore, the journal contained a long, equally "objective" article about anti-Semitism on the Left in the Federal Republic.

Unfortunately, all of the above goes hand in hand with certain recent international developments, for example, when Israel not only begins to deepen its friendship with South Africa but provides the South Africans with a warplane by the name of "Kaffir Interceptor." "Kaffir," originally an Arab word for "unclean" persons, became the term the Boers applied to the blacks. In other words, it is a warplane to stop the blacks. The name may be accidental, but it is just as unfortunate as the statement that one actually does not have to be an anti-Semite at all in order to criticize Israeli politics and Zionism.

In leftist circles I often hear that German philo-Semitism is basically only a kind of anti-Semitism. It is true that I, being Jewish, am also opposed to philo-Semitism and hold that a Jew ought to be treated like any other human being. Nonetheless philo-Semitism is based on significantly nobler motives than anti-Semitism. It can, however, if it results in the preaching of uncritical approval, become in time just as dangerous as any uncritical attitude and then might indeed revert to its opposite. Moreover, right-wing philo-Semitism is conducive to acting as unfairly and ruthlessly toward

others – such as toward Palestinians or leftist students – as anti-
Semites did and do toward Jews.

Notes

1. One must not forget the laws that were passed in the late 1940s regarding
the "confiscation and use of the land and property of absentee owners."
Every Arab who during certain critical times was absent from his property
for more than three days was considered an absentee owner according to
the law, even if he had returned immediately after the skirmishes between
Zionists and Palestinians had stopped in and around his village. For this
reason the persons affected by this law, that is, those whose lands were
expropriated because they were absent although they were present, were
called "Nifkadim Nokh-him" (present-absent ones). Their property is
placed under the direction of a commissariat and leased to Jewish Israelis.
The original owners receive income from the lease, less administrative and
maintenance costs; since, however, the lease amounts only to 5 or sometimes even 1 percent of a conventional lease, the owner's annual compensation is usually less than the bus fare needed to pick up the money.

Georg Kreisler

Georg Kreisler was born in Vienna in 1922 as the
only son of a lawyer. He studied music at the Vienna
Conservatory of Music and later became a well-
known political writer, musician, actor, political satirist, and cabaret artist. In 1938 Kreisler and his parents emigrated to the United States, and he became a
U.S. citizen. While living in Hollywood, he continued
his studies at the University of Southern California.
Kreisler refers to his U.S. citizenship when discussing his political orientation, linking it to no specific
political party or nation. In general, his viewpoints
are best understood as those of an author who has
lost his native culture as a result of the Shoah. His
bitter irony is often directed at the Austrian public.
Kreisler has proven himself as a successful arranger,
pianist, and conductor for musicals and film scores,
including Charlie Chaplin's *Monsieur Verdoux*. In 1942
he was drafted into the U.S. army and sent to Europe
as a translator, and, as the successful author of a musical for soldiers, he was given permission to form a
group to entertain the military. In 1946 he moved to
New York City where he performed his own songs in
cabarets and night clubs, worked as an author and
actor on Broadway, and wrote songs for radio and
television. In the 1950s he began traveling to Europe,
and in 1955 he moved to Vienna. Kreisler has lived in
Munich and Berlin; in 1992 he settled in Basel,
Switzerland. He was married to his colleague Barbara
Peters. He published numerous volumes of songs,
short prose texts, satires, novels, and recordings, in-
cluding *Nichtarische Arien* (1967; Non-Aryan arias), *In
Rhythm* (1976; In rhythm), *Worte ohne Lieder* (1986;
Words without songs), *Ist Wien überflüssig?* (1987; Is
Vienna superfluous?), *Der Schattenspringer* (1996; The
shadow jumper), and *Das Auge des Beschauers* (1996;
The eye of the beholder).

Georg Kreisler

Bundschuh the War Criminal

One has to be able to make do without explanations. The truth is different. But the paths are covered with snow, an ill-tempered dog is waiting, and everything is rather uninviting. Perhaps one should simply smile. Surely, help is on the way, struggles through the undergrowth, shouts gray perjuries through the fog. Those who say gray have to prophesy as well. I shall now prophesy the past.

I am innocent. Even then there were no pleasant people, one had to be satisfied with the familiar faces. Besides, one was young, wanted to have confidence, not feel abandoned, and what was one supposed to talk about if not one's own risks? Nowadays one encounters nothing but helpless looks, nobody allows a person to take shelter, the present is always present; none of that was different then. It was merely a different present.

I cannot start with the beginning, I lack the memory. Question and answer, cause and effect, those are children's games. Just imagine, you sit in the store and a lady walks in. Ten years later it turns out she was no lady, it was no store, you were not even there. That's exactly what happened to me.

I have a sister, does that disturb you? She doesn't talk much, she does the dishes or laughs a little. I don't know why she's laughing. There's no explanation for it, one can either laugh or not laugh. One can also kill or not kill. What I oppose is the routine answers. At the start of day everyone has to get along as best he can. One always says that children are not to blame, but I am not to blame either. Once I was a child too; nothing has changed that fact.

Now I write my memoirs. But I explain nothing and tell nothing, I only write. I have a bathroom and a bed, I take a lot of walks, and my memoirs are not important to me. I have been silent for a long time and shall remain silent because life is an enigma. There's nothing science can do about that. Everyone I know says the same thing.

Georg Kreisler

The Unknown Nation

I am a German, but I am a descendent of a nation you probably don't know. My nation lives scattered across the oceans, one finds them entrenched on every island in the world. We are a peculiar nation, no one recognizes us, but we recognize each other. That's enough. Unfortunately no one appreciates us very much, most people even despise us. The fact is that we are very unreliable. My nation's history can be told in a few words.

Our forefathers emerged from a shipwreck, that was a long time ago. This shipwreck became our religion. We believe that there is still a ship circumnavigating the world that one day will take all the members of my nation on board. However, we are pessimists; we also believe that the ship will only save us after the rest of humanity perishes. At that time the ship will dock wherever our people live, and it will take them on board. Once our entire nation will have gathered on the ship, the captain will embark on one last voyage and take all of us to an unknown country. That captain is our god.

Not a particularly attractive religion, I know, but, after all, what religion is all that attractive? Nonetheless, we arrange our lives according to it and try to avoid the mistakes that people nowadays make everywhere. As I have already said, we are unreliable, we even consider reliability a sin. We also oppose punctuality, a sense of duty, and the love of truth, to mention just a few things. Punctual people waste time, dutiful people are unbending, selfish, and cruel, and those who love the truth chase after a chimera, for there are many truths.

Much more could be said about this topic, but I know that you consider your time valuable. My time is valuable as well, but in a different sense. We hold that the only time not wasted is the time one uses to interact with other people. We even have numerous missionaries among us, who attempt to convert our fellow human beings to human neighborliness. In the last two centuries we have converted thirty-four human beings, not many, but nonetheless.

The conversion is complicated, although it can be summarized in one single sentence: one must renounce power. When our ancestors experienced the aforementioned shipwreck, they recognized through it not only the disastrous power of nature, they also recognized that power, no matter what kind, implies death and destruction. Death is a power, and whoever disavows power also disavows death; in other words, he will not die. For that reason our nation will continue to live after all other nations will have died.

It is only natural that all this appears confused to you, but it only does so because you have not learned to manage without your familiar thought patterns. Your thinking is based on the notion of power. The notions of family, marriage, state, profession, and achievement do not function without power. Therefore you consider it impossible for my nation to exist. You cannot imagine that there is a nation nobody knows about, you consider the story of the shipwreck and of our salvation a figment of our imagination, and figments of the imagination are powerless, thus they are of no value to you, but they are to us. I know that I cannot change your mind, in that respect you are no different from most other people, and since I am not a prophet, I cannot tell you when the day of our salvation will come. One thing I can tell you with certainty: that day everyone, including you, will recognize all of us because of our powerlessness.

Unfortunately I cannot provide any concrete pieces of advice. Concrete pieces of advice are concrete pieces of manslaughter. The growing autonomy of political and technological constraints can only be abolished by the emancipation of people, but that is a truism, you are quite right. But the entire world consists of truisms, and so does our nation. Our entire nation is a truism.

Eva Deutsch & Brigitte Schwaiger

Eva Deutsch, née Chawa Fränkel, was born in the shtetl Brzezany in Galicia, Poland, in 1924 into a Polish-Yiddish-German-speaking cultural environment. One of six brothers and sisters, she grew up within the eastern European Jewish tradition, of which she paints a vivid, albeit not uncritical, picture in her autobiographical account *Die Galizianerin* (1982; The Galician woman). Deutsch was the only one of her immediate family who survived the Holocaust. Her story recounts the experience of extreme deterritorialization: in order to survive, Deutsch had to move from place to place, change her identity, and pose as a Christian. After the war she and her husband moved via Bratislava to Vienna. Not a native speaker of German and an outsider to literary circles, Deutsch was not in a position to produce and publish a book by herself about the experiences of her childhood, the Shoah, and her lost culture. *Die Galizianerin* was written by the Austrian writer Brigitte Schwaiger, an established Austrian mainstream author. Deutsch was the resource person for Schwaiger's historical-biographical novel, but ultimately Schwaiger is in control of the text, which inadvertently reflects the power relations between an Austrian postwar author in full command of her native German and a Jewish Shoah survivor who so obviously struggles with the linguistic, conceptual, and ideological patterns superimposed on her perceptions and memories by the German language and the Austrian author. In other ways, however, Deutsch takes charge of the narrative, although Schwaiger emphasizes Deutsch's Yiddish accent and syntax, a symbol of linguistic incompetence, so that the speech ascribed to the Jewish woman comes close to the idiom German and Austrian authors attributed to Galician Jews. In certain cases, one may even wonder if the views expressed by the Jewish first-person narrator are not in effect those of Schwaiger. Tensions such as these are characteristic of the relationship between Austrians and Jews after the Shoah, and Deutsch is certainly aware of them, hence her half deferential, half ironic address "gnädige Frau" (madam, dear lady). Mocking Schwaiger's position of privilege, Deutsch is aware of depending on this Austrian woman – the daughter of a man whose views were far from incompatible with Austrofascism, even National Socialism – to have her story published and distributed. Yet, there are limits to the degree to which she conforms to her collaborator's and readers' expectations. Throughout the text Deutsch insists on her Jewish identity, and her reinterpretation of the New Testament according to which Jesus is the son of a good Jewish woman and himself a suffering Jew positions her close to other Jewish and Jewish-identified authors such as Else Lasker-Schüler and Nelly Sachs. Moreover, the decidedly rebellious, feminist tone of Deutsch's voice distinguishes the "ghetto" stories in *Die Galizianerin* from the more nostalgic ones by male authors such as Arnold Zweig or Isaac Bashevis Singer. Deutsch's assessment of her childhood world is reminiscent of Esther Singer Kreitman's *Der Sheydim Tunts* (1936), translated as *Deborah* (1946). Topsy Küppers recast Eva Deutsch's account into a play, with which she went on tour. Eva Deutsch died in Vienna in 1990.

Brigitte Schwaiger was born in 1949 in Freistadt, Upper Austria, as the daughter of a physician. She studied psychology and Romance and German literature and language at the University of Vienna. In 1968 she married a veterinarian from Spain and lived in Mallorca and Madrid, where she taught German and English. During this time Schwaiger became involved in painting and sculpture. Her marriage having ended in divorce, she enrolled in the Linz Pedagogical

Academy while working as an actress, dramaturge, and secretary. Gradually, writing became her full-time occupation. Since 1975 she has lived in Vienna. Her first novel, *Wie kommt das Salz ins Meer* (1977; Why is there salt in the sea?) was an immediate success and established her as a major woman writer of the postwar generation. Her novel went through fifteen editions within the first year of publication and was followed by a collection of poetry and prose texts entitled *Mein spanisches Dorf* (1978; My Spanish village). The volume deals with the topic of childhood and youth in rural Austria. Schwaiger's second novel, *Lange Abwesenheit* (1980; Long absence), deals with the generational tensions between the prewar and postwar generation in Austria, particularly the rift between the narrator and her father. Schwaiger's critical attitude toward her own roots and her interest in women's issues and Austria's recent history provide the common ground between her and the Holocaust survivor Eva Deutsch, with whom Schwaiger coauthored *Die Galizianerin*. Despite these shared concerns, however, there is a great deal of tension in the narrative, which is ultimately controlled by the German-speaking author. Deutsch's irony, her ostensible subservience vis-à-vis the well-known younger writer, and the emphasis she places on her Jewish identity throughout the text alongside statements that seemingly exonerate Germans, even Nazis, suggest different underlying assumptions and agendas on the part of the two collaborators.

Eva Deutsch & Brigitte Schwaiger

EXCERPT FROM

The Galician Woman

Madam, not even a picture of my family remains in my possession. And after the war, in Preßburg [Bratislava] – I was already married – my husband brings home a credenza. At that time such pieces were somehow available. People were trying to furnish their places, and my husband had a credenza with a marble plate taken upstairs to our place. Surely it came from a very rich family, from a Jewish family. After the Jews of Preßburg had been annihilated, their entire furniture was piled up in a big temple, and after the war it just stood there. Any Jew who needed a piece of furniture hauled one off to his place. So my husband picked the beautiful credenza.

He cleans it quickly and pulls out a drawer and in this drawer he finds a postcard. And he's about to throw it away because he has no particular use for it, although he came from an orthodox family and had an education. When he's about to toss it out, I pick it up. And I look at it closely. Since I know how to read the Hebrew letters, I say: How about that, you want to throw this away? I am a descendent of this family! This is my tribe! It was a photograph of a tombstone. And it fell into my hand. I had it enlarged. You can take a look at it, it's on the piano. On my mother's side of the family the Fränkels are descendents of Shabsai Cohen. The cohanim are the priests. There are also the leviim, they are the attendants. And then there are the Israelites, the people. At the time of the Temple the priests, who served God, performed the ceremonies. According to the Bible they had no claim on real property and lived off the things the people gave them, off the donations. It was ordained that way in the Book of Moses. And the leviim were their attendants. They helped them to wash their hands. Also the glass had to be cleaned, and the sacrifices had to be prepared. Well, the Temple no longer exists. The Jews ended up in the Diaspora. Hence there is no Temple, there is nothing at all.

This Shabsai Cohen was a great scholar, so that everything, his deeds, his knowledge, and his achievements were recorded on his tombstone. In secular terms his rank was comparable to that of a professor of philosophy, only in Talmud. He was a rabbi. My father, my grandfather, all of them had been schooled privately! The boys did not attend the public school; it was a secular school, after all, and a Jew was not allowed to uncover his head. And at school they were forced to hand in their kipa. I come from such a family. They belonged to a community that is called Hasids. I am thirteen generations removed from that Cohen. Approximately in 1664 he fled from Poland to Moravia because of the pogroms. He was buried in Czechoslovakia, and it was mere coincidence that this photograph remained in my possession.

Do you know what was being discussed today on the radio talk show where everyone can call in and take part in the conversation? We, all of us, are crazy, a certain professor, a psychiatrist, said. So I called in and said, Mister Professor! Because he had said: We are all crazy and realize that something is wrong. I say, It can't be true that all of us are crazy. All I intended to say, dear lady, was the following two words: It can't work out, because we are not perfect. But the moment I call, my brain had a flashback. And I said, Our religion was taken from us. Do you know why I said that? I lived in a Communist state in Preßburg. And my husband thought that since I had such a Christian appearance I should deny my religion. I say, Are you serious? I have experienced such a horrible war and now I am not supposed to profess my religion? And I did profess it and was penalized. That serves you right, my husband said. And I say, Too bad, earlier it was a matter of life and death, now it's only a matter of my livelihood. In the case of the professor in the radio show my memory suddenly clicked that I had been supposed to deny my religion. Somehow I articulated that too fast. But at that point I could no longer retreat. And he claimed that somehow the religion had not been taken away but the church had failed to come through.

Well, I have digressed. There you go. But I want to give you an idea of how it's done, even though I'm not even allowed to. This is the way the priest positions his fingers to give the blessing, he puts them together like this, but we are not supposed to watch. One has to keep one's head lowered. Only the priests have the right to see the people. And of those priests, since we are already on the topic, a certain high priest is mentioned in conjunction with Jesus. What was his name? A certain Caiphas. In my opinion Jesus was a Jew through and through. A scholar, a good person. He only wanted the best for the entire population. The population was oppressed by the Roman government. What was his name, the other one? Herod! Well, and Jesus, to keep the people from despairing about their situation, he comforted them. He promised them Heaven and everything possible.

You know, in despair and about to perish, you will make promises. And Holy Mary, Miriam, had the honor of being his mother. But leave Jesus out of this. I tell you how things were with the Christian religion. The Christian religion was introduced by a ruler by the name of Constantine. It was meant to be unintelligible. He was a leading heathen who converted! And you must not take offense, but the Christian religion has a lot of heathen elements. Consider Jesus a Jew who was, to use the modern term, a revolutionary, a reformer. And the old Jew with all his shortcomings was unyielding. He had no other choice but to denounce Jesus. At first Jesus was asked to stop subverting the established laws, because they are sacred and people must not exclude themselves from the community. He was supposed to remain a devout Jew according to the ancient law. Jesus didn't want to. He, too, was unyielding, insisted on his views, and preferred to die on the cross. Crucifixion, however, was a Roman practice. Jews don't crucify. You have a law in the Book of Moses that a guilty person must stand trial. The elders in the council tried peaceful means to change his mind. If a person commits a sin, the community stones him to death. An eye for an eye, a tooth for a tooth. That's the law of the Bible. You must take into consideration that the Israelites were desensitized, having been slaves in Egypt. They had to be kept strictly in line. To prevent them from becoming villains and murderers. And there is an urging in the Bible for fathers to discipline their sons when they are disobedient. This way he saves the child from becoming a brute. The child must obey others, including his parents. So that he is productive and lives happily. If the father does not discipline his son, the father will be beaten by his son in his old age.

Matters of religion are a very sensitive issue, madam. Many intelligent people failed when it came to that! How can we two women assume to be smarter? We can only do one thing: that both of us uphold our convictions and be fond of one another nonetheless. Mean well. Be honest. Believe me, I had no intention of going into the gas chamber cheerfully.

Let's assume a man had come and said, I shall save you and take you for my wife, but you must become a Christian. Without thinking I would have said no. I would have preferred the gas chamber. I'm sorry, but it's true. What would Jesus have done in that case? I believe he would have gone into the gas chamber as well. He would not have abandoned his Jewishness. He was born a Jew, he died a Jew. It's not his fault that the Jews were murdered in his name. The others did that after his death. He would have wept terribly about the gas chambers. God is there for all of us, madam. We are supposed to seek rather than study him. A faithful Jew has no doubts. He believes. The "Eternal Jew" stems, I believe, from professing one, the eternal God. Only later it became a derogatory term for the Jew because he had no country of his own. Being driven from country to country, hunted, robbed, raped, strangled. But the persecutors did not succeed!

Madam, if the story is too stressful for you, take a breath of fresh air! Eat well. You are even allowed to take medicine in case you are nervous. If I get on your nerves, just take the adhesive tape! Tape my mouth shut! I talk too much. If you can't sleep, take a pill. In fact, you ought to take medicine.

Listen, a child born to Jewish parents was very sick and threw up everything he had in his stomach. He did not tolerate any medication. So the parents went to the rabbi. The rabbi told them to hold the medicine in front of the child's nose, so that the child would take in the aroma. And he got well again. You see, in every situation the Jew finds a remedy.

Madam, everything I'm telling you is true. How could I tell you things that are not true. And I have to add something regarding my brother Samuel. It haunts me. I had to write it down. Just wait until I put on my eye glasses. After all, I'm half blind!

Well, then.

The story is: He did not become *kalle*, he became smarter. *Kalle* is a Yiddish expression. It means: bad. Perhaps it was even derived from the Hebrew. I really have no idea. That's how they say it in jargon.

Well, as I have already mentioned to you, madam, I had a brother named Samuel. He was the firstborn. He was very gifted and had a good memory, this child. He was also a mathematician. You know, when he was still at our parents' home with us, he calculated exactly how many cigarettes would fit into our room. He was so involved in math that he calculated such nonsense. Give him the height of the room and the size of a cigarette, and he figured so much of this will fit inside. He carried his heart on his mouth just like Eliezer. But Samuel was not a whistler! He was a scholar. And he was hard-headed in the Jewish sense. He was very religious. As a boy, before you go to bed, you say your prayers, just like the Christians do. He was praying a special prayer, after which you were not allowed to speak anymore. And this child was not even yet required to adhere to this rule, because he was less than thirteen years of age. He did not even have to say the prayer. But he would sit down in his bed like a Turk, his legs crossed, and recite the entire prayer from memory. And it was not short!

Afterward he would turn to the wall, and you could have beaten him to death, you would not get another word out of him! Regardless if there was a fire and whatever it would be, he would not budge. As if one had taped his mouth shut with adhesive tape, yes, yes. At fourteen or fifteen he already studied with men who had beards and *paies* (sidelocks). Some of them were even married, and he sat on the same bench, at the same rabbi's house. Our rabbi's name was Halberstein. The *rojte* Mottel was his *chosed*, which means "a young man."

Our Samuel, the Talmudist, did not wear a tie but a shirt front made of black silk. And he wore the caftan over it. At the age of twelve he was sent to the yeshiva to study and be devout. Following this training he was supposed to become a rabbi. For his celebration at the age of thirteen, for his bar mitzvah, my mother sent a big package with pastry as well as tefillin, his philacteries, to the yeshiva. And these tefillin were from our grandfather. They had been kept especially for him. My mother requested them from her brothers, because her brothers actually had the rightful claim on the tefillin. My grandfather had owned several other pairs, and she asked for one of them. In other words, my mother was proud because Samuel was a very good student. He kept up with the men and often was even smarter, according to the rabbi's report. His memory worked so precisely, you know, that for every question he had an answer. He must have been brilliant.

Well, all that happened in Biecz. Now, one day the two boys come home, my brother and a neighbor's son. They were sick, the doctor was called, and he said: that's pleurisy. It was in the middle of summer. Samuel had a high fever. He hallucinated! The second boy died. They were only sixteen or seventeen, my brother and his fellow student. Now my father blamed my mother for sending the child to that yeshiva. Maybe he had not had enough to eat there! Maybe the air was bad or something! And now we shall lose him! My parents had arguments because of all that. But in that situation fights did not help.

Doctors came and brought different medicines. I went to the river, cut branches of a willow tree, sat for hours by his bedside, and fanned the air. I also chased away the flies, because there were lots of flies, although we had flypaper everywhere. They were a real nuisance, those flies! But God did help! My brother survived the crisis, and my mother sent him to her sister, who lived in a city where the air was much better. This aunt had a son who was much older than my brother. And modern. Educated in the Jewish sense, but modern. And his influence on my brother was such that the latter no longer wanted to return to the yeshiva. Well, the entire family was in despair. Now he had to learn something so that one day he would be able to provide for a family. That's what his cousin had talked him into!

My father had relatives in Biecz, owners of a cloth towel factory. He sent Samuel to them to learn weaving. But my brother was not handy. For that reason they transferred him to the warehouse. Thereby, somehow, he will develop into something, there, with the fabrics.

But the war comes. My brother packs two suitcases full, takes a train, and wants to go home. The trains stop because the Germans are bombing. So the people had to walk. The suitcases became too heavy for him. So he throws one of the suitcases away and keeps the second. His wardrobe was inside, madam. In both of the suitcases. Then the second one becomes too heavy to carry as well, and he throws it away also. Now he is left without anything and walks. But he was not the only one to walk. Masses of people were fleeing. Only that the Germans caught up with him and put him into a camp, where several hundred Jews and Christians were thrown together, boys and young men. One suggested to my brother to escape from the camp. The other boy had somehow looked around more closely and noticed a possibility somewhere. If they had been caught, they would have been shot dead. But Samuel went along with the boy. I don't know who the second one was, Samuel told us the story as I tell it. He ran away together with the other boy and came home.

There were barracks boarded up with wooden planks or whatever they had available, and this other guy must have found a hole somewhere. The Germans had rounded up everyone, Jews or not Jews, young folks: Let's go! Our Samuel was a tall, slender boy. And how he arrived home: in rags, bruised, his head uncovered, exhausted, without money, without everything. But underneath his shirt he carried the tefillin! And he came back home with the tefillin. The boy was so religious, he even turned his face away when a girl passed by.

Until I was twelve years of age I actually wanted to become a teacher of religion. However, girls are not allowed to study the Talmud. Meanwhile, in the city an old gentleman was taken ill, an attorney. He suffered a stroke, which left him paralyzed. Gradually the family started to be ruined. There were two daughters in the house. Although they were elegant, they were so very emaciated. They were decked out like parrots. Such parrotlike girls. And they were not even young any longer. The third one was missing. Rumor had it that she was studying. One day the third daughter returns and takes over the attorney's practice. And people talked about it all over town. And I saw her. She was athletic, well-dressed, not made up, and had straight hair as I do. And she was an attorney. She provided for her family and remained single. I don't know what happened to her later. She rode a bicycle and wore a pants skirt. You know the kind, when she walks, it looks like a skirt. When she gets on the bicycle, it's a pair of pants. And it occurred to me, for God's sake! I could become such a person! But I did not end up becoming an attorney.

But I am no longer as narrow-minded as my upbringing; I am a worldly person now, but one who is even more religious. I light candles and keep the Sabbath.

This Aron, this brother of mine, he was a born singer. I used to get Bs in singing. But he was a very talented singer. Would you imagine such a boy to play cowboy and some such things? He would pull a tablecloth over his head, jump on the chair, small as he was, aged seven, place the prayer book on the chair, the siddur, position himself properly, and begin to recite prayers. Just as if we were at the temple. And he knew the melodies. I was the attendant. He took the tablecloth because he was not allowed to touch a tallit. Father told him that, right? In our parts Jews have a tallit. A prayer shawl. My father had one too. You must have one. It is worn on the head. And the boy had seen that at the temple. So he took a tablecloth, a white one, put it on his head, and prayed exactly as it is printed in the prayer book. He sang the melody like a cantor.

I sang along, madam, I knew how to as well. I can sing a melody to you because every Saturday evening I went to the rabbi's with my father. Also, my father most likely had a talent for singing. I must have been still very young. There were approximately fifty men over there, married and unmarried, and this rabbi by the name of Halberstein. There he sat in a baroque *fauteuil*, which was surely very old, perhaps two hundred fifty years. There he sat so elegant. He was also very beautiful, this rabbi. Oh, how beautiful he was! And before the end of the Sabbath some of the men who had the talent to sing gave a presentation. Such men were greatly admired.

But there were also men who could not sing a tune. They had no talent. And they were not, as they say, admired. They could pray, but they could not hold a tune, they did not have the aptitude. My father did sing. He sang one particular song, and I was so proud of him.

That was a real honor, you know. I can sing that melody to you, if you like, but not as beautifully. I know how to sing everything, but it does not come out so well because of my throat.

Actually I had wanted to study. You know, I was a lecturer. I did not recite, I lectured. Madam, the schoolteacher gave us the topic "The Journey into the World" and I spoke from memory for the entire hour! Then she said to the students: Please, who has any criticism? One boy raised his hand. His name was Schlank. His father was some sort of privileged person, some intellectual. He raised his hand, saying that this and that had been missing. That's beside the point, the teacher told him. Imagine, she brushed him off, just like that. And he was one of the protégés and I was a Jewess. I came to school speaking in jargon and gave such a presentation!

When it came to history, geography, or religion, subjects where you must know something, I was usually surrounded by several students in the hallway during the longer breaks. Oh, I beg you, Chawa, do you know the lesson? I was so ambitious! Madam, I spent the entire break making presentations to them. And they listened and this way got some idea.

But I must have been peculiar when I was a child. I could not get over the fact that I was not a boy. I would have gladly accepted a boy's life and characteristics. Because boys had better opportunities to pursue their studies. I wanted to study the Talmud, just like my brothers. To keep up with them! They were, after all, my playmates. And I can sing the Jewish prayers, because I grew up with my brothers. The cantor sings, and the congregation repeats after him. Then there is the choir. They help him. And they add the harmonies, which make it all beautiful, you understand, so that it pleases the ear. After, we rock back and forth. And you don't care for it to be likeable. Women do not rock, only men do. But I rock. When you watch the wind, the leaves, as the trees are gently rocking, that's how the congregation rocks. And I cannot keep my body quiet. My nerves are worked up so much that I rock along with the congregation. It is not fitting for a woman, I am aware of that, but I cannot keep myself in check. I rock with them. I have always done as my brothers did.

My second brother, Elias, broke my nose when we were playing. I jumped into his fist, and he had such strong hands, Elias. He was a tinker. And we played in the street, I was five, and he somehow lifted his fist, I jumped, and he smacks me in the nose. I was all covered with blood. Supposedly I used to have a Greek nose, a thin nose. None of us children had a bump on their nose. Only I did. But my mother said: You had the most beautiful nose of them all, and this had to happen especially to you! My bone is broken here, you see? I got such a spanking. My mother took it so much to heart. Because I was a girl. I was disfigured. Well, there it is, the bump. After the war I could have had an operation, but I no longer wanted one. As you can see, I got married anyway. I did not place much stock in beauty. Only my mother thought: A girl with a broken nose, you know what I mean. She was not indifferent to that. But I did not notice anything, because I had no idea what I had looked like before.

And this Elias, the tinker, carved a chess game for us, a big one. I still play chess to this day. But I must not. I am already too weak. Thinking hard causes my heart to beat fast – after all, that game requires one to speculate. Our father taught us the game of chess. And my brother carved it. I tell you, the king was big, at least fifteen centimeters. My father traced it for him and he carved it. The black figures were painted with ink, the white ones were left in their natural wood color. And then he built the chessboard.

Elias also made cards. He colored them magnificently, jack, spades, hearts, and the queen. All we played was Forty-Four. Our father did not teach us that, he did not know the game. But Elias had somehow found out about it.

He also built the joiner's bench himself, and I assisted him. And he weaved whatever you might like of leather, he weaved belts using differently colored leather, and then he sewed, using clasps and whatever else, and I helped him. Not always, only when I had time.

As for me, I did not play with dolls. I did sew clothes for my sister's dolls, and I made scarves, dresses, aprons, bed sheets, and whatever was needed. Give me needle, thread, and material, and I put it together. But my sister was very motherly. She had a doll in each arm. Then she came to me to have outfits made. And she began to complain: My poor doll, her stomach hurts! She has a fever! And then I played the doctor and gave her a prescription. And I told her what to do, so that the doll would get better. I recommended, for instance, to administer aspirin. And that she should make a warm compress and put the doll to bed.

She was such a motherly child, you know, but she was not a good student. I took such trouble with her, you have no idea. Sometimes I got downright mad. But at play she was so playful, so caring, so thoughtful, and I played supersmart. I wanted to make beautiful things for her. So I decorated her cradle, made her a hat, a cloth-covered board made of cardboard, a *kaschkett* (casket). And I sewed ornaments on it.

The very little one was still a baby. Oftentimes, my mother placed her in her basket when she wanted to have peace and quiet. You understand, she did not want the child to get scalded in between the pots. Her name was Sießel, sweet as sugar. Sweety. That's the name of my great-grandmother on my father's side. And I continually tied her bows and dolled her up quite a bit.

The name of the motherly sister was Hindele. She was a fat little girl, like a barrel. According to the registry her real name was Hendel. Hindele. What I'm telling you right now happened when we were already in the strange city, at the time when all of us were still in that place called Brzezany. Late one evening, when I was at the shop, she was walking home from a friend's house, and a dog followed her, quite a big dog, and she was very frightened. She came home yelling. A dog, a dog, a dog, she screamed and became so ill she was taken to bed. So the doctor was called. There was something wrong with her heart. Just a few days later the child was dead. She was so pudgy, such a fat little girl. When she ran, she overexerted herself.

Jakov Lind

In a *New York Times* book review of 24 January 1965, Jakov Lind was called "the most notable short-story writer to appear in the last two decades." He was born in Vienna in 1927 as the son of Jewish parents. Eleven years of age at the time of the Nazi invasion of Austria, Lind fled to Holland where he found a foster home. His parents went into exile in Palestine. When in 1941 the Germans conquered the Netherlands, Lind managed to change his identity. With a forged ID card he survived the war years in Germany, working as a farm laborer, gardener, and sailor. His education includes two years at the art academy. Lind describes the conflicts and identity crisis he underwent during these years in *Counting My Steps: An Autobiography* (1969). After the war he moved to Palestine, where he met Edgar Hilsenrath. The two aspiring authors worked odd jobs and discussed their literary plans. Via Amsterdam Lind returned to Vienna. Since 1954 Lind has lived in London, New York, and Mallorca. A frequent visitor in Europe, he has taken an active part in Vienna literary life since the postwar years. Lind writes in both English and German. His experience of a complete loss of trust and certainty is reflected in his literary as well as in his autobiographical works, such as *Landschaft in Beton* (1962; *Landscape in Concrete*), *Eine Seele aus Holz* (1962; *Soul of Wood*), *The Silver Foxes Are Dead, and Other Plays* (1968), *Numbers: A Further Autobiography* (1972), *The Trip to Jerusalem* (1974), *Der Erfinder* (1988; *The Inventor*), *Crossing: The Discovery of Two Islands* (1991), *Vienna 1938: Return to a Distant Land* (1992), and *Nahaufnahme* (1997; *Close-up*). Bawdy, cynical, and satirical, Lind's texts undermine the notion that anti-Semitism and the Shoah represent aberrations from an otherwise sound moral and legal system. Rather, he portrays the profound corruption of his native Austrian society, suggesting that the tendencies that made the genocide possible continued to prevail after 1945. In his more abstract short texts he examines the phenomena of power, loyalty, and exploitation in such a way as to reveal the failure of modern civilization in dealing with the innate cruelty and competitiveness of the human species.

Jakov Lind

The Story of Lilith and Eve

Before God created Eve, legend tells us, he created Lilith, but Lilith left Adam, as she could never agree with him in smaller and larger matters, and Eve became Adam's true wife, that is, a woman who is always in agreement with her man. Lilith left, but Lilith didn't leave for good, for she returns to haunt Adam as lust, legend tells us.

Once upon a time there was a man who was haunted by Lilith. The demon had disguised herself in the clothes of an ordinary, simple, agreeable woman and came to visit Adam when he was alone.

"Why are you on your own?" Lilith asked. "Where is your woman, the one who came to replace me?"

"She is out in the country where she went to visit relatives. She will return soon and she will not be pleased to find you here, for she fears you."

"Why should my sister be afraid of me?" asked Lilith. "I am as simple in my heart as she is, I am as good and kind as she is, I love my parents and I love my children just as she does. But we don't think alike – our difference between us is in our minds, not in our bodies."

"I believe you," said Adam, "and I love you, but I need a peaceful life."

"Have it your way," said Lilith, "have your peaceful life. I am just your other woman. I will not leave you but love you as I always did."

Adam looked into her eyes and said no more. Her eyes were like doors wide open into a world he had nearly forgotten, and he stepped inside.

They were in each other's arms and mouths when Eve returned. "Lilith and Adam are united," she said. "Stay with me, sister. I will bring food to your bed." She brought to their bed food and drink both, and retired to a far corner of the house, where she crouched beside the stove to keep herself warm and went into a trance. She left her body and entered the body of her sister Lilith, and thus she embraced and kissed Adam and felt his love for her as she had never known it before.

"But I am your Eve," said Lilith, "why do you love me so passionately, as you have never loved me with such passion before?"

Adam laughed and said, "You will leave with dawn and I will not see you for a while. If I am passionate, it's because our happiness is for but a short time."

"How can you say that?" said Lilith. "I will be here tomorrow and the day after and so forth for the rest of your life. Why do you love me so passionately? Do you think I am who I appear to be? I am Eve, speaking through my sister's mouth."

"You are joking," laughed Adam. "I know you will leave at dawn and will not be back for a long time."

Lilith (who was now Eve) kissed him and said, "I wish this were so, but alas I cannot leave you. I will stay with you because you are full of fire for this other woman whose body I have taken over. Look at me carefully and tell me whether you don't see that I am your wife, Eve?"

"Eve sits in the far corner of the house," said Adam, but when he looked, he could not see his wife. What he saw were merely the flames from the stove.

3. The Generation of Austrofascism, World War II, and the Shoah

Ruth Klüger Angress

Ruth Klüger Angress, born in Vienna in 1931, survived the concentration camps Theresienstadt and Auschwitz-Birkenau. After the Shoah she moved to New York. She studied at Hunter College and the University of California at Berkeley, from which she received a Ph.D. in German in 1967. Klüger, a professor of German at the University of California at Irvine, specializes in Kleist, nineteenth-century literature, Stifter, and Holocaust literature. She also taught at the University of Virginia and chaired the Department of Germanic Languages and Literatures at Princeton University. She received the Rauriser Prize for Literature (1993), the Grimmelshausen Prize (1993), the Marie-Luise-Kaschnitz-Prize (1994), and the Testimonial of the Heine Society (1997). In addition to *weiter leben* (1992; Continuing to live), she published *The Early German Epigram: A Study in Baroque Poetry* (1971), *Katastrophen: Über deutsche Literatur* (1994; Catastrophes. On German literature), *Von hoher und niedriger Literatur* (1996; On highbrow and lowbrow literature), *Frauen lesen anders* (1996; Women read differently), and numerous articles on Lessing, Kleist, Grillparzer, Stifter, Thomas Mann, and Schnitzler. Klüger has been a guest at Marcel Reich-Ranicki's *Literarisches Quartett* and participated in the TV production *Reisen ins Leben – Weiterleben nach einer Kindheit in Auschwitz* (1996), together with Gerhard Durlacher and Yehuda Bacon. Klüger lives in both California and Göttingen, Germany.

Ruth Klüger Angress

Halloween and a Ghost

I

Unlike real people, ghosts are obvious,
Thinly disguised and come when most expected.
Is that why you stand at my door on Halloween,
With a sheet over your head like the other kids,
Asking for candy, Brother?

Ripples of water where you are swimming,
Your questioning voice saying "Ampersand?"
These I recall and your sailor hat and
In a wintry school yard the shape of your breath,
But I forget the form of your death,
There being so many ways of killing.

Dead boys shouldn't walk the streets.
Real ghosts should wear real sheets.
The heart may break of tricks and can't give treats.

II

You are the skipped sentence in a book I'm reading.
You are the kitchen knife that slips into the thumb.
Memory: the autonomous twitch of an aching muscle.
You are the word that is always mistyped
And, erased, defaces the page.

Tonight your two nephews play host here.
Apples and peanuts are theirs to bestow
With squeals of delight, for they do not know
That it's always you who is ringing the bell,
Changing the house to a pumpkin hell.
("There is no such thing as a ghost, dear.")

Spilled ink I give.
Tears have run through a sieve.
Wine and milk are for lovers and children who live.

Ruth Klüger Angress

An Admonition

Choose of the many spirits
A companionable ghost.
Walk by his side in silence
Along the brown coast.

Don't blurt out your fears and forebodings,
Though the antechambers of Hell
Deafen your ears with their roaring –
Hold your peace and don't bore him,
Where sound is whorled in a shell

Among driftwood, stranger to handle
Than table or bed,
And sand shifts like time in your sandal,
And you know you can't keep a candle
Burning all night for the dead.

Keep all words in abeyance
Along this brown coast.
Hold for a while in silence
Converse with a ghost.

Ruth Klüger Angress

Vienna Neuroses

I

They say:
In the executioner's house
do not mention
the noose.
I know –
and with every step I take I mention
executions.
Remembrance offends
against good manners.

I was born in the executioner's house.
Naturally I return.
In crooked hiding places
I search for the noose.
A thread remained stuck in the back of my neck.
My perseverance was my luck.

But the noose was lost
and the executioner died.
Lilacs bloom at the site of the gallows.

II

A bridge-saintly Nepomuk
stands in the courtyard at Bauernmarkt One,
where I live.
How on earth did he get here?
Aren't there enough bridges
that require something saintly

and don't get it?
Here, he appears like a mockery.

Here, he is wasted.
Many people perish
in torrential rivers,
and he greets you
between the elevator and the garbage bin:
Who needs it?

Or is there a bridge here, after all,
one just as invisible as the river?
No tourist in the Jasomirgottstraße
has an idea of his travail,
for he is the one who guards against evil,
he (his wood) fills the gap
and subdues the danger.
We see him next to the wastepaper,
but he knows to what end
he was hauled to this place.

Saint Nepomuk, pray for us, especially
for me, so that I do not fall into the waters
that I can't see and therefore can't watch out.
Dear sanctimonious one, do a good turn:
Look after the Jewish customers,
so that I won't drown at Bauernmarkt One.

Ruth Klüger Angress

Lanzmann's *Shoah* and Its Audience

I

At one o'clock in the afternoon on a weekday, at $10 a ticket for Part I of a nine-hour "documentary," the cinema on Broadway is packed. Some in the audience are obviously survivors, myself included, but there are also many younger people, an overwhelmingly though not exclusively Jewish audience.

Shoah is in several languages, spoken with a variety of accents and accuracy.[1] There is German and English, translator's French, Polish, German again, sung and spoken, Yiddish, Hebrew, and more German, a little Italian and more English and the final words of the film in Hebrew, by a man who remembers his thoughts in the silence of the Warsaw ghetto after it had been evacuated: "I am the last Jew. I'll wait for morning and for the Germans."

Shoah is interviews, faces and voices of victims and guards and onlookers. It is people remembering, and shots of Auschwitz and Treblinka and Chelmno (Kulmhof), as they are now with only words and no pictures to recall what they were. For example, Lanzmann has interviewed in front of the church of Chelmno, where Jews were once kept before their deaths. The camera shows a procession emerging from the church, very colorful, with genuflecting, mini-skirted girls in white. The camera lingers. The words about mass deaths still reverberate like a subtext, while the eye is pleased to take in images that are ghoulishly inappropriate. The present superimposes itself: a church in Poland, picturesque.

Renais's *Night and Fog* also juxtaposed the present and the past.[2] The thrust of Renais's film is an admonition to remember in order to prevent future catastrophes. There was a beautiful lyric text, written by a survivor, which now sounds too poetic, too idiosyncratic. For Lanzmann memory is a festering trauma in the minds of the survivors on screen whom he invites us to join in an act of exorcism with no discernable message.

I don't believe in going back. Lanzmann does. The museum culture that has sprung up around the concentration camps is based on a sense of *spiritus loci* which I lack. What was done there could be repeated elsewhere, I have argued, conceived as it was by human minds, carried out by human hands, somewhere on earth, the place irrelevant, so why single out the sites that now look like so many others? I don't go back to where I've been. I have escaped. Lanzmann goes back to where he has never been. No landscape, I have always believed, can recall what happened, for the stones don't cry out. Lanzmann believes they do. Standing on a rutted road where the dead and the dying once accidentally fell out of the killer vans, and if the exhaust fumes hadn't quite choked them, they were shot while crawling in the mud, he reminds us that those who have knowledge of these things haven't really escaped. As the hours pass the audience will have that knowledge too, and some will try to escape it by letting their attention drift. The "boredom" of this film is of a very special kind.

Like all survivors I know that Auschwitz, when the Nazis killed Jews there, felt like a crater of the moon, a place only peripherally connected with the human world. It is this "otherness" of the death camps that we have such difficulty conveying. But once the killing stopped these former camps became a piece of our inhabited earth again. When I was a child there in the summer of 1944, a former teacher showed me a blade of grass and said, "You see, even in Auschwitz there is grass, things grow." He meant it as a life-affirming statement, and I understood it as such and in my hard-boiled, childish way I despised him for it. He was a Central European humanist, steeped in a gentler tradition than I, who had lived all of my short conscious life under Hitler and the last 18 months of it in starving, crowded, disease-ridden Theresienstadt. I felt contempt and bitterness that a grownup should tell me as a kind of comfort that here in Auschwitz the grass might survive while we didn't. The teacher was probably killed, for few survived the June 1944 gassing of B II b, the "family" camp that in its earlier stages figures prominently in the second part of *Shoah*. There is plenty of grass in Lanzmann's long shots of the camp site today. I look at its technicolored image and I think of that middle-aged man who was trying to tell me something about the resilience of life in general when I felt only naked 12-year-old terror for my own particular life. If I could, I would take back my rejection of him by filling in a blurred memory. And so, after a full six hours of film, I begin to understand why Lanzmann cares about place.

Every one of the languages spoken in the film is understood by someone in the audience. People react before the subtitles come on. They laugh, scoff, whisper to each other in argument, in short, they participate in the interviews. They refuse to be passive, as if the weight of this collective memory were too great to be borne without some reaction that breaks the spell somewhat. One man who has endured in stony silence finally pays for it when he gets up and walks out, muttering that he can't take any more. The rest of the audience work off the tension by reacting audibly. I have come with some students and practice academic restraint. Once in a while I correct a subtitle for them or point out a detail they might miss. I come back the next day alone for the second part. Now the theater is more than half empty; I sit by myself with no neighbors to distract me. During intermission a woman complains to the management that the theater is cold. It isn't: the film has drained her of warmth. After intermission I, too, start shivering and huddling and talk back to the screen as a way of warming up.

At that point Rudolf Vrba,[3] who escaped from Auschwitz in 1944, was talking about the death of a man whom I knew. Fredy Hirsch (sic: not Freddy, as the printed text has it – let his name stand as we knew it) was an idol of those children of Theresienstadt who lived together in "children's homes." Fredy was thirty, Vrba says (I interject that he seemed younger) and he had "a very close relation with the children." This time I turn to Lanzmann and begin to explain why or how Fredy was charismatic to children though apparently not to adults. Vrba recalls that Fredy was to be a leader in a planned uprising, but that he failed because he worried too much about the children and ended by committing suicide. Like many incidents in the film, this story ties in with another one, told by the historian Raul Hilberg, about the death by suicide of Adam Czerniakow, of the Warsaw ghetto *Judenrat*, who could not bear to abandon the ghetto's orphans.[4] But Fredy was different, he was not a strong personality, the adults did not trust him, only the children adored him. Vrba does not know this, and my impulse is to fill in this information for the two men talking up there, as if the barrier between screen and spectator had been abolished. At the same time the exercise of memory is so complete that I grieve for my community's lost opportunity to act and, resurrecting Fredy Hirsch, I try to convince him that the children would have followed him, that he could have had a crusade of children with everyone over six obeying his orders.

Another survivor takes up the story and tells of the death by gas of these two convoys from Theresienstadt. They had arrived in September and December and were killed in March, knowing exactly what was about to happen to them. Filip Müller, whose mind is stocked for the rest of his natural days with the details of the deaths of some of my childhood friends, tells about it with the Czech-accented German that a part of my family spoke.[5] I sit slumped in my seat and offer his brightly colored image the irrelevant facts of my own survival.

I have described my reaction in such detail because the peculiar power of this film depends on the extent to which the viewer is willing to let himself be drawn into Lanzmann's enterprise. The tendency to respond vehemently and directly seems to be widespread. People say and some reviewers have written that they wanted to get up and interfere with Lanzmann when he was pressuring his interviewees too much. And although Lanzmann does not inflict himself unduly on the audience but keeps pretty much in the background, viewers often express a strong reaction to him personally.

It is the peculiar merit of Lanzmann's art that it engages us more than the printed word docs and overwhelms us less than do the usual documentaries which show footage from the original camps. Lanzmann invites us to pass judgment on everything, including his interviewing technique, and thereby creates a cinema of participation, of active engagement with the immediate details before us. For example, he makes it clear that he is interviewing Nazis who don't know they are being filmed. He leaves it to us to validate or reject the deceit. He pushes survivors who are emotionally overwhelmed by their memories to continue when they want to stop. He doesn't cut where tact would require a pause; he invites us to judge him. The viewers understand this perfectly and make up their minds in every instance. This may not be new: in a sense every talk show has some of the same effect, and there are obvious predecessors which are frequently mentioned, especially Marcel Ophuls's *The Sorrow and the Pity*.[6] But Ophuls himself has commented on the fact that Lanzmann differs from him in that he "never tries to ingratiate himself with the audience, hardly ever tries to charm or entertain . . . because of the unique nature of his task" (*American Film*, November 1985, p. 22).

This "task" demands our confrontation with absolutes, even though we hear only of details. And thereby it provides a different experience from what we have come to expect of cinematic entertainment, including its documentaries and its avant-garde offerings. It depends on us how much we want to give this film and by the same token it makes it possible, even easy, to refuse cooperation. I have talked to a number of people (though a minority) who saw the film and rejected it as boring, as unfair, as repetitious of what is known anyway, as too long. Pauline Kael's negative review of 30 December 1985 in the *New Yorker*, which roused so much indignation, is a case in point. Given the nature of the subject, it is obvious that many movie goers won't want to give it their attention, and some may not be able to give it more than half their attention at a sitting. A woman who assures me that the film left a lasting impression on her, nonetheless dozed off at intervals and at other points found her attention straying to her wardrobe. And even if one focuses intently, there is plenty of room for trivial responses. A colleague of mine, a professor of literature at Princeton, returned from a trip and complained about the lack of leg room on his charter plane by stating that having seen *Shoah* he felt he was in a cattle car to Treblinka. In other words, we should not assume that a serious film that moves the imagination will move all imaginations seriously. Precisely because it depends so largely on the cooperation of the viewer, this film is bound to evoke a wide spectrum of acceptance and rejection.

What is at issue here is the furniture of our minds. It is easy for me who remembers the bottom of the maelstrom to be fascinated by every detail. I am at one end of the scale at the other end of which Pauline Kael complained of boredom and fidgeting. I saw the film twice, 19 hours in all, and had no difficulty concentrating. And unlike viewers who felt that they had learned nothing new, I was amazed at how much I did not know. But there is also a generational problem. I think that young Americans, who bring only hearsay and a scant knowledge of the events to the film, are more willing than their elders, who during and after the war were notoriously unwilling to think about the fate of the Jews, to follow Lanzmann all the way to those limits of violence which he explores. This happens to one of my students, who suddenly hisses, "It's absurd; the whole thing was so absurd. Nobody got anything out of it, it didn't make sense." The exhaustive testimony has transmitted to him an insight that he will not forget, a sense of how the Holocaust transcended anyone's self-interest.

Shoah deals with nothing but what the title says, that is, annihilation. It is not about life in the concentration camps, about suffering, survival, and escape. It is relentlessly about one thing only, about the process, the details of extermination. Only when it is absolutely necessary do we receive a scant bit of information regarding the fate of the witnesses. In other words, it focuses on what matters by speaking unremittingly about what the myth-makers call the "unspeakable." (In that sense it is not about us, the survivors in the audience.) Once one accepts this premise and does not expect the film to move on to other themes but to continue to recover and make known what it can about the massacres, one finds that Lanzmann does not simply pile up details, but that he has organized this material carefully and effectively.

There are the progressive refinements in the technology of extermination, from the vans using exhaust fumes in Kulmhof (I prefer using the German place names where Germans made a place infamous), to the early gas chambers in Treblinka and the later efficiency of Auschwitz. Lanzmann often illuminates the story of a convoy or a camp by having it continued from several points of view, and he weaves his witnesses in and out of the account, as continuity or a different angle requires. Toward the end he interviews for contemplated or real resistance, and therefore fittingly ends with survivors from Warsaw. Viewers who are too over-

whelmed by the details may lose sight of these connections and
wonder why the next witness enters at a given point. In conversations and even in reviews, I found that viewers make gross mistakes
about what they have seen because they saw it in disjointed bits, not
realizing that this film follows any scent like a dog on a trail.

Cinematographically Lanzmann, as has been pointed out, may
indeed be somewhat clumsy in his repetitive showing of trains or
the slowness with which he manages those interviews for which he
needs a translator. On the other hand, this slowness is also part of a
technique aimed at drugging us less than cinema normally does.
Listening to the maneuver between the languages we come a little
closer to the Babel of tongues that the camps often were and the
uprooting of European populations that was involved. Watching
the trains provides a pause for thought, which can help prevent the
usual passive consumer's trance that cinema induces so much more
easily than any of the other verbal or pictorial arts. Shoah is not
effective unless we bring our recollections, and even our resistance,
our willingness to contradict, to bear on it. For straight information
it is better to go to the books. For in a sense viewers who find
nothing new here are correct. While most of us who are not historians, certainly including myself, are not likely to know all the facts
the film presents, these facts are readily available. The witnesses
don't tell their stories for the first time. Vrba's testimony, though
without his name and not in quite the same words, about the convoys of 1943 and even about Fredy Hirsch, had been familiar to me
from H. G. Adler's book on Theresienstadt.[7] But I read and registered these facts with the stupor with which I, like others, assimilated the Holocaust after the war. It had not affected me so much
before. My student, who was suddenly struck by the "absurdity" of
the Holocaust, had been reading up on the economics of murder,
but the force of illumination was none the less real, "a lasting
thought" which, as Yeats has it, one "thinks in a marrow bone."

Even Raul Hilberg, whose function in the film is presumably that
of the objective commentator, is "cast" in such a way that he seems
to preside like a recording angel over the annals of the damned.
Asked about the fascination of a typed sheet of train schedules, he
says: "Well, you see, when I hold a document in my hand, particularly if it's an original document, then I hold something which

is actually something that the original bureaucrat held in his hand. It's an artifact. It's a leftover. It's the only leftover there is."[8] On screen, with a voice and the faces of a speaker and a listener, these rather flat, unrehearsed words have the force and depth of poetry. I had of course read Hilberg's work and have even heard him lecture, but on neither occasion had I felt the anger and passion that Lanzmann elicits in interview. Whether Hilberg speaks of the uncanny precision with which the trains ran on schedule and which implied an uncommon measure of cooperation on the part of railway officials or in his elegiac near-identification with Adam Czerniakow, the president of the Warsaw ghetto's *Judenrat*, the camera captures the historian peering at the world, or perhaps at God, like an avenging spirit, clutching the evidence that proves the existence of evil in the form of typed office documents.

II

Lanzmann speaks German fluently and with complete disregard of the finer as well as the coarser points of grammar, as if the language merited only contempt. There is a great deal of German spoken in *Shoah*, but the only native speakers are Nazis. They all share one characteristic: detachment. They share it not only on screen, but it keeps recurring in the witnesses' accounts. When Filip Müller describes how the gas chambers functioned, he tells of victims who just before they were murdered implored the ss to let them live and to send them to a labor camp as they had been promised. But the ss, says Müller, "waren wenig beteiligt," not much involved, hardly participating. (The subtitles translate, they "remained impassive.") And that is the pervading German attitude in this film: "wenig beteiligt," the detached perpetrators. Where the survivors recall with obsessive precision what happened to human beings, the German interviewees either employ a technical vocabulary to describe a process or they shake their heads and use the easy small coins of emotional interchange, "sad," "terrible," "schrecklich, schrecklich."

The second part opens with a view of a neat German street, followed by Lanzmann's crew inside a parked van monitoring the pictures that a hidden camera is taking of Mr. Suchomel, a former guard at Treblinka, who has no knowledge that he is being filmed and has earlier expressly voiced the wish not to be identified. While he is still out of sight, we hear Suchomel's voice singing a ghastly variant of the famous Buchenwald song. The SS at Treblinka, it seems, had poetic aspirations and forced the prisoners upon arrival to learn these verses and sing this "Treblinka song," which is heavy on obedience and duty.[9] Lanzmann urges his subject to sing it a second time; Suchomel complies with gusto. Then he sighs and comments how sad it all is, "and here we are laughing." Lanzmann's voice, gravely, "Niemand lacht." He is right, of course, neither of the two men is laughing. Suchomel presumably means to say that he is having a good time remembering and that he feels a little bad about it. But, after all, he is doing it for the sake of history, so it must be all right. There is no Jew alive who remembers the Treblinka song, he assures Lanzmann, it's a unique offering. Lanzmann is duly impressed. Suchomel fails to realize that, apart from his intimate knowledge of the camp, what is of truly historic interest is not his abominable verses but his sink of a mind, which he is offering his interviewer for inspection.

Suchomel describes naked women in Treblinka waiting in the winter cold to be gassed. They knew what was about to happen, and their bowels opened. Housewives for the most part, I think as I listen, mothers who cleaned and cooked and raised families. As Suchomel speaks I visualize them, which is easy, because I worked with women like them and knew them to be kind to children like myself, even when they were starving and frightened. No amount of yelling on the part of the guards could ever make them march in step. I remember what must have been the first feminist thought of my life: that we were more assertive, less slavish and therefore "better" than the men, because we could walk as we liked once the SS realized that it was simply impossible to make us adopt anything resembling a military gait. And here on screen an insignificant little man mouthing clichés with a Southern accent conjures them up, or their likes, in a scene of ultimate disavowal of human fellowship: women to whom modesty was second nature, trained in domesticity, whose worst act of violence might have been an occasional outburst of anger or frustration, now stripped of their clothes and moving their bowels involuntarily in the freezing air as they waited in lines of five to be gassed. One knows so much and yet never enough. I am struck by the full significance of Hannah Arendt's dictum that the Holocaust was a crime "against the human status," not only against humanity.[10]

Suchomel illustrates Arendt's other, and more famous postulate as well, that of the perpetrator who is too shallow to have regrets, so that there is an unbridgeable chasm between the deed and the doer, the enormity of the crime and the banality of the criminal. After telling in detail what I have just summed up, Suchomel normalizes it with a "medical" disquisition about the physical effects of fear of death and cites the death of his own mother at home in bed as if this were an apt analogy. He has deflected from the scene of exposure at Treblinka with the skill of someone used to subsuming harrowing images under the comfort of 'umbrella generalizations.

This is the secret of all the Nazis Lanzmann interviews: they normalize, they trivialize, they hold at arm's length. They claim not to have known, even when they were there, they are masters of repression, and when all else fails they express a conventional regret that such terrible things occurred. One thinks of the Frankfurt Auschwitz trials, where the accused laughed and the witnesses wept, a phenomenon that impressed Peter Weiss, who effectively wrote it into several scenes of his *Investigation*.[11] Their minds have a different compartmentalization from those of the survivors. They operate on a different wave length. It was all very sad and very terrible, and one shouldn't laugh about it. Not so much as a hint of antisemitism crosses their lips.

To be sure, sandwiched between the interviews with survivors, the German interviewees are bound to be repulsive to the spectator whose ears still ring with the blow-by-blow account of massacres. But while the interviewer deceives them with his hidden camera, he does not manipulate their answers. They all have a common way of shocking us through their business-as-usual detachment, the absence of a sense of nightmare. So much so, that it becomes an open question whether they are lying or telling the truth when they say they didn't know. Of course one thinks they must have known, and Lanzmann makes it pretty clear that he thinks so. But it is possible, even though extraordinary, that bureaucrats like Dr. Grassler of the Warsaw ghetto administration closed their ears to the "rumors" of the Jews' destination. And whatever he believed or knew at the time, he may well, in what passes for all sincerity, have persuaded himself since then that he was trying to do his best for the ghetto.

Walter Stier, head of the Reich Railways Department in charge of Eastbound Traffic, the man who arranged for the human cargo, actually has to grope for the name Auschwitz. "Like that camp – what was its name? It was in the Oppeln district." Only then does he remember the place name that for decades has been synonymous with genocide. Lanzmann confirms the name with just a trace of irony in his voice. It is such scenes that reveal the workings of a mind in ways that are beyond the printed page. I feel a twinge of envy for these people, including Mrs. Michelsohn of Kulmhof, to whom 400,000 murdered in her backyard are like 40,000. (She knew it was something with a four in it.) Essentially the interviews with the ex-Nazis show us minds at peace. They harbor no grudges. They talk to a Jew who doesn't speak German correctly. They con-descend to him. "We are going in circles, Mr. Lanzmann." They set him straight. "Believe me, Mr. Lanzmann, 18,000 [murders] a day is too high a figure, 15,000 at the most."

Only the Jews are damned. They, too, reveal themselves beyond their actual statements. For example, when the barber Abraham Bomba, who has so far spoken in measured English about cutting the hair of doomed women, breaks into tears, Lanzmann continues to film as he suddenly speaks a few desperate sentences in Yiddish. And we realize, as we wouldn't from printed testimony, how the foreign language has been a necessary defense for him. "If you could lick my heart, it would poison you," says a survivor of the Warsaw ghetto. The Germans, for their part, hold emotions at bay. We have always known that the Holocaust was our nightmare, not theirs, but the film brings home graphically the difference between guilt and guilt feelings. The perpetrators have innocent minds and are fond of fresh mountain air; the victims speak of their poison-ous hearts. The ex-Nazis act like people who once worked in a slaughterhouse, no more. Sad and terrible, to be sure, but what was one to do?

On reflection I could forgive Mrs. Michelson her difficulties with numbers. Who hasn't mixed up their statistics? When it comes to casualties and especially where tens of thousands are involved, most people, including reporters and historians, are apt to make mistakes. But Mrs. Michelsohn felt that the whole enterprise of killing Jews shouldn't have been imposed on her, that she should not have been made to witness it. It was, she says literally, "eine Zumutung," an imposition. (The subtitles say, "gets on your nerves.") Mrs. Michelsohn also mixes up Poles and Jews, and when she gets them straightened out with some prodding from Lanzmann, she points out that they disliked each other. No hint that she, too, may have disliked or despised Jews in those days. There is a veneer of civilization as the consistent and prevalent Nazi attitude. "Wenig beteiligt," as Filip Müller's understatement puts it so well.

The Poles are different again. There is a real sense of *Schadenfreude* apparent in their accounts. All viewers come out of the cinema somewhat or greatly shocked by the up-front, almost cheerful antisemitism of the Polish rural population whom Lanzmann interviewed. But these attitudes are not new. What Jew doesn't know that antisemitism has been and is a prevalent attitude in Poland, especially among the uneducated?[12] Timothy Garton Ash has written sensitively and persuasively on this issue in his review of *Shoah* in the *New York Review of Books* of 19 December 1985 and given Poles what credit they deserve for helping Jews.

I was more struck by the myth-making ability of the population. With the dead Jews still vivid in their memories, these good Christians made up implausible stories about them and turned them before our eyes into the stereotypes that populate the minds of hostile or fearful non-Jews. From the Poles we heard of Jews calling on Jesus and Mary, we heard of a rabbi telling his congregation that they should be content to atone through their deaths for the death of Jesus. Before our eyes, or rather ears, the Gospels turned into a source of hatred. And here were the stories of the beautiful Jewish women to whom the Gentile Poles made love and who were so beautiful because they did no work and the ugly Jewish men who stank. And Jews being transported to their deaths in trains with dining cars, and all of them so rich, until they were wrenched by thirst and gave away all their jewelry for a drink of water. The degree of antisemitism in a country virtually without Jews may be astounding, but it is this mingling of fact and fancy that is truly fascinating. Obviously nothing that Jews do or that happens to them makes a difference to the age-old notions about them. We are like props in a scenario we never wrote. The emotions of these country people were similarly mixed up. While they were quoting scripture to prove that Jews are not worthy to live, they seemed genuinely delighted to be photographed with a Jewish survivor who had returned to them. They remembered him with pleasure as a boy with a beautiful voice who had to wear chains on his legs.

I come out of the movie house, shivering a little but not much. Broadway superimposes itself on Poland. I hail a taxi.

There is a legend about a horseman who one cold winter night rode across Lake Constance, when the huge lake was frozen solid, something that never happens. When he arrived on the shore and had the firm ground under his feet again, he looked back and realized where he had been and how unnatural was his trip and his survival. Tradition says he died on the spot of the shock. I read that story after the war and it struck me with the force of a sick joke. I think of it now, as I ride up Broadway, where I used to take long walks at night as a teenager, mourning the dead in a strange country, where everyone then said, forget, forget. Oddly, the shock has not become less. It's as if the intervening years had cleared our perspective so that now nothing obstructs our view of an arctic region of the mind and of the past. The film Shoah, a look back, is memory that feels, in the words of the poet, like "zero at the bone."

Notes

1. For the film book, see also Claude Lanzmann, Shoah: An Oral History of the Holocaust (New York: 1985).

2. Alain Renais, dir., Night and Fog. France, 1955.

3. See John S. Conway, "The First Report after Auschwitz," SWC Annual 1 (1984): 133–52.

4. The Warsaw Diary of Adam Czerniakow, ed. Raul Hilberg, Stanislaw Staron, and Josef Kermisz (Briarcliff Manor NY, 1979).

5. Filip Müller, Eyewitness Auschwitz: Three Years in the Gas Chambers at Auschwitz (New York, 1979).

6. Marcel Ophuls, dir., *The Sorrow and the Pity*, France, 1970 [originally produced for Lausanne, Switzerland's Télévision Rencontre].

7. Hans Günter Adler, *Theresienstadt 1941–1945: Das Antlitz einer Zwangsgemeinschaft*, 2nd. rev. ed. (Tübingen, 1960); Adler, *Die verheimlichte Wahrheit: Theresienstädter Dokumente* (Tübingen, 1958).

8. Raul Hilberg, *The Destruction of the European Jews* (Chicago, 1961); Hilberg, "German Railroads, Jewish Souls," *Society* (Nov.–Dec. 1976): 60–74.

9. See Shoshana Kalish and Barbara Meister, *Yes We Sang! Songs of the Ghettos and Concentration Camps* (New York, 1985), pp. 106–13.

10. Hannah Arendt, *Eichmann in Jerusalem* (New York, 1965).

11. Peter Weiss, *The Investigation* (New York, 1977).

12. See Earl Vinecour, *Polish Jews: The Final Chapter* (New York, 1977).

Peter Henisch

Peter Henisch was born in Vienna in 1943. After
working as a volunteer at the Socialist *Arbeiter-Zeitung*
(Workers' paper) in Vienna, he studied philosophy,
history, psychology, and German language and literature at the University of Vienna. He is one of the
cofounders of the sociocritical literary group Wes-
pennest (Wasp's nest), which published a high-
profile journal by the same title. In 1971 he joined the
musical ensemble *Wiener Fleisch und Blut* (Vienna flesh
and blood), for which he also wrote texts. He is the
author of fifteen novels and collections of poetry and
short stories, among them *Hamlet* (1970), *Die kleine
Figur meines Vaters* (1975; *Negatives of My Father*),
Hoffmanns Erzählungen (1983; The tales of Hoffmann),
Steins Paranoia (1988; Stein's paranoia), *Morrisons Ver-
steck* (1991; Morrison's hideaway), *Vom Wunsch, Indi-
aner zu werden: Wie Franz Kafka Karl May traf und
trotzdem nicht in Amerika landete* (1994; About the desire
to become an American Indian. How Franz Kafka
met Karl May and did not end up in America), *Kommt
eh der Komet* (1995; The comet will come, regardless),
all of which are rich in social criticism. Henisch is
the recipient of the prize of the Theodor Körner
Foundation (1973). A preoccupation with Austria's
Nazi past permeates Henisch's writing. In the autobiographical novel *Negatives of My Father*, which appeared during the presidency of the notorious Kurt
Waldheim, shortly after the Waldheim scandal, he
discloses the autobiographical motivations for his intense concern: his own father's work for the Nazi regime and his Jewish background. In *Steins Paranoia*
Henisch explores the problematic of an Austrian who
becomes conscious of his Jewish roots and must consider the options open to him: assimilation, which in
the increasingly anti-Semitic atmosphere of the
Vienna of the 1980s requires concealing his back-

ground, or emigration to the United States as the most likely option. Although Stein decides to stay, it is obvious that he can only do so if he reconfigures his life and makes the attempt of fashioning an identity appropriate to his new awareness.

Peter Henisch

EXCERPT FROM

Stein's Paranoia

To the
President of the Republic of Austria
Vienna 1, Hofburg

Dear Mr. President:
To avoid any misunderstanding, let me make it perfectly clear in the
first sentence of this letter that I respect (I *have* to respect, for what
else remains for me and my ilk?) the democratic election that made
you the representative of the Republic of Austria. Nevertheless, the
election took place under such unfortunate circumstances, and the
year that just passed likewise brought with it (perhaps, more appropriately: called forth) such disastrous effects that I, a citizen of this
country, which is now in disharmony (at odds?) with itself and the
world, cannot but profoundly regret its outcome. All the more,
since you and I have valid, even if (what does this "even if" mean?)
personal, reasons to make this assumption that are impossible to
detail in a few lines – all the more, mind you, as you, much es-
teemed Mr. President, would probably not even have been elected
without me. In any case, not under the awkward circumstances
under which you *were* elected.

    Not that this – and here, too, there should be no misunder-
standing – has anything to do with my voting habits: I did, as you
probably have figured out by now – if you've even read this far – *not*
vote for you. Rather – and with these words I admit to an, if anything, criminal omission – I simply forgot about the election. This
(this forgetfulness), to be sure, occurred for reasons of a different
forgetfulness, a real sin of omission, of which I honestly indict
myself bitterly by writing to the highest address of this country. The
truth is in fact this: All of this was triggered by a lack of good

reflexes and possibly also of the courage to stand up for my beliefs in a certain (both highly personal and highly historical) situation. Quite possibly, other comparable omissions also took part in the matter, so that the sum (no: power!) of such omissions results in the current, sad situation – but I am aware of my omissions.

In a sense, dear Mr. President, I have guilt feelings concerning you, and for that reason I would like to apologize to you for the time being in this (postal) fashion. Because this much is clear: Had I (and had under the right circumstances all the others, my brothers and sisters, who are similarly slow on the uptake, all my lazy and faint-hearted comrades of the Austrian species) reacted affirmatively at the proper time and in their respective places, you wouldn't have ended up in the situation in which you are now. Dear Mr. President, I could, as you are probably reading with astonishment, exonerate you (I wouldn't want to be, if I may allow myself this observation, in your shoes). If you're interested, I am (one-on-one would be best) available for further comments and explanations regarding the aforementioned observations.

Dear Mr. President, let us attempt a common endeavor, a common effort! Let us try to rectify what has gone wrong; perhaps it is not yet too late. Let us, both citizens of this country about which we have reason to be concerned, set forth a civic resolution. In the hope of your cooperation in this matter I remain,
With the greatest respect,
Max Stein.

What exactly Stein had in mind with this civic resolve that he and the President (together?) were to set forth, we don't know. The intern who was to treat him later felt that a more exact concept was improbable anyway. The sketchy character of the letter, By the way, the intern continued, supported the assumption that this letter was not intended to be mailed. The president's office would have denied receipt of this kind of letter in either of these two possible cases.

It is beyond doubt, nonetheless, that Stein continued to be ready for action. For example, he appeared a second time at the district museum. He had come, he said on this occasion (a partly solemn, partly worried tone remained in the memory of the professor entrusted with the collection), in order to make a suggestion. He did not want to, as he had done the last time, simply read something; he wanted to write something.

The professor was not at all adverse to this. It so happened, he said, that a memorial tablet for the synagogue was already planned. Yet, that the inscription would be done by a private individual would certainly require a discussion with the public authorities. On the other hand, . . . why not? Nobody would be scrambling to do this delicate task anyway.

Stein was, at the time, calm and ready for action.

Besides, he checked the letter box at his house every noon when he came home from leafleting with a fearful, excited, throbbing, red-white-red heart. The answer from the president to his surely well-intentioned suggestion remained a mere anticipation. Instead of his reply, Stein found one day the following letter:

Dear Max,

Since you decided some time ago to leave us and obviously have no intention of returning to our conjugal and familial relations, you need to be informed about the following. I have been married to you for ten years – most of the time, I would have to say, happily – and in the eyes of the law we are still man and wife, but I am in favor of clear-cut relationships. One glance at the calendar will perhaps jog your memory to realize just how long we've lived apart. I've been patient and hoped that your crisis, your confusion, or whatever it is would pass within a reasonable period of time. But I'm afraid, as much as I regret it, that I've generally misjudged both the situation and you.

Max, my dear – I don't know exactly what's the matter with you. That means – and, of course, I've picked up on a few things – that despite all of my requests that you tell me what has influenced you so deeply, you apparently consider me to be too dumb to discuss the matter with me with any degree of openness and honesty. Apparently, you could and can do this better with someone else – and not only talk – well, that's your business. I mean, it will soon be only your business.

I have – and actually this is the only thing I need to share with you – hired a lawyer to begin my divorce proceedings against you; you'll hear from him in the near future. For my part, I am no longer

interested in a reconciliation. Regarding your meetings with Marion, I'll have to ask you to maintain a distance for the time being and to wait for the legal ruling. I wish you much luck in your new life.
Brigitte

(Difficult-to-read notes from a restaurant)
Normally not my style to drink in public. Embarrassing. Undignified. Disgusting. Cold. Humiliating. But at home (*at home?*) I can't stand it. The horror of the mirror, the howling misery of the bed. Grandfather with his talks: unbearable. Maybe he means well, but it drives me crazy. When I'm dead, I'll be clever too. I don't like this inn, I don't like it at all. On the walls: cadavers, heads, antlers, tables with spotted tablecloths (couples in national costumes). Smell: very unkosher. But the wine helps.

At the next table, two people talk entirely too loudly for my taste. That is to say, only one of them speaks too loudly for my taste. According to the dialect, from Burgenland (commuters?). Or East Styrians. Apparently colleagues. Try to write along: The Jews, the Jews. Precisely. Did I really hear correctly? Already heard that before (suspected/imagined).

I used to feel sorry for them, but not anymore.

Why not?

Because they always malign our kind! They always have to malign our kind, our brothers. They're always making Austria look ridiculous. And from foreign countries to boot! They can't give it a rest!

In that case he (the older one) wouldn't give it a rest either, he says, if he were in their (in *our*) position.

Oh well, all they do is criticize Austria!

Now then, is that a surprise, considering what's happened to them?

(Us.)

Nonsense, the young one interrupts him – what happened, happened. What took place took place. And what's over is over. Over must be over. An order is an order. Weren't you, he asks the older man, in the military?

Of course he was.

Right. If you receive an order there . . . just as an example . . . okay, you're a first lieutenant and the order is given by a major . . .

Shoot at that man or that man or that woman or that woman . . .
You get the order – okay then, what are you supposed to do?

That is really the worst, that you're trained for such things.

Yeah, but that's the way it is. That's the chain of command.
That's the way it was and that's the way it still is in every army.
Because without a chain of command you really can't win no war.

We did, in fact, said the older man, lose it, no matter what.

Who? asked the younger one.

Um, said the older one, the Nazis.

Yeah, but only because they didn't know when to quit! If Hitler
hadn't attacked the Russians, then we would've won the war for
sure!

He's in his early twenties, the guy who says those things. And in
those days, he says, they were all for it. Because, he now explains
eagerly, of the unemployment. Much worse than today; but also
today . . . You can see how things are!

What?

Well, the most important thing for most people is their job. And
I'll tell you this: If a Hitler were to come today, and I had my little
business . . . It makes no difference who they strike out against: the
Gipsies, the Croats . . . Austria is German for the most part, so the
others have to act accordingly; I have not the least bit of patience in
these things!

(Sentences for a memorial tablet)
Here stood the synagogue built by the architect Max Fleischer in
1903. Here stood the synagogue, attended by many believers and by
a few less believing Jews from the neighborhood as well. Here
stood the synagogue, set on fire and burned in the morning of the
so-called Night of Broken Glass. Here stood the synagogue; its
walls also were blown up one year later. Here stood the synagogue;
above the Ark of the Covenant there was a votive tablet for Empress
Elizabeth. Here stood the synagogue, set on fire and blown up in
the years '38 and '39, and no one did anything about it – what could
one have done? The cardinal-archbishop of Vienna, Dr. Innitzer,
paid a visit to the Führer at the Hotel Imperial on Tuesday, 15 March
1938, to express his joy at the unification of German Austria with
the Reich as well as at the determination on the part of Austrian

Catholics to cooperate energetically with the German construction effort. Immediately after the liberation of Austria by the Führer, the Lutheran Synods AB and HB joined together and agreed unanimously to a church law passed by the Lutheran Superior Church Council.

Here, where a public building stands now, stood the synagogue (even the Socialist Karl Renner, who would later become the first president of the Second Republic, expressly welcomed the annexation). It is understandable that the people's anger was directed specifically against the synagogues in the individual districts, and finally the fires started. That the Jewish temples were the primary targets of the national comrades' resentment is totally understandable; after all they were the homes and educational establishments where teachings of the Talmud or Schulchan Aruch, both of which were hostile to the state and the people, were cultivated and disseminated. On Thursday, 11 November 1938, the majority of them went up in flames, including the temples in the Schiffamtsgasse, Neue-Welt-Gasse, Tempel- and Stumpergasse, the synagogues in the Untere Viaduktgasse, Schmalzhofgasse, Hubergasse, Siebenbrunnengasse, Große Schiffgasse, Kluckygasse, as well as in the Neudeggergasse, Malzgasse, Schopenhauerstraße, in the Zirkusgasse, Steingasse, and Müllnergasse, and in the Pazmanitengasse, at the Humboldtplatz, and in the Turnergasse.

Even if, as in most cases, the bare buildings remained, the interiors were so badly destroyed by the flames that there is no reason to assume that in these buildings any foreign and subversive elements would ever again be capable of using the camouflage of "religious gatherings" to discuss measures that then in various foreign countries will be taken against the Reich and the German people under the slogan "boycott movement" and "anti-Fascist demonstrations." But it didn't stop at the temples. In the streets and neighborhoods where in spite of the Aryanization of many shops there is still more than enough ongoing "Jewish activity," the closing of the businesses had to be undertaken as a protective measure. In the process various distinct summons were directed at the proprietors, suggesting Palestine among other places of destination. Until 8 May 1945, with the direct or indirect participation of many Austrians, sixty-five thousand citizens of Jewish descent were murdered – here stood the synagogue.

Morning – the night, despite the pulsating sleepiness I felt running through my veins and arteries, was sleepless. I gathered my energy and went shopping – I must, although I have absolutely no appetite, indeed, am disgusted by the thought of food, feed myself. Bread, milk, margarine, yogurt, and, not to forget, schnapps. I had them wrap the bottle to prevent Grandfather from immediately noticing it again.

On the way back I pass the community center. And there I notice something that on my way to the store I hadn't seen yet because I was hardly able to notice anything at all. But it might also be that it was put there in the meantime: exactly on the spot for which the memorial tablet was planned, a large – even though drawn only in chalk – swastika, which I, using my hand and scraping the skin off in the process, erased as well as I could, but it remains spinning before my eyes.

Afternoon, in the subway: A young man. After boarding the train at the university, he gave a quick glance around, with gently flexing nostrils, as if he wanted to test the scent, and then sat down on a bench across from me. Something about him bothers me. Maybe it's his haircut (extremely short and shaved around the ears), maybe the haircut in combination with the broad-shouldered, green army-surplus-store pullover that seems all too militaristic to me.

The boys of 1939 we saw in the newsreels that were once shown to us in school (for historical reasons) . . . as they, a happy tune on their lips, went skipping off to war so blithely. . . . Yet: Pointless, I think, prejudice, I think, paranoid. Now he even smiles at me, this young man of 1987, and now (what do I want?), now he even opens a book! Someone who reads is immediately likable as far as I am concerned. And a beautiful, old book as well! Clothbound, deep blue, the spine with gold lettering . . . What's he reading, the guy across from me? I'm interested.

I bend forward (discreetly) in order to decipher the lettering. (I notice lately that my eyes, with which I've never had any problems, are deteriorating.) What would he be reading, the young man, maybe Dostoevsky? I probably come up with this idea because now,

in the beautiful light of belletristic associations, so blond and so
pale with that hectic red around the cheeks, he reminds me of
Prince Mishkin. And then I decipher the lettering: *Mein Kampf.*
Leaning back in my seat, I think instinctively: Where is the emergency brake? The young man opposite me lifts his blond lashes.
And I know which part he has just finished reading, and he knows
that I know, he compares me with Hitler's description – and smiles
again: derogatory, disparaging, in agreement.

At the movie theater at the Graben: *Rambo IV* or something like
that. The evening is damp and heavy, a red sky hangs over the
Stephansplatz, I wonder what is in the air. A horde of supporters of
the soccer club Rapid is moving up the Kärntnerstraße; they are
wearing their uniforms, green-and-white-striped vests, hats, and
shawls. Their motto (increasingly audible): *We don't want any Jews!*
I avoid them, turning in the other direction: Rotenturmstraße,
Schwedenplatz. In front of the ice-cream parlor, two boys try to
trample on a tiny frog; only God or the devil knows how it got here.
With helpless jumps the frog tries to flee. Three girls, who obviously are with the boys, are standing nearby and watch, half
bored, half amused, licking their ice cream.

That night Stein decided to emigrate. Early the next morning he
took his suitcase, which stood in the kitchen still unpacked, turned
the apartment key in the lock twice – he had never been in the habit
of doing that – and left the house. He needed to go only a few steps,
he was barely on Lerchenfelderstraße, when he saw and hailed a
taxi. Wow, look here, said the taxi driver, an old acquaintance!

To the airport, Stein said. Yes, said the driver, that's what I
thought – where are we flying off to this time? Hopefully not, said
the driver, to Italy. Great, said the driver, satisfied, that's excellent.
As they say, it's all a question of mentality – those southerners have a
different mentality than we do. We, said the driver, are a different
breed. "The Merry Lumberjacks," isn't that true, the "Mountain-
eers," don't you think, on the Island of Crete in wind and rain. We
were stationed before Madagascar, right, we were standing at the
gates of Moscow. What doesn't break us, makes us stronger, am I
not right?

And those guys over there, pampered, coddled by the climate.

Actually it's unfair. The common good goes before personal gain, there's something to that. There, no, but here, where the workers in terms of the gross national income, from a business point of view . . . one for all and all for one; jobs: work, work. Those guys over there, on the other hand: Striking is the one thing they consistently do. But, said the driver, when they have one of their constant strikes again and I am stuck – just as an example – in a traffic jam on the Brenner Pass, shall I tell you what I would like to do most of all? No, said Stein, but obviously too softly. Grab the revolver that's under my seat, get out of the car, bend my finger and: Bang!

It would be a relief and hardly cause any damage! Because all these people: they're not worth anything. Turks and southeast Europeans, for example: they're not any better. They send their people to us, so that they can take away the jobs of our people. What would they do, asked the driver, without us? Without us they would already have starved to death. And it would serve them right – because one shouldn't interfere with nature. All of those people: one should simply starve them.

Yeah, talk to me, thought Stein, the things you say! You help me to abide by my decision. You really can't say anything else that would validate my decision more. In any case, you indirectly validate me.

The south and the east, said the driver, have nothing to offer me. He's more for the north and the west. Two years ago he was with his family in Scandinavia and last year – no, this year – in Belgium and Holland. There people like us feel more as if we were among relatives. . . . Although those in particular, they, too, have just recently disappointed us. The Belgians, the Dutch, the Scandinavians – even the Swiss. Even the Germans – the West Germans, mind you, not the East Germans. But the Eastern block – with them you don't want to have too much to do either. The French – hum, the French always seemed a bit suspicious to me. And the English – well, the English, it's been a long time since they were what they once were. But the Americans – nice friends they are! Of course, as one knows, not all of them, only the ones from the East Coast, right, the names they've got, I'm asking you, you can tell right away!

Yes, the names they've got: Mandelbaum, Kirschbaum, Birnbaum. Rosenfeld, Bienenfeld, Sonnenfeld, Schönfeld, Herzfeld. Gut-

mann and Seligmann, Sinnreich and Ehrenreich. Karpeles, Jeiteles,
Abeles, Kindeles, Kohn . . .

Central Cemetery, Israelite section: Stein had instructed the cab
driver to wait. The flow of traffic on Simmeringer Hauptstraße was
anyway at a standstill – why not cast anchor on the banks of the
cemetery? He had come to bid farewell – there lay his dead. Born in
Prague, in Budapest, Czernowitz, Cracow, died in Vienna.

Died "peacefully," were mourned "leisurely" until 1937. From
then on one died less peacefully and mourned more quickly. March
'38 was an intense month, followed by November. Died on the fifth
and the seventh, and especially on the ninth . . . *Man is / in his life like
grass* (those who died between 1939 and 1945 were buried here only
in exceptional cases). *He blossoms / like a flower* (many of their names
were, in the end, chiseled into the stone register). *On the field / When
the wind blows over it / he is no longer there.* (Died in Dachau, killed in
Buchenwald, murdered in Auschwitz.)

Very few dates after 1945. Died in New York, deceased in Phila-
delphia, passed on in Jerusalem. Many graves in disrepair, some
with overturned tombstones, lying open under a canopy of overgrown vegetation. Many by the name of Stein. On the grave of one
David Stein, Stein placed a pebble.

Robert Schindel

Robert Schindel was born in Bad Hall, Austria, in 1944 as the son of Jewish Communists. His parents moved to France but returned to Austria after the Nazi invasion in order to join the anti-Fascist resistance. His mother was arrested four months after his birth. The Nazi children's welfare took charge of Schindel under the name Robert Soël. Schindel's father was murdered in Dachau in 1945. His mother survived Auschwitz. Schindel grew up in Vienna, where he lives today. He did not complete his philosophy degree at the University of Vienna and took courses to become a therapist. He worked as a librarian, a night reporter, an actor, and a scriptwriter. He collaborated, among others, with Nadja Seelich on the film *Kieselsteine* (1982; Pebbles) and took part in Ruth Beckermann's *Die papierene Brücke* (1987; Paper bridge). In the 1980s Schindel, who had begun to write at the age of eight, began to publish his poetry in the collections *Ohneland: Gedichte vom Holz der Paradeiserbäume* (1986; Without country: Poems of the wood of the tomato trees), *Geier sind pünktliche Tiere* (1987; Vultures are punctual animals), *Im Herzen der Krätze* (1988; In the heart of the scabies), and *Ein Feuerchen im Hintennach* (1992). Like his poetry, Schindel's novel *Gebürtig* (1992) and the narratives in *Die Nacht der Harlekine* (1994; The night of the harlequins) reflect the ambivalence and identity problems of a Jewish intellectual socialized in post-Shoah Austria, and the wariness and simultaneous, passionate interest in the way in which Austria deals with its past. *Gott schütz uns vor den guten Menschen: Jüdisches Gedächtnis, Auskunftsbüro der Angst* (1995; May God protect us from the good people: Jewish memory, Information Bureau of Fear) deals with problems of the current interest in Jewish issues and the Holocaust. Schindel was anthologized in *Jewish Voices, German Words: Growing Up Jewish in Postwar Germany and Austria* (1994).

Robert Schindel

Prologue to *Born-Where*

Double Lamb

You can't get out of your head
You can't get into the dream
Your heart takes a walk
You can't get out of your heart.
—JAKOB HARINGER

I

The majority of the Double-Eagle's children were sheep who spent their life rolling in blood and shit so that their ultimate butchery wouldn't sate anyone but God. We are their children, editor De-mant said to his heart as he trotted off to a bar at the end of April around eleven at night. These lambs occasionally are semi-wild and most of them have long since grown two heads through their lambskin. One of them bleats, the other pretends to bleat. One neck has a goiterisch bell dangling from it, the other a knocker that looks like a necktie.

Demant took a long stride so as not to step into a woman's lost laughter whose puked-up remnants were splattered on the side-walk; and, besides, he was thinking of Christiane, his girlfriend in February, July, and November the last two years.

Christiane was sitting in the bar and thinking how she could communicate her momentary fantasies to her girlfriend without blowing her totally out of the fabric of their conversation. Finally she drew a laugh out of her stomach which then wafted forbid-dingly around the bar and slowly dripped down on the rest of the clientele. These fantasies were indescribable; outside the air had cleared up. At the bar itself stood the unemployed sociologist Masha Singer from Ottakring and the designer Erich Stiglitz from Mauthausen. A snowblown hamburger with ketchup belonged just as much to Christiane's momentary fantasy as did yesteryear's sound of nipping at shoulders, a yesteryear in Lilienfield on the River Traise. Christiane Kalteisen had started working as a psycho-therapist last winter. Now she sits next to her girlfriend, but from among the various faces she is able to put on she now selects the one with which to greet the approaching Demant.

Otherwise, aside from me, there were another fifty-odd folks at the bar, so that except for Danny Demant everything was well appointed. But as long as he isn't here yet, I have the time to listen to the stories taking place in back of me. Besides, I'm pretty well distributed all over the bar, 'cause I write down whatever comes my way, so that the diverse forms of speechlessness acquire traces that you can follow. My name is Sasha Graffito.

Demant stepped into the bar. Christiane raised her head, and used the sides of her mouth to model the prearranged face of a derisive bluejay, so that Demant would stop talking to his heart, by saying to it: "These lambs, you know, the Double-Eagle's progeny, they are very inward human animals at certain levels, as woundedly sensitive as deer in their body language, and have positively charged ski-poles in their pupils, but are totally ruled by a solemn sensuality. When they raise their heads and gaze out at the lord-godly open sky, then their fear of bombs and poison rain comes from that sky and gets them to toll the alarm bells, to sing the slogans, while the intestinal joy and trickery of life moistens their wool. Belief and superstition infest heart and lungs and express themselves in the brain as IDENTITY and BEING-I. In the event that the lambs then give themselves names, each of them will bear a HEAR HEAR or a NEITHER RELATED TO NOR IN-LAW as a title in front of their given name."

"Here's looking at you," he derisively greeted Christiane, and because he could just barely stop his depression from slipping out from behind his teeth, he kissed her elegantly and easily, yet not fleetingly, between the restless corners of her lips, pulled the sweater off over his head and sat down.

2

The two-headed lamb of innocence
Grazes on the meadows of inwardness
Carved out of the mud of ages
Each head must want to be inside the other

What might the thirty-five-year-old Stiglitz, blond and from upper Austria, have to say to the Jewish Viennese chanteuse [*sic*: Michael Roloff's erroneous translation of the name Singer] from Ottakring, I ask myself, and Stiglitz must be asking himself the same thing. Yet the two know each other. They have mutual friends, Danny Demant and me, for example, they see each other at parties, now as always, at Demos and always at the bars. They know this, that and what not about each other. Stiglitz is standing here because there's no one at home, and, drinking wine, gives the women the eye. Masha is waiting for friends and acquaintances while letting people look at her. She has noticed Demant out of the corner of her eye but first will jive with Erich before going to Danny's table. Erich nods at Demant but will stand on his spot a bit first, because they're talking at Danny's table, talking, and you're better off going home alone in that case.

Because Masha is transitioning from jiving to the pauses that punctuate jive-talk, Erich notices that she wants to leave. The acid level in his stomach rises, he looks into the eyes of the dark-haired girl and says: "Mauthausen is a pretty nice place."

Masha is nodding even as she stops nodding. That's going to take my breath away, she thinks, people saying things like "I had a good time playing ball at Auschwitz," always made her go rigid. She could really never make up her mind whether sayings like that enraged her, because she simply always got upset.

"Listen," she says, "saying something like that is not in good taste."

"Come off it," he says, "I grew up there. I know it. The region is real nice. As a child I played all the time in the concentration camp. A super playground. Do you think I gave it any mind as a ten-year-old? I only found out when I was twenty that they kept my uncle prisoner there."

"Fine," Masha rages, "fine. Children are children. But now

you're three times that age. How can you talk like that, so blue-eyed, as though nothing happened there, and so uninhibitedly."

"Incidentally, 'cause of miscegenation," Erich goes on, " 'cause I don't have inhibitions." Stiglitz puts the glass down behind him. Now he sees that there's no way he's going home now. Rooted to the spot, the snooty sociologist is standing on his children's playground. The butcher who supplied the ss with meat is now retired, yet Stiglitz knows him well. He grew up with Murner's son, and Murner was in the ss camp.

"Well, so what?"

Masha's eyes rage at him: "You think you're not responsible for any of it?"

"How can I be responsible for any of that?"

"Because you talk without any compunction about it. You talk in such a blue-eyed fashion."

While little Erich hops up and down the Mauthausen stairway to death, time passes, and it is as though Masha would be tossed once more from the rock quarry. She wants to darken his filthy sky for him in the ice-cold metropolis Vienna. He can see how her outrage is belittling him. Without the least compunction, without saying even a word, she drags one dead relative after the other out of her lap, so that the glass marbles fall out of little Erich's hand, but instead of hopping down the steps of the rock quarry, merrily, they disappear in the open maws of those smashed cadavers.

Masha doesn't see it like that. Once again she is beside herself and yet also sunk deep into herself, as though her sandbox were filled with ashes. Even before she can raise her hands in defense, little Erich leaps caboom into big Erich's stomach, and Stiglitz's lips become razor thin: "Asshole," he says, "get lost! This is the last time I talk to you! You want to say that I am a fascist? Get lost."

There stands the two-headed lamb
Wants both to blanch and blush
But to do that, and not exhaust itself,
It needs both heads.

3

As I finish my beer, I see Masha, her shoulders lowered, run to Demant and Kalteisen's table. Erich Stiglitz stares at her back, before he lowers his eyes, reaches in back of him and takes a look at his empty glass, dissolves off the wall, against which he has been leaning, and turns the corner to the john.

Masha is now sitting next to Danny and reports, while he doesn't even look at her, merely lending her his ear. Christiane Kalteisen talks and laughs at her girlfriend who is caught up in their carefree to and fro, so that this table breaks into two halves for me, as though a glass wall were erected between the two twosomes, mute, invisible, hermetic. Stiglitz comes back and reestablishes himself at his old place, orders another beer, and observes the quartet just the way I do.

Masha's eyes are moist, but Demant's eyes are gone from this room, and perhaps also from time; his ear seems to be his deputy in each and every respect. Even during the pauses that Masha now makes, and into which Demant dips his face, no intellectual presence is to be detected. The ear disappears behind his cheekbones, his eyes register the gradual changes in Masha's face not any differently than any old face registers the passage of time in another face.

Of course, now she's going to sob on the shoulders of her Jewish friend, thinks Stiglitz. There sit the Viennese and shit on him because all he can do is drink wine and stare at the floor. He won't even deny that Masha exerts a certain fascination on him in which his obscene place of birth has combined in the crudest fashion with her – from his point of view – Jewish brouhaha. This fascination motivates him to produce a list of evidence, especially because he has long since overcome his status as a provincial. The same fascination, however, also justifiably tempts him to insist on his origins and to behave accordingly. Perhaps they have to be intellectual women who might accept him as a man, and he hopes especially for suchlike whose broken pride makes them appear desirable. On the other hand, it seems laughable to him, after ten years in Vienna, to feel like an upstart from Muehl, not to feel effortlessly at ease here as he deserves to after putting in all this time here. One might assume that Jews especially have developed some delicacy for discrimination; but instead of uniting with him, since his foreignness possibly mirrors their foreignness, they preen themselves on being the incarnation of urban sophistication. They especially, as though they hadn't been humiliated in the most ridiculous fashion in this city back then before being taken away.

Masochistic until they were gassed, but then playing the victim
for him. Then letting him stand there. For Masha I belong – Stiglitz
is drilling these thoughts into his soul – to the eternal victors in this
country; which is why I invariably lose in this city.

But Masha talks a bit at Demant. At the moment she doesn't even
want to know what he thinks of this business, but she is talking
against a feeling that is eating her, obscurely. It is irrelevant
whether self-justifications course through her rising sadnesses. At
the end of each of her words, vague feelings of failure darken the
penultimate syllable. That is why her speech is becoming more and
more birdlike, ambiguous, draws pauses out of itself, whereas her
eyes are becoming moist.

It seems as though Stiglitz could provoke her at will, without
addressing her directly, personally, even once. It isn't that he interests her, but at least she had been able to detect how she fascinated
his movements at one time. Yet her Jewishness, as she realizes once
again, has taken on a maddening existence of its own which is
totally cut off from her usual powers of expression; due to this cut-
off-ness, those of his movements which are directed at her simply
move of their own accord, at least that is how it seems to her.
The independence of her breasts and legs, her voice and eyes has
become so habitual for her, is woman's business through and
through, but such special attributes have a special effect on mothers' boys like Stiglitz, as though they were specially treated, these
attributes, as though they were sedimented bone-Hebrew, that is
what she feels. The attributes have long since broken out of the
Masha time-space continuum and are what really make the upper-
Austrian landscape into a thoroughly upper-Austrian one. If it
weren't for her accidental Jewish pussy, the landscape around
Mauthausen would be a matter of complete indifference. Since
Masha sees herself excluded, but is being desired and lewdly so,
she must at least be allowed to express her upset.

If he can talk about it as though it were nothing, he is actually
deporting me; he is foisting an inheritance on me that I have not
assumed, and assumes his own without the least compunctions.

All of them, uninhibitedly and innocently stepped out of this
butchery of Jews and of all the other homebody feelings, and stand

around with the kind of self-assurance that resembles their region in which they are regionalized like that.

"He says," Masha says to Demant, "that I must fuck him, 'cause Austria lives from intercourse with foreigners."

"Go on," Demant motions.

"At any event, he disregards how touchy I am. I won't let him get away with it. He hasn't changed. Their fathers stuffed ours into the ovens, their mothers recited their rosaries, and their sons, magnanimously, would like to make us part of the community, they simply disregard what happened, uninhibitedly claim to be victims themselves."

"Aren't they?" Demant's question extends beyond time and space.

"They remain locals. The victors. And me they cut off. And I exist in fragments. And what I am is foreign to me. That is what they want! I won't let them do that to me anymore."

"I, too, consist of nothing but fragments." Demant dipped his face into a long pause before uttering that admission.

Masha regards him pathetically: "But the Danube connects them," she hisses bombastically. "You know, Danny, his fragments constitute the country. That is what I am supposed to sink into. That's what they would like, these blue-eyed mommies' boys."

I'd like to too. It means they'll sink no matter what. Shouldn't we sink together, topsy-turvy?'

Masha Singer now replies to him softly, her next to last syllables again become obscure: "I know that I am incomprehensible to you."

Demant smiles. "What's the use if I understand you at once? If that guy thinks Mauthausen is a pretty region, why do you have to knock him for that?"

"Oh, you want to be like him! Once again. Or like her." And Masha looks with a closed-off face at Christiane Kalteisen.

Demant tosses his head back, his voice crickets a little at the starts of each syllable: "Can't our Jews be a little bit dead now and then or do they have to be constantly sharpened even when they are nothing but bone meal?"

Masha shakes her head, opens her lips, but nothing comes out except for the dark-silvery words, her tears fall back into her mouth.

Far off in the sky the airy grave
Of the six million lambs
The double lamb now asks advice
The land of the sons, the land of hammers.

4. The Post-Shoah Generation

Elfriede Jelinek

Elfriede Jelinek was born in the Styrian town of Mürzzuschlag in 1946 as the daughter of the chemist Friedrich Jelinek and his non-Jewish wife. Her father survived the Nazi period in relative safety from deportation because his work was considered vital to the war effort. While still a high-school student, she studied music at the Vienna Conservatory of Music. In the early 1950s Jelinek's father experienced bouts of mental illness. In 1964 Elfriede Jelinek enrolled as a student of theater and art history at the University of Vienna. Because of a severe nervous disorder she terminated her studies, and she began to write poetry. Her condition worsened, and in 1968 she had a nervous breakdown and remained housebound for a year. In 1969 Jelinek's father died in a mental hospital. Around that time Jelinek became involved in the student movement, participated in literary debates, and associated with the Forum Stadtpark in Graz and the journal manuskripte, which reflected the literary program of this experimental literary circle and which in turn had received decisive impulses from the Wiener Gruppe. The influence of both groups is most clearly reflected in Jelinek's early prose, notably in *wir sind lockvögel, baby!* (1970; we are bait, baby!) and *Michael: Ein Jugendbuch für die Infantilgesellschaft* (1972; Michael: A book for adolescents fit for the infantile society). In 1971 Jelinek passed her final examination as an organist at the Vienna conservatory. In 1972 she lived in Berlin, in 1973 in Rome. In 1974 one of her most highly acclaimed radio plays appeared, entitled *wenn die sonne sinkt ist für manche schon büroschluß* (1974; For some people it's already time to close the office when the sun sets). In 1974 Jelinek married Gottfried Hüngsberg, an information-science specialist and former member of Rainer Werner Fassbinder's circle. The same year she joined the Communist Party of Austria (KPÖ). Her political views are reflected in her literary works, including the radio play *Die Bienenkönige* (1976; The king bees) and the novel *Die Ausgesperrten* (1980), on which Jelinek based a film script with the same title, which was released in 1982. In the satirical sociocritical novel *Die Liebhaberinnen* (1975; *Women as Lovers*) Jelinek combines the motif of class struggle with that of the battle between the sexes. In *Lust* (1989; *Lust*) psychoanalytical perspectives are combined with sociological and feminist narrative approaches to unmask and link the phenomena of pornography, sexual exploitation, and power. Together with Werner Schroeter, Jelinek authored the film script *Malina* (1990) based on the novel by Ingeborg Bachmann. Jelinek is also a notable translator. Her musical interests are reflected in the novel *Die Klavierspielerin* (1988; *The Piano Teacher*). In 1991 Jelinek left the Communist Party of Austria together with the two party secretaries Susanne Sohn und Walter Silbermayer. Elfriede Jelinek received numerous prizes and awards, including the poetry and prose awards of the Youth Culture Week (1969), the poetry prize of Austrian students (1969), the Austrian state scholarship for literature (1972), the Roswitha Medal of the town of Bad Gandersheim (1978), the prize of the Federal Ministry for Education and Art (1983), the Heinrich Böll Prize of the city of Cologne (1986), the literature prize of the city of Vienna (1989), and the literature prize of the city of Bremen (1996). Aware of her Romanian, German, Czech, and Jewish descent, Jelinek works in the tradition of Jewish satire, which links her work with the prewar tradition of Karl Kraus, Elias Canetti, and Friedrich Torberg.

Elfriede Jelinek

EXCERPT FROM
Wonderful, Wonderful Times

Shut Out

You have to shrink back from me as you would from a demon. Fear is seen in the eyes, hunger in the physique, ill-treatment on the skin, often it's more than skin-deep. It extends into the very soul. That is expressed in a look too. A woman recoiling from the man who's about to rape her. The man she knows is her master in this situation. There must be submission in her gaze. Static. Putting on one expression after another is pointless, this isn't a movie camera, it only takes still photographs. Concentration, Gretl, please. A tenant comes in, imagine this situation: contrary to expectation he finds his landlady, who is still young (which you of course aren't), about her toilet, all alone, he gives her a look that tells her immediately that her hour has come and that no power on earth can help her now. He won't hesitate for a moment to use force. What on earth are you doing with that duster, Gretl, now of all times, get rid of it and show your stuff. You have to ease the lingerie down slowly, try to keep your hand over it, but like everything else of this woman's her hand is in the wrong place, you can see everything.

Herr Witkowski talks like a waterfall yet again, which unfortunately is only silver, Frau Witkowski preserves her silence, which is golden. Herr Witkowski has been familiar with the saying since childhood, he is also familiar with it from the prisoners' quarters at Auschwitz, likewise the statement that honesty is the best policy. Ever since History forgave him he has been honest, it has been his policy for quite a while. After 1945 History decided to begin again from scratch and Innocence, after much hesitation, forced itself to take the same decision. Witkowski started over, at the very bottom, where normally only young people with everything still ahead of them start; the climb is a more arduous one if you have only one leg, indeed everything is tougher with only one leg; walking for starters. And even more gold is silent (for ever): the gold from teeth, spectacle frames, chains and bracelets that were saved up for, coins, rings, watches, the gold remains silent because it comes from silence and to silence it has returned. All that comes of silence is silence.

Don't leave me standing around stark naked so long, it's cold because of saving on the heating, says Margarethe Witkowski. First I've got to think about how to shoot it, there has to be some violence in it. Double up in pain, imagine you've been hit. That's fine, even you get the message, little by little. If only I knew what angle to choose so as to get everything in. The panties have to be at your feet. And now step out of them. Slowly! That's the discarded skin of an animal you're leaving behind, say a snake, and up you rise, as snakelike as possible, to your reluctant but compelling desire.

Frau Witkowski does this as she imagines a snake would do it, and up she rises, but not to her desire, a stench is filling her nostrils and she has to race to the kitchen, where the rice pudding has burnt. Thus she destroys her husband's delicate artistic mood. The genius was inspired and his prosaic spouse has destroyed it all, totally. I have to see to the cooking, it's high time, too late, in fact. Meanwhile her husband abandons himself to his own thoughts, which are somewhere far down, in the Polish lowland plains, Russian plains too, where Communism is constantly coming from these days. Back there he was still somebody. Who is he now? Nobody. A porter. Herr Witkowski is pleased that the putsch was foiled back in 1950. He too was one of the little wheels (though not a very handy one, given that he lacked one foot) in the ranks of those who did the foiling. Because he tirelessly drew attention to places infected with the bacillus of Communism. You couldn't be too careful. This is how it was: Communist raiding parties received 200 schillings per man per raid from the Russians, it said so in the paper. The Western occupying powers intervened and prevented the putsch. Restrictions had to be imposed on the circulation of newspapers (not the same newspapers that reported the 200-schilling payments) on the grounds that they had spread unfounded rumors. No one troubled to call in the public prosecutor. In this way, a

socialist home secretary by the name of Helmer circumvented the
freedom of the press, quite effortlessly. This was good, since no
one grows heated over things they know nothing about, and staying cool was the order of the day, to avoid clashes. Once a paper
starts peddling untruths it has to be disposed of. The Socialists
aren't exactly number one party in the Witkowski book, after all,
he's not a worker, but this time they kept in line, there's no denying
that. Perhaps they will learn something from history at last. Perhaps they will lend their support to the right powers from the word
go, that is to say: the powers of high finance, they are the only
powers that count anyway because money rules the world (thinks
the invalid, who has none himself and so, consistently enough,
rules nothing), money can rule all by itself, everyone knows that. In
consequence, those who have nothing are left with their nothing,
more is given to them that have, and a modern monopoly system is
set to begin. Capital reaches out its helping hands from foreign
countries in the West, swamping our *Heimat* with foreign money
and influences and linking hands with our people to form a chain
as strong as the caterpillar track on a tank. Herr Witkowski es-
pouses the cause of Capital, which he does not possess, and this
enables him to gaze with confidence from the Past into the Future.
With confidence, because in days gone by he gave Capital his personal protection, and now it is again in full control, personally
showing its gratitude to him. By allowing him not only his full in-
validity pension but also a job as a night porter in a hotel, where he
gets to see important representatives of the middle class, travelling
in the course of their work as industrial sales representatives. So it
goes, with the one representing the other, even if he doesn't know
who exactly it is he's representing. It goes without saying that Herr
Witkowski still represents the National Socialist Party, as he always
did, he knows exactly who's in it and what the people in question
stand for. After all, it was that very party that made him so big that
he surpassed himself. No one else would have enlarged him in that
way. Nowadays he enlarges his nice photos. He looks not only to
the well-being of the individual but also of the group he oversees.
Since he always bears in mind that he represents a whole group and
not merely himself in his spare time, he always behaves accordingly. He sets an example. To teach the youngsters. Just as others
also represent their companies with dignity in their spare time.

When he considers his children, he has his doubts about the fruits of his upbringing. Strangers are well brought up but his children are not. At the time of their conception he was still an officer. But what was the result? Two children who give him the shivers. In the old days you never used to see children like that, but nowadays there are a lot like them. The wife makes a pig's ear of everything, including the milk pudding, which she stirs; this doesn't make it any better.

He goes to get his pistol, to clean and grease it, you have to do this even if it happens not to be needed just now. Be prepared. The steel is a cold weight in his hand. In the case are his favorite photos of Gretl, the gynecology photo (which will soon have to be taken anew, the photographer is more experienced now), the brothel photo, the schoolgirl photo with the apron and cane. The pistol is kept in a secret drawer no one knows about in the kitchen cupboard. It wouldn't interest anybody anyway, his son is unfortunately only interested in literature.

Taking an abrupt decision, the ex-officer (the things an officer has to be capable of, such as decisiveness!) goes into the kitchen to rape his wife, since he suddenly feels like it, but the cow makes an awkward movement, as usual, and he slips on the tiles and falls to the floor with a crash. Where he flounders to and fro, his remaining leg twitching. However badly he wants to, he can't get up. Getting it up is usually a problem of another kind, in fact, but this time he'd have been sure of a hard-on because he was so full of desire. So much for that. It's his belief that the cause of the trouble is that the powerful stimuli he was flooded with as a young man in the occupied eastern territories have been far weaker in recent years. Once you have seen mountains of naked corpses, women among them, the charms of your housewife back home offer no more than a paltry temptation. Once your finger's squeezed the trigger of power, you slacken off rapidly if squeezing strangers' hands at the hotel is all the force you can exert. Regulars greet him with a shake of hands and a slap on the shoulder. Along with popular salesman jokes and anecdotes. He tells them at home to turn Margarethe on if his prick isn't enough, which is often the case. Damn thing, there are times when it simply won't get up.

Times are growing weaker and softer and so are the youngsters of today. He does not know where it all will end. In half-hearted mediocrity, plainly, if not in something worse. His son is afraid of that mediocrity too.

Papa is still floundering, revolving helplessly, because he keeps paddling on one side only and not on the other one as well, which is a mistake. Recently, to crown it all, he's been tormented to extremes by sciatica and rheumatism too, as if having a leg missing weren't enough of a problem. He revolves on his axis and tries to get up on his foot. Which he can only manage with the assistance of Margarethe's patented lifting-up grip, heave-ho, that it? Now he's standing again, crutches jammed under his armpits, there we are, he'd imagined that he'd be able to do without crutches when ravishing Gretl, at one time he didn't need propping up like that.

Poor little mouse, why don't we go to bed, it's more comfortable. But the bed gives and I'd really like to drill you into the hard unyielding ground. Well, but still, it'll be snug and warm and cosy there, dear, and I've got a drop of rum left, come on, duckie.

Various parts of Otto's body hurt badly when he props himself up on his crutches and swings his remaining leg, to and fro, to and fro, but he doesn't betray the fact. The charismatic authority he once had drags his wife along behind him yet again. I'm always so tired nowadays, I'll have to get a check-up. Poor dear, yes, why don't you do that. And instead of giving it to Gretl good and proper, seeing that she's right next to him, he buries his greyed head at her breast and can't help crying. She is very moved by this. Because she does not know the reason and mistakenly supposes it's because of her. Poor little fellow, it'll be all right, she says softly, comforting him. It does not comfort him. The lumbering man sobs, he's coped with so much, he's killed so many, and now there's so much he can't handle himself. What bad luck.

I can't help crying just now, I hope the children don't see me in this state. They won't be home so early, they've been out the whole time recently, I don't know where. What they need is a firm hand, which I have, I even have two, though only one leg.

My poor poor Otti. Stroke stroke pat smack.

It's all right, there there.

We'll have a drop to drink, then we'll have a nice cup of coffee, and this evening we'll listen to the Maxi Böhm quiz show. There are valuable prizes to be won by listeners at home, sometime or other we're sure to win. If I don't know the answer we'll just ask Rainer or Anni, children learn so much these days. But we're sure to know the answer, because we're the parents. There we are, now my Otti's laughing again, there's a good boy.

He tells her to pour it out, but not to be so stingy as the last time, after all, he gets quite decent tips. Even if it's fundamentally humiliating. But things have changed, and incompetence is making the running. Drinking brings the gift of forgetting and is good for the gastric juices. Seeing how rarely there's meat on the table. Herr Witkowski gives a comforted snuffle, looking forward to his good coffee, which he will take with a massive amount of sugar. There are good things in life, there really are, as long as your expectations aren't too high. Of course, he could demand a good deal if he cared to. Since he's entitled to it all.

Today he even gets more than usual. Because he cried so much.

Café Sport is another scene. A scene, because that is where the artists and intellectuals go to be seen. Taking part is what matters, not winning. It is like sport, which is where the café got its name. Many have already lost their faith in Art, in spite of the fact that it was they alone and no one else who were predestined for it. They practise Art because it earns them nothing and they are therefore unsullied by filthy lucre. If they did earn anything from Art they'd gladly be sullied. But they would never have recourse to an ordinary middle-class profession, not because they can't master one but because the ordinary would master them and there would be no time left for Art. You can't express yourself aesthetically, man, if some boss is expressing himself by means of sports cars and villas at the expense of the afore-mentioned artist. Anyone whose cigarette is only a single notch above the cheapest is immediately a target for cadgers.

At the table where the Holy Foursome are passing their time today, two other people are busy trying to prove Pythagoras's theorem by purely graphic means and failing in the attempt. As far as Rainer is concerned, mathematics belongs in the realism sector and is therefore uninteresting to him. If they were discussing literature he would long since have butted in and annihilated somebody, which he has a right to do.

Elsewhere some Greeks are sitting round, practically pushing their dark heads into each other as they joke about women and occasionally chat one up. All this happens close by the Ladies, just where the women have to pass by.

Whenever something is said that isn't to Rainer's taste, and at other times too, irrespective, he will stand up abruptly and stride thoughtfully off into a corner, where he stares about blackly till Sophie or Anna solemnly fetches him back. What's up? Tell me please, please. You get on my nerves, stupid cows. I have other concerns, at a different level, the level I live at. You bore me rigid. Please, please come and sit down again, Rainer. You lot don't understand anything at all, how can anyone take action together with people like that, they'll run away from everything because they're cowardly mediocrities. Rainer wants the others to get their hands dirty on his behalf so that he can stay clean. Let the others take action for him. He'll keep clear. But he'll egg the others on. And he'll take his share of the money, he needs it to buy books. He sees himself as a spider in the background of their net. But he's going to go about things without the safety net of petty middle-class security. He will pull that net away from under the others' backsides so that they have to rely completely on each other and on him.

Rainer gapes at the cigarette butts, scraps of paper, red wine stains and crumpled paper handkerchiefs (and other, worse things) on the floor and waits for the inevitable nausea. Sometimes it comes, sometimes it doesn't. Right now, this very moment, nausea has seized hold of him at last, so that he drops the pen with which he was about to jot a line of a poem in his notebook, the ink squirts out, wasted. Now, was that nausea or wasn't it? No, on the whole it probably wasn't. The place looks as philistine as it always has done. You could hardly say that space looked even slightly heavier, thicker or more compact. But (like Sartre) he has realised that the past does not exist. And the bones of those who have died or been killed, even those who passed away in their beds, have an altogether independent existence of their own and are nothing but a little phosphate, calcium, salts, and water. Their faces are merely images in Rainer himself, fiction. At this moment he has a very strong sense of this. It is a loss. But he doesn't tell anyone that Jean-Paul Sartre had already sensed that loss in exactly the same way before him, he pretends the loss is his own.

Hans, who lost his father, is not thinking of phosphate, calcium, salts and suchlike, which is what his father is now, instead he is humming an Elvis hit, without the lyrics because they are in English, which Hans never got to grips with. Generally speaking, there are few things he has got to grips with. Though he'd be happy enough getting to grips with Sophie.

Another scene is the jazz club. Rainer wants the others to commit crimes. When the musicians take a break he strolls over to the saxophone and tries out a few fingerings he thinks are right, though maybe he wouldn't produce a single note if he were to blow in it. All that counts is that the people who see him imagine he can play the saxophone. When the musicians return he hastily lays it down so no one will smash his gob in for damaging a musical instrument. Then he orders a raspberry soda, the cheapest drink there is (they haven't bagged a wallet yet!), and starts a poem (he'll write the beginning today and the end tomorrow). Nothing out there can distract him from it. It doesn't matter what she looks like. Even Sophie has to accept this. Though one isn't as severe in respect of her, because she is the woman one loves. Love is only a small component in Rainer's life, because he knows that Love can only ever be a small part, Art makes up the rest. In the poem, Rainer expresses contempt for all fat people, with their poncy flash rings, nothing but money-making in their heads. True, he's never seen people like that close up. Sophie's father is on the slim, wiry side, really. He is a sporty type too. Rainer would not care to despise the father of the woman he loves, so it's fine that he does not need to. He has the image of fat rings on white fingers from Expressionism, which has been forgiven and forgotten. He despises them all, daytripper obesity, caryatids in tails, it wasn't for that that his mother pushed him out of her (so he writes and so he feels, intensely). But his mother would also protest at the thought of having pushed him out for these good-for-nothings in Café Sport and Café Hawelka. She did it so that he could have a decent education. Which he at present doesn't care a shit about.

Even in here, in the unvarying gloom, Rainer is wearing his fashionable diamond-shaped perspex sunglasses. His hair is combed right into his face. This is supposed to be a Caesar haircut, but he does not look as if he were from ancient Rome, he looks as if he's

from modern Vienna, which is incessantly whispering that he
should go on helping to rebuild his home town and make it more
and more beautiful. This, however, he has no intention of doing.
Vienna, the City of Flowers: a perennial favorite for school essay-
writing competitions, Rainer has already won a prize twice, once he
won a rubber plant, the second time a handsome fern which has
already died because loving Mummy watered it to death, ferns tend
to prefer it dry, as the nursery gardener confided to the young essay-
writing competition winner. (He came third, so did nine other high
school pupils.) The advice was ignored. His school always partici-
pates in things of this kind and then shows off about it afterward.
All those flowers, springtime blossoms and others, burgeoning in
every corner, on every square, are now decidedly improving the
city's appearance, fresh greenery, replacing the foreign uniforms
that vanished when the Treaty was signed. At last. Even the Russians, the worst of all, vanished too, though as a rule they do
nothing of their own free will, they prefer forcing others, particularly women, to do inexpressibly awful things. They enjoy that.
Now they're gone, and the Nazis, both the neos and the old guard,
can come out of their grey nesting boxes into the daylight again,
like flowers. Hail fellow, well met.

Oh and, while we're on the subject of blossoms and leaves,
Rainer has only ever seen grammar school pupils among the other
competition winners at the awards ceremonies in the Vienna school
board offices, which is because grammar school pupils can express
themselves, they can write down what they feel when they see a tulip
or a lilac bush. What they feel is Joy. And Hope for the Future. Even
if someone else is capable of feeling Joy, it doesn't mean he can
write it down, without making any mistakes, not by a long chalk.
The language they speak isn't the language of high culture, it is the
language of their own, which is not recognized. In Austrian usage
there is a vast and gaping rift between these two linguistic levels,
which comes from the inequality of Man. And will continue in
perpetuity. Not Man, the inequality. All it takes is for one speaker to
use the imperfect, and lo, the other no longer understands him.
That is what happens to Hans with Rainer. Hans is awkward,
Rainer is articulate.

Rainer's talent for writing was already recognized back then, now he is out to make it his definitive profession. In his case, his profession will also be his hobby, which is ideal. Many people claim that this is how things are with them. Usually that is untrue. If a plumber or a butcher claims his profession is also his hobby, it is undoubtedly untrue. Nor do you believe it if a tram driver or brick-layer claims as much. If a doctor says his hobby is healing and helping people, you're more inclined to give credence to the state-ment. Healing and helping can be both leisuretime pursuits and jobs at one and the same time. Hobby is a word that is rapidly gaining currency. The Yanks have gone, their language remains, hooray.

Reluctantly Rainer now notes that Hans, the jerk, is not his own tool at present but the jazz musicians'. Hans is zooming hither and thither, zealously folding up music stands, cramming double basses in canvas wraps, alternately closing and opening the piano depend-ing on what he's told, wiping out trumpets, stacking the scores in piles and distributing them once again when he's given the order, picking up chairs and putting them down and scraping them along, undoing everything he's so carefully accomplished simply because one of them snaps that he's done something wrong, asking how long it takes to learn to play the flute, sax, trombone, bass, etc. Piano takes longest, no doubt, learning to play the piano is the best policy, like honesty, which this Rainer is about to make an end of. I'd like to do something like that some day too! Being able to play an instru-ment must be nice. Perhaps even nicer than being a gym teacher or an academic. In a minute, after the last number, "Chattanooga Choo Choo," he'll lug a whole lot of heavy things outside along with a crowd of other idiot volunteers, where another good-natured fool will let his car be misused for the transport of instruments, just to be part of it all for once, which is all that counts (see above) because winning isn't everything. A number of questions remain unan-swered: Is it difficult? How long does learning to read music take? What is the correct way to tune a violin? Who do you approach if you seriously want to learn to play an instrument? I'll volunteer first thing in the morning. The things you like doing, you do voluntarily. Working on heavy current is something you have to do, though. That will have to be given up.

I can't stand it any more! explodes Rainer, breaking out of his thoughts and into Hans's. What he was just thinking was: I spit on you all! With your packed lunches and fat bellies. I am gigantic, I walk on the ceiling, you can all see me, clear as day, right, that's me! He snatches the clarinet case which eager Hans is about to help carry outside out of the lackey's paws and smashes it down on his head, it makes a roaring sound and the wind instrument inside it howls. Hey you, yells the musician in question, have you gone crazy?

The amateur clarinettist, a law student, does not understand the expression this prompts on Rainer's face (impenetrable, expressionless) and so ignores it. If he only knew what Rainer is thinking about him right now! Rainer is thinking: I'd like to rip your throat open with a meathook. The chemist's son has no idea that this is what he's thinking and thus has no occasion to be afraid, but Rainer is proud of having thought something so brutal. Soon it will be done, for real. At Rainer's table the plotting and planning is begun in earnest. I can't be saying everything four times, that goes for you too, Anna, though you know about it in rough outline. Being my sister. Sophie must know, since she is the woman I love, and Hans, seeing that he's the one who'll be doing the dirty work, will be put in the know as well, always assuming he can grasp what it's all about. Which is by no means certain. Are you coming, Anni, or aren't you? She is not coming yet because, perceiving a unique opportunity, she is casually trickling off Chopin's étude for the black keys at the piano, casually but a great deal of practise has to be put in at home if something like this is to result, and she's about to start on something from *The Well-Tempered Clavier* when the jazz pianist (a medical student) comes up: Kid, you're in the wrong groove, why not forget it and go on home to Mummy and keep up the practising, but not here, not in a cool joint like this. This isn't a music school, you come here when you've finished music school or you've taught yourself to play. But if there's anything else I can teach you, honey, I'll be glad to, stop by again when you've got some tits. With Annamother around, teaching yourself anything is quite out of the question, you have to have expert tutors, nothing else will do.

A cold shiver goes through Anna because she has discovered that possibly she is not quite perfect and has to go on developing further, a notion she rejects. She has already reached the finish and has nothing more to lose. The fact that there might be something else ahead of her drives her crazy, because as far as she's concerned she's done it all, and murderous feelings surge within her. There must be nothing more to come, only absolute nothingness, where there are no moral standards, such as this student no doubt still has, even if he talks to a woman in a way that seems coarse. As he goes by she knocks a half-empty glass of beer and splosh, there go the contents all over the know-it-all young academic's brand new blue jeans, they'll have to be washed, which will mean a little more wear and tear, which will hurt the student's finances. Fine.

Rainer is going on at Sophie, who is sipping lemonade, she shouldn't gabble, she should listen, though she isn't saying anything anyway. What Hans thinks is that if she doesn't want to listen to him (to obey him), she ought to feel (him). But Sophie does not want to listen (or obey), she wants to see. She wants to see Hans lift the heaviest objects, and even heavier ones, with the greatest of ease. There isn't a single soft spot on his torso, though hopefully there are soft spots inside him. Rainer's torso, by contrast, has something of a chicken about it. A chicken that has been totally starved of sun and almost totally of feed for a long time. Still, he doesn't just cluck, that's true.

Hans flings himself into an armchair and describes in broad outline (the details are yet to come) his future music studies, which will enable him to give pleasure to people and help them relax and will make him successful. Down, boy, says Rainer. But he goes on to say how the old woman gets up his nose with her stupid envelopes and the work she did for the Party when she was young, that is why I want to get my distance from all that, maybe musically. Rainer says he'll hit him in the gob in a moment. In a low trawl, Sophie says: Leave him alone.

Anna: You could bore the pants off the Goethe memorial on the Ring, Hans.

Sophie: Don't be so arrogant.

Hans: See that, Anna? When a woman loves a man and she can't show it and doesn't want to show it either, she'll stand up for him in front of other people. In doing so, she realizes what her own feelings are, in spite of herself. I've seen it in films, time and again. Anna zaps her hand between his legs, not a bad spot. Are you two at it again, breezes Sophie. Hans shoves away the unloved hand, which he nonetheless still needs from time to time, and is ashamed. Sophie is not supposed to know. Though she is supposed to suspect. And to want it herself. On the one hand, Anna now wants to punish him, and on the other she is afraid that he doesn't want to do it with her any more. Although she was good, no doubt about it.

Hans is my concern, defending him is no business of yours, he can defend himself and I'll tell him now. And anyway I don't give a toss (which is of course not true). Hans knows that a woman who stands up for a man in front of other people may often look as if she's doing it against her own will, but it is stronger than her will. Gentleness conquers toughness. The last impression in the world that Sophie gives is the impression of inner turmoil. She orders a rum and Coke. This is too expensive for the twins and they look away when the waiter comes, but the waiter is used to that kind of thing. Hans orders something even more expensive, his mother back home in her old kitchen chair would take leave of her senses if she had any notion of it. His secret overtime.

Anna says that the weak are defeated by the strong in the world of Nature. A reed by the north wind, for instance. And silence by the forest. Rainer: So this is going to be robbery and assault.

Hans: I'm not crazy. You don't know what you're all talking about. It's madness.

Rainer: Madness? Categories such as that do not exist – as far as I'm concerned, *everything* is healthy, except for fruit and vegetables. In art, too, madness comes in handy, in the art of the insane, and soon there will no doubt be artists who inflict wounds upon themselves, they will be the most modern of all modern artists. For example, you're injured and you go for a walk along the street and display your injury to a police inspector, calling it a work of art, he does not understand this, and the gulf between him and the artist (who is at one and the same time his own work of art) becomes immeasurable, never to be crossed. Submission to something you didn't preach yourself is no good, I quote. Because Man must burst his ridiculous bonds, which consist of what is supposedly current reality with a prospect of a future reality of scarcely any greater value. Quote: Each and every full minute bears within it the negation of centuries of lame, broken history. End of quote.

Bah, goes Hans, gurgling down a drink. That's one of the few jobs I wouldn't care for. Policeman or artist. Though maybe an instrumentalist. He will also see that the woman he loves (Sophie) is not exposed to disagreeable things, Beethoven and Mozart may be allowed once he's subjected them to close scrutiny.

Anna turns her listening apparatus windward because there was a heart-felt inflexion in the name Sophie that she did not care for. It is shitty that, in obedience to a natural law, you no longer like what you already have quite so much and instead strive after the unattainable. She herself would like to be the unattainable, but Sophie has already picked that role for herself. Shit. For all she cares, Sophie can die. Sophie promptly notices, she raises her eyebrows.

Rainer says to Sophie, doesn't she think that of all of them Hans is the one who ought to want to be extraordinary most of all, because in the way he thinks he is the most ordinary. Don't you agree? Anna says that every sentence Hans utters comes out exactly how it's been uttered at least a thousand times by other people before. Is Anna at the helm or at the rudder in this love affair? We shall see. Perhaps we shall see in the next few fractions of a second because she is out to grope Hans's thighs again, where there is certain property she is interested in acquiring. But the thigh in question is removed, you don't do things like that in public, least of all with Sophie present, and so the hesitant loving female hand reaches smack into some old chewing gum that's been stuck there. It's sticky, and where Love has found its place, there Love sticks.

Hans is against violence on principle. You only believe this if the one who says it is physically very powerful and thus does not need to use force. He bought a book by Stefan Zweig, an important writer, and liked it a lot, but he'd still like to ask a thing or two about it, since it is literature of a more complex kind. Sophie, do you think you could give me some information about this book? Rainer says that Sophie might be able to answer his questions but he will do so himself because literature is his field, not Sophie's. Sophie's exclusive field is his own literature, she has to concentrate on that twenty-four hours a day. If Hans tries his hand at simpler stuff first, that's fine. Hans says that Stefan Zweig is one of the most difficult writers there are, though. Rainer says that the mental bonds linking him and Sophie are far stronger and more enduring than any physical bonds could ever be. Intellectual ties last your whole life long, physical ties last a week or so at most. At present I'm reading Camus's *Outsider* together with Sophie. The hero doesn't care about anything, just like me. He knows that nothing is of any importance and that all he can be sure of is the death that awaits him. You have to get to that stage, Hans, where you don't care about anything and nothing is important. At the moment everything still has to be important to you, so that you have a position to build on.

The assaults will be a powerful experience. Which one can subsequently discuss.

Hans wants to save Sophie from herself and be there for her. Sophie says she doesn't need him to be there for her. Rainer says he quite deliberately does without support of any kind, that's why he is so strong, because nothing bothers him. Hans says that getting ahead in his career does matter to him.

Anna: The best thing you can do is to imagine there's nobody else but you. Then you won't be judged by anyone else's standards, only your own. That's how I do it, for instance.

And now the Annahand, sticky with chewing gum, wanders over for a third time, and Hans, flattered, lets it stay. The bird in the Annahand is worth two Sophies in the bush.

Rainer is pondering how to incite the others without getting his own fingers too dirty. First he'll need an elevated position to command an allround view, the view from the Hohe Warte is better than that from the Elisabeth Memorial in the Volksgarten. There are born leaders and there are the rest. He'd rather be the bellwether than the sacrificial lamb, that's for sure.

Nadja Seelich

Nadja Seelich, née Stibitzová, was born in Prague in
1947 as the daughter of a Bohemian and Viennese
Jewish family, Shoah survivors and resistance
fighters. In her immediate family she was the first
native speaker of Czech, the language that her grandmother Josefa Stibitzová, who refused to speak German after the liberation, had adopted. Seelich
studied cultural sociology at the Prague Charles University. From 1966 to 1968 she worked on a research
project on children's leisure-time activities and co-
edited the literary journal *Divoke Vino* (Wild wine) of
the Klub Mlada Poezie (New poetry club). Her contact Jana Cerna (1928–1981), the daughter of Milena
Jesenska and the Jewish architect Jaromir Krejcar,
prompted her to undertake the editing of Cerna's
Adresat Milena Jesenska (1968; *Kafka's Milena*) and it inspired her highly personal film on prerevolution
Prague, *Sie saß im Glashaus und warf mit Steinen* (1992;
She sat in the glasshouse and threw stones), which
was awarded the 1993 prize for Austrian documentary films and was featured at the film festivals of
Rivertown, Montréal Nouveau Cinéma, and Duisburg
and at the Berkeley Women's Film Festival in 1994.
While a student in Prague, Seelich also published
short stories, radio plays, and poetry, including the
anthology *Akdar Ajdan Leporello*, which was written in
1969 and is scheduled for publication in Prague. In
1969 she emigrated to the West – the United States,
Switzerland, and Austria. Since the mid-1970s
Seelich has lived in Vienna. She lives together with
Bernd Neuburger. Her daughter studies in Prague,
where Seelich has a second residence. Seelich has
written the scripts for *Kieselsteine* (1982; Pebbles), *Ein
Spielfilm für 2 Berge, 3 Schauspieler und einen Feuersala-
mander* (1983; A feature film for 2 mountains, 3 actors, and a salamander), *Nett* (1984; Nice), *Jonathana*

und die Hexe (1985; Jonathana and the witch), *Ferien mit Silvester* (1987; Vacation with Silvester), *Mein Name ist Egon* (1987; My name is Egon), and *Who is Who in Mistelbach* (1989). Together with Bernd Neuburger she produced *Sie saß im Glashaus und warf mit Steinen* and *Theresienstadt sieht aus wie ein Curort* (1997; Theresienstadt looks like a resort), which was featured at the 1997 Viennale [Vienna film festival]. The film is based on the Theresienstadt memoir of Seelich's grandmother, taped in 1948, and her observations on life in the Theresienstadt concentration camp from 1942 to 1945 from the point of view of a woman who was deported in 1942 at the age of sixty-nine.

Nadja Seelich

Film, State, and Society in Eastern and Western Europe – and I

I spent the years of Stalinism in Bohemia, attending kindergarten.

There we studied the poems of Pavel Kohout, who later became a Burgtheater author: "What is it that smokes over there behind the mountain? No! That's not the smokestack of a factory! That's Comrade Gottwald's pipe!", and under the Christmas tree at the kindergarten we sang: "We thank you, Comrade Gottwald, for the beautiful Christmas tree!"

In the evening my education was gently readjusted by my parents. Soon I learned that I had better keep the parental corrections to myself, for when I tried to explain to my kindergarten teacher that "people's democracy," just like lemon lemonade, was a pleonasm, she did not praise me but summoned my parents to the director's office.

Thus began my INTERMONDIAL LIFE, a life between different versions of the universe. My later emigration was only a logical and consistent radicalization of this mode of living.

The phenomenon "child" was traditionally valued extremely highly in the Czech culture and society.

More than three hundred years before Bohemia was afflicted by Marxism and Leninism, Jan Amos Komenius, the founder of modern pedagogy and an advocate of *schola ludus* (playful learning), lived and worked there. By the way: when the Habsburg dynasty had ascended to the Bohemian throne, he fled to Sweden.

One of the basic texts of classical Czech literature is a children's book of 1855 by the title of *Grandmother*, a rural novel. In it the writer

Bozena Nemcova depicts the loving relationship between a little girl, Barunka, and her wise grandmother.

Most of the major Czech authors have also written for children. Children's literature is not considered inferior literature, nor are children considered inferior people. The fact that this is not the case in other countries, including, for example, Austria, was an important aspect of the culture shock I suffered in the West. But I shall return to this topic later.

Outside the kindergarten we read primarily the children's books by Karel Capek (1890–1938, an author, dramatist, and journalist). He was a representative of Czech humanism, which envisions human beings not as heroes without blemishes and defects but as loveable creatures with weaknesses and faults.

All of the "true heroes" came to us from the Soviet Union, for example Comrade Meresjew. Comrade Meresjew was a hero who had lost his legs during a mission in World War II. Every November he traveled from the Soviet Union to our school to tell the same story every time – how he had lost his legs and became a hero. In the end, his chest decorated with medals, he danced a legless *kosatchot* to instill courage in us.

Every 7 November, the anniversary of the October Revolution, we went to the movie house, rather than to school, in order to see *The Battleship Potemkin*.

Approximately three times a year we went to see movies as part of our school curriculum. Every time we saw the same Russian films.

I was especially taken with a film the title of which I have unfortunately forgotten but whose final scene I shall nonetheless keep fresh in my memory for the rest of my life:

A small room in a one-room *dacha*. Black-and-white. Gloomy. She (young, buxom, with long, blond braids) stands at the fireplace and stirs the contents of a pot with a long soup spoon. She looks at the loudly ticking clock. She looks through the small window. Gradually it is getting dark. She stirs the contents of the pot. The clock ticks. Outside snow begins to fall. She looks at the window. She looks at the clock. The clock ticks. She takes the pot off the fire, lights the kerosine lamp. Looks toward the window. A snow storm starts. The clock ticks. She sits down and looks at the clock. Behind the small window the snowstorm rages. The clock ticks. Then, finally, the door opens, and from the howling snow storm a male figure emerges. He enters the room, closes the door behind him. She jumps up, he sits down. Slowly he removes his snow-covered beret. His radiant eyes look into the unknown. "Would you like to eat?" she asks. He shakes his head and stares into the unknown with radiant eyes. "Alyosha," she says, "you have another woman!" Slowly, he nods, his eyes are radiant, "Yes!" She moves her hand to her heart, glares at him, while he stares into the unknown, "Alyosha! Say! Is she more beautiful than I?" He nods and slowly says, "Yes!" "Alyosha! What's her name?" For a while he remains silent, then he turns his radiant eyes toward her and states in firm voice: "REVOLUTION!" At these words she lights up as well and throws herself into his arms.

Every time during this scene the movie house, crowded with fifteen-year-old students, was in an uproar. Everyone howled with laughter. The teacher's anxious "Shush!" was completely drowned out.

At least superficially I looked like the ideal Young Pioneer: at the age of ten I had the required long braids and possessed the radiant look. As a consequence I was sent to the podium during the May Day parade to hand a bouquet of flowers to the erstwhile minister of culture. Full of excitement I gave my father an account of the event later that evening: "And imagine, he gave me a kiss!" My father looked at me in horror, "God forbid, I hope you did wash already!"

In the 1960s the movie scene was flooded by the films of the Czech New Wave: Mencl, Forman, Chytilova, Jasny, Herz. These films were so much more intelligent and humane than any of the French, Italian, German, and American films that were offered us at that time; they were so close and familiar, made exactly for us.

The notion that Czech films are much better than any other films, which is widespread among the Czechs, goes back to that

time and continues to persist stubbornly despite the disastrous
situation of the Czech film during the 1980s and the embarrassing
commercial revitalizing attempts of the 1990s. To this day the older
Czech films are the ones that are sold out for weeks in the Prague
movie houses.

It is a known fact that in Bohemia Communism lasted for forty
years. Of those years I experienced the first twenty in close physical
proximity. These first twenty years differed in a decisive aspect from
the second twenty: We were firmly convinced of the impermanence
of Real Socialism. We considered the situation in which we lived
abnormal, and for this reason we did not try to establish ourselves
in it.

In all likelihood one reason was that the brutality of Stalinism
in the 1950s resembled very closely that of the protectorate of the
so-called Thousand-Year Reich of the Nazis, which had just been
overcome.

In the 1960s the dictatorship seemed already rather tired, and to
oppose it did not seem like a heroic battle but rather like a playful
outmaneuvering. Of course, I am not speaking for the entire Czech
nation but only for myself and my friends, a handful of Prague
students of my generation.

At that time the censors were sleepy and paid little attention; they
were much more easily persuaded than the Austrian film commissions today.

We wrote, published, put on plays, discussed for nights on end,
and listened to jazz. Jean-Paul Sartre came to Prague and told
us about Marxism, and we howled with laughter – the anxious
"Shush!" of our professors was completely drowned out.

Then came Allan Ginsberg and we liked him a lot.

In the spring of 1968 a discussion between students and members of the government and the Central Committee of the Communist Party was organized by the philosophical faculty. One of
the ministers at that time, Smrkovsky, declared: "Young friends! I
would like to explain to you what the Communist Party was for us:
for us it was both the midwife and the worker with the hammer!" In
response the student leader Zdenek Zboril stated: "Allow me to tell
you what the Communist Party was to us: to us it was the midwife

with the hammer!" We howled with laughter, and no professor was in the least anxious to shush us.

August 1968.

I lived in the attic of a turn-of-the century villa in Prague-Strasnice.

A brass bed, a small desk, an art-nouveau lamp, a poster of Einstein sticking out his tongue. Above the poster the inscription: HE HAD LONG HAIR, and below: Don't act against your convictions, even if they force you!

The room was full of yellow roses that my friends had filched for me in a park the night before.

"We're at war! Get up! We're at war!" Next to my bed stands my landlady, a tiny, white-haired, ninety-year-old woman in a black dress and yells, "We're at war!" I try to calm her down, probably she has had a bad dream and, "War! We're at war! Don't you hear the tanks?" "Tanks? Those are the milk trucks; they always come at this time." "War! This is war!" she screams. "You will not be able to study!" Finally I get up and go over to the window. A rosy summer morning, dew on the magnolias in the gardens, everything quiet, the streets deserted. But at a distance a strange, constant rumbling can be heard. Across the horizon an endless row of tanks roll by, so unreal and heavy, like a herd of dinosaurs.

I put on my clothes and ran to the closest large intersection. A tank was positioned there. Gigantic, green-gray, dusty, with paint peeling off in some places. On top of it a soldier, motionless, silent, covered with dust, wearing a fur beret with a little red star. A few people stood around the tank, touched it with their hands. A woman inquired, "What kind of film are they shooting here?"

This is how on 21 August 1968 the Soviet Republic of Absurdistan was established.

New Year's 1969 I spent already in Vienna. In a large, sparsely furnished student's apartment. On the wall a poster of Marx and another one of Lenin. I found it humorous and winked at the man of the house. He looked at me without having a clue.

At midnight the Internationale was played. I found that very

funny – in Prague they play Vienna waltzes on that occasion. So I
laughed. A girl shushed me.

He did come through and produced my first screenplay, *Kieselsteine*.
It was the story of a love-hate relationship between a Jewish woman
and a German man in today's Vienna.

Because the leftists were at that point fed up with Israel, my
producer took advantage of the opportunity the subject offered and
took certain liberties with the script. Against my protest he had a
dialogue entered into the script that exposes Israel as a Fascist
country.

Strangely enough, at the Moscow film festival this scene did not
prevent Soviet journalists from attacking *Kieselsteine* as a Zionist
concoction. The Czech party paper *Rude Pravo* adopted this verdict,
mentioning not only the producer's name but mine as well. The
bureaucracy in Absurdistan was shoddy and did not possess much
imagination. Hence they failed to make a connection between the
name of the Austrian scriptwriter and the name recorded in my
Czech emigration passport. I considered this extremely kind, otherwise I would have hardly been granted another entry visa for the
CSSR.

A few years later I was punished for the "Zionist concoction"
nonetheless:

At that time Bernd Neuburger made a children's film based on
my screenplay *Jonathana und die Hexe*. The film was acquired by
diverse countries, including, much to my enthusiasm, the former
CSSR. Because the bureaucracy over there was so shoddy and as a
consequence unpredictable, I did not dare undertake the Czech
dubbing.

The film ran in Prague in several movie houses, including the Bio
Illusion, the theater of my childhood.

Sentimental as I am, I went to Prague, and for the first time after
many years I once again went with my father to the movies. The
dubbing was a catastrophe: the role of the old witch was spoken by
a young actress; that of Jonathana, a sensitive and shy seven-year-
old girl by a sassy, rebellious, twelve-year-old. The punch lines had
for the most part been eliminated, some words were translated
wrong, some not at all, and others too literally (the latter resulted in

unidiomatic expressions styled after the German, offensive to the Czech ear). After the film my father sat silent for a long time. Then he said, "But the camera work was beautiful." I felt like bawling.

The distance between Absurdistan and Vienna was less than a hundred kilometers, but none of the Austrian producers of critical documentary films ever had the desire of making it the subject of a film. Of course I told them that the films they could produce there had the same potential for suspense as those about Africa: labor camps, psychiatric wards, university professors working as night watchmen. They smiled knowingly and explained to me that by doing so they would play into the hands of the enemy, and that would be dangerous.

The fact that the enemies of my friends on this side and the other side of the Iron Curtain were each other's enemies made my situation more complicated rather than simplifying it.

The Velvet Revolution was a "Once-in-a-Lifetime Festival." At nighttime I strolled through Prague; there was a light snowfall, at every street corner music was played, and people sang in every imaginable language. People who did not know each other from Adam exchanged pleasantries with one another, hugged, and danced. The baroque saints observed us from up high above the Charles Bridge and smirked. "We, the generation of 1968, have wonderful children!" was written on one of the many banners.

The Vienna generation of 1968, my friends, were for the most part childless. They sat at the restaurant Oswald und Kalb, griping: "No doubt you will see where all of this is going to take you! Just wait and see!" Only the most optimistic ones among them hoped that after the collapse of Real Socialism true socialism would finally come.

The critical-documentary filmmakers immediately dropped Africa and rushed to the neighboring countries. Day in and day out the same old and new clichés about my homeland flickered across the television screens: beginning with the statement that the Charles University had been the first German university altogether (I do not know whether the House of Habsburg had already spread this nonsense or whether it took someone like Hitler to invent it) all the way down to images of paint peeling off factory walls behind which the concerned voice of the commentator suspected a progressive breakdown of the economy. Scattered in between baroque, beer, Kafka, and "Trabis" (popular short form for the East German car model Trabant). An everyday story, filmed by Toni Spira, represented a marvelous exception. In his film travelers on a train between Austria and the CSSR were interviewed.

"How can I know what to think if I don't see what I speak of?" I thought in a slight variation of a statement by E. M. Forster, and together with Bernd Neuburger I produced the film *Sie saß im Glashaus und warf mit Steinen* in Prague. It is a journey through the Prague behind the greeting cards, the Prague that is the home of the daughters and sons of the golem and not of Orwell. It was the most beautiful film shooting I have ever experienced.

I was particularly curious about the New Czech films.

Unfortunately it turned out that most of the scripts that were written there in the last twenty years and could not be produced because they were outlawed had become outdated, and there is no need to produce them at this point. In other words: although the drawers are full of scripts, there is nonetheless a great shortage of filmscripts.

Nonetheless, films are being produced. Unfortunately, decades of Sovietization had crippled the rich, charming, absurd, surreal-witty, human, and caring film discourse of the sixties. What remains is a kind of heavy-handed social satire that follows conventional patterns of criticizing the new political and social abuses.

There are, thank God, exceptions, primarily among the very young directors. Many of the established masters no longer live in Bohemia (Forman is in Hollywood, Jasny in Canada, Herz in the Federal Republic of Germany, etc.).

As far as Czech literature is concerned, the situation is fundamentally different, because books apparently age less rapidly than filmscripts. Luckily almost the entire oeuvre of Bohuman Hrabal has by now also appeared with Suhrkamp Publishers (some of the novels by this author had been filmed by Jiri Mencl, including *Lärchen am Faden* (Larches on a thread) – an outstanding film, which for twenty years was kept in a safe in Absurdistan and was shown even by the ORF (Austrian Television) three years ago. But this is only a fraction of what Czech literature has to offer at this point.

Austrian literature continues to be represented in Czechoslovakia primarily by Simmel, in other words, by works that confirm the Czech prejudices about contemporary Austrian culture.

As far as Austrian films in Bohemia are concerned, the film that is shown most frequently continues to be *Jonathana und die Hexe*.

CONCLUSION

In the late sixties we who lived in Prague wore the same bluejeans and the same long hair and listened to the same Bob Dylan as the members of our generation in Vienna. The forms of antiestablishment protest were the same, but the content was different.

"In the West everything goes and nothing matters, in the East nothing goes and everything matters," Philip Roth wrote.

A rapprochement between West and East is only possible if we become acquainted with the history and roots of the longings and dreams of the other – and if we understand that this otherness is a prerequisite for a dialogue. A dialogue between people with identical experiences, views, ideas, opinions, and dreams is pointless.

Finally, as Jan Werich said: "Only stupid people live in paradise. Those who think live in the hell of eternal questions and doubts."

Nadja Seelich

Farewell to Jana Cerna

From 1966 to 1968, while studying, I worked for the publishing house Klub Mlada Poezie (New poetry club) in Prague. There I became acquainted with Jana ("Honza") Cerna, the daughter of Milena Jesenska. Cerna's work was often published in the club magazine, Divoke Vino.

Her book Adresat Milena Jesenska was also published by the Klub Mlada Poezie. Subsequent publication in the Federal Republic of Germany followed, and this year (1992) a film version of the book was made under the title Milena Lover.

Jana Cerna's life is just as dramatic and tragic, just as indicative of the time and degree of latitude at which it unfolded, as the life of her mother. Jana was born in Prague in 1928 as the daughter of the journalist Milena Jesenska and the architect Jaromir Krejcar. Her parents' circle of friends consisted of left-wing orientated Prague artists and intellectuals. Her mother was addicted to morphine, and this finally led to her parents' separating. Krejcar, enthused by the idea of Communism, went to the Soviet Union. Milena Jesenska moved in with her lover, the translator Evzen Klinger, taking Jana with her. Jana got on very well with her stepfather and idolized her mother, although her mother's drug dependency constantly caused difficulties, not least from a material point of view.

Krejcar returned from the Soviet Union deeply disappointed and talked bitterly of Stalinism – of arrests, poverty, and the grandiose cult of personality. Milena was horrified, and the young Jana, who had always been treated by her parents as an equal, took everything in.

In 1938, Milena successfully completed treatment for her morphine addiction. Just before Hitler came into power, Jana's stepfather emigrated. Milena could not make up her mind to emigrate and stayed behind with Jana. She wrote for an illegal newspaper, and Jana, her youthful innocence rendering her inconspicuous, served as a messenger. Indeed, this is what she was engaged in doing when her mother was arrested in 1939. Milena Jesenska was deported to the concentration camp at Ravensbrück, where she died in 1944.

Jana went to live with her grandfather, Jan Jesensky, a well-known Prague dentist. Formerly a dandy, he was now increasingly becoming a tyrannical eccentric. Jana at first attended high school, and later a school of graphic art. Her grandfather, unable to come to terms with the death of his daughter, called Jana "Milka," as he used to call Milena. He died in 1945, after the war, and left a fortune to the seventeen-year-old Jana. Jana succeeded in squandering her whole inheritance with a friend within a year. All her life she was unable to manage money.

After the Communist putsch in 1948, Jana too came to feel the hatred of the Czech Communists for Milena, whom they had heard openly announce her loathing of Stalinism in Ravensbrück. She never had a permanent job and lived on temporary work and writing, frequently in dire poverty. Occasionally, having nowhere to live, she slept in attics, cellars, or in strangers' beds in return for payment. Jana spent her time among a group of significant literary figures of her time, impressing and influencing them with her views on art. She married four times and casually bore five children. She paid them scant attention, and this resulted in her being sent to jail at Pardubice in 1963 and 1964. The final years of her life were more tranquil. She lived, almost contentedly, with her fourth husband and occupied herself with ceramics. She died in a car accident at the age of fifty-two.

Jana Cerna, when I got to know her in 1966, was a large, solid woman with a fat stomach and sagging breasts, dressed in men's trousers, with straggly dark hair, soft full lips, a squint, and wearing spectacles. She did not fit any ideal of beauty, least of all the moral concepts of the nineteenth century that have marked the century thereafter.

Yet she was a fascinating woman whose spell was impossible to escape. She radiated an animal motherliness; one wanted to be loved by her, knowing

*only too well that her love was a trap and that she, like the revolution,
devoured her own children. She never kept a promise, lied, stabbed her friends
repeatedly in the back, was elusive, incomprehensible, full of wonderful plans,
and filled one with excitement.*

*Although she was born a few years after the death of her mother's famous
lover, Franz Kafka, she considered herself in a certain sense to be his daughter.*

*We, the editors of the Klub Mlada Poezie, were all scarcely twenty years of age,
and Jana Cerna, who was much older and in every respect more experienced,
treated us with a certain disparaging condescension. She repeatedly attempted
to trick us; again and again, we got annoyed and swore that we would never
again have anything to do with "that woman." Then, a few days later, we
would again be sitting at the table in the kitchen of her small dilapidated
apartment in Prague-Letna, a table piled high with dirty crockery, laundry,
manuscripts, and bottles (I always cast a quick sideways glance under the
rumpled bed, searching for a shoe box containing a freshly stabbed fetus), and
there we would listen to her, spellbound. Her velvety tones hovered between
surrealism, Marxism, and obscenity, and it was impossible not to believe her.*

*It was not only us, with our postpubescent, lyrical naiveté, whom she held cap-
tive, for significant literary and philosophical personalities such as Bohumil
Hrabal, Dr. Zybnek Fiser, and Ivo Vodsedalek were also captivated by her.*

Most of what was published during her life (two novellas and several short stories) she wrote specifically and consciously for money,
and such writing therefore belongs more among the superficial
works of the period, which remained faithful to the party line.

Her seven short stories written from prison, which appeared in the
magazine *Divoke Vino,* and the novel *Adresat Milena Jensenska* (1968)
are an exception.

At the time, her novel attracted hardly any attention. Only a very
small number of copies were printed, and further printings were
then no longer possible for political reasons.

The novel was published in Frankfurt in 1985 and was later made
into a film. The metamorphosis that the title has undergone is in

itself tragic and indicative of the commercialization that has taken place. In the Czech original it was *Adresat Milena Jesenska*, in the German translation, simply *Milena Jesenska*, and in the film version, *Milena Lover.*

A small volume was recently published in Prague with the title *Clarissa and other writings* under Cerna's maiden name, Jana Krejcarova.

Clarissa is a fragment of a novel or, rather, notes for a novel. The volume also contains a letter to Dr. Fiser ("Egon Bondy"), which is one of the most beautiful and impressive love letters published in this century – romantic, realistic, humorous, obscene, and philosophical, written with remarkable ease.

Anna Mitgutsch

Anna Mitgutsch was born in Linz, Upper Austria, in 1948. After university studies in German and English literature, she moved to Boston, where she taught German language and literature. Her scholarly works include *Metaphorical Gaps and Negation in the Poetry of W. S. Merwin, Mark Strand, and Charles Simic* (1980) and *The Image of the Female in D. H. Lawrence's Poetry* (1981). Mitgutsch holds a doctorate in American literature from the University of Salzburg. She taught American poetry at the University of Innsbruck and has recently undertaken a research project on medieval Jewry. Her novels *Die Züchtigung* (1985; *Three Daughters*), *Das andere Gesicht* (1986; *The other face*), *Ausgrenzung* (1989; *Exclusion*), and *In fremden Städten* (1992; *In Foreign Cities*) have been translated into other languages. She was awarded the Anton Wildgans Prize (1993) and the Advancement Prize of the Austrian Federal Ministry for the Arts (1996). Mitgutsch currently lives in Linz Fricoenegg. She has held visiting professor's appointments at Lafayette College, Oberlin College, Tufts University, Allegheny College, and Amherst College. Throughout her career Mitgutsch, who converted to Judaism in a conscious effort to regain part of her Jewish heritage, has addressed issues of otherness, many of which she experienced herself: the otherness of an Austrian woman in the United States, the otherness produced by autism, a problem with which she is familiar as the mother of an autistic child, but most of all the pervasive otherness felt, but not fully comprehended, by an Austrian woman of Jewish descent. In *Lover, Traitor* (1997), a semiautobiographical novel set in Jerusalem, Mitgutsch explores the multiple levels of alienation of which an Austrian Jewish convert becomes aware as she interacts with different ethnic, religious, and social groups in Jerusalem.

Anna Mitgutsch

EXCERPT FROM

Lover, Traitor: A Jerusalem Story

Farewell to Jerusalem

I walked back past the Russian Church and stopped for a moment
in front of the police station. Then I went down Jaffa Road, making
a conscious effort not to bolt like a criminal on the run. Once I
reached the corner I turned to look behind myself, but casually, as if
I were just trying to orient myself. No one seemed to be following.

So I headed straight for my hotel and was overcome by relief
when I reached my own room and locked the door. I peered out
between the slats of the shutters to see whether anyone was standing in the street below looking up at my window.

What am I thinking? Why would anyone be following me? True,
I've stayed a little longer than most tourists do. The men who hang
around the Old City walls, standing in the shade waiting for tourists, I'm sure they all know me by now. I look at them out the corner
of my eye when they call to me and I watch them from my rusty
wrought iron balcony – how they walk by with a nonchalant swag-
ger, pretending to be idle but always with purpose etched on their
taut, focused faces as they make their way to the Arab bus station or
the Jaffa Gate. The air in East Jerusalem is thick with tension. It
covers the Old City like a blanket, heavier on some days than on
others but never lifting completely.

Most of the people in this part of the city are Palestinian. I don't
really know anyone here and in any case, I can't tell one face from
another; if someone were shadowing me twenty-four hours round
the clock, I still couldn't pick him out from a crowd. The men stare
at me, sizing me up, but I just can't look them back in the eye. The
fear that someone will recognize me drives me back to the Jewish
side of the city, to West Jerusalem, where I'm treated with indif-

ference. Nobody takes any notice; I'm just another woman out shopping. But I can't seem to keep away from the Old City, where the ironic smiles hint that my secrets are showing, out on display for everyone to scoff at.

I don't know where I belong, in East Jerusalem or West, and I don't want to make a choice. It's time for me to change hotels again. Jumping from one address to another like this will only make my case look worse, but one more day here or there won't change the fact that I'm on the run. I can't go underground and deep down I suppose I want to be caught. Why else would I keep walking past the police station?

Sooner or later, I'll have to talk about what's been going on these last few weeks. I want to be ready, to explain how it started, to have good reasons for what I did and convincing answers for the questions they might throw at me. It'll all depend on how I present the information – how skillfully I stretch the things I will tell them to cover up the gaps, the missing parts that I'll keep to myself. There can be no cracks in the story. They'll say I should've reported it right away. They'll want to know why I waited. How can I answer without giving away my shame and showing my longing?

My fear is surely groundless. No one's paying attention to me. And if they are they probably think I'm just one more crazy tourist lost in Jerusalem. But even my friends were amazed to learn I was still here. "I thought you'd gone," Nurit said a week after I was supposed to fly home. I lied. I told her I had an open ticket and had decided at the last minute to stay a while longer.

I should've told them. This way, I can't find out what happened, so my dread just intensifies. But talking to Nurit or Eli I clam up after the first sentence.

"I met a young Armenian," I told Nurit.

"Where? In the Old City?" She looked skeptical. "Be careful."

"He's not like the men who hang out at the Jaffa Gate."

She eyed me with pity. "And how long did it take you to find that out?"

"About four days."

We laughed and moved on to something else.

Sometimes I imagine that it's all on tape – every humiliation, all our silly conversations, his awful friends, our lovemaking – every little part that I'm too ashamed to tell my friends. I can't bear to think of it. But when I do, when I picture the whole thing on-screen, I cringe, mortified. There's no excuse. Do what you want with that woman, I think. She's not worth defending.

One Friday afternoon, I met Anahita in the Old City. I'd decided to tell her. I thought I'd feel less embarrassed talking to her because she herself is Armenian. Anahita ran a bright little tourist boutique in the Cardo, the ancient Roman arcade excavated in the Jewish Quarter. The light in her shop was dazzling, reflected in her mirrors and glass and gold and silver trinkets; it made the street outside seem like a dark tunnel. A few steps away, the Muslim Quarter languished in the lifeless hues of an inhospitable twilight, the stores dark and shuttered every afternoon in protest. Only the rivulets of rainwater gave light, glistening as they trickled through the cracks of paving stones. On the walls, graffiti blossomed in riotous colors. My shame was written there, glaring and obscene. "We fuck your women," it said, an insult to humiliate the enemy. But the enemy no longer goes there, not without a weapon. Even the tourists keep away, preferring to spend their afternoons down at the Dead Sea.

I sat on a stool and watched Anahita sell a menorah. She seemed bored by the transaction, naming the price in such a soft voice that I couldn't hear what she said. Her smooth face gave away nothing, not her thoughts nor her age. She always greeted me with such indifference that I'd wonder whether she wanted me there. Although she had volunteered her life story the first time we met. She'd even told me about her parents and how they'd survived persecution. She'd asked me to come again and gave me the feeling that I'd found a friend.

Her customers, two wiry Frenchmen in gray tones from their carefully trimmed hair down to their tasteful slacks, turned to go, undecided and discouraged. Anahita took a half step toward them and announced a new price. One pulled out his wallet in relief and resignation.

"Tourists are dumb," she said once the two were out of earshot. "They'll buy anything from Jerusalem, even useless bits of rock."

I liked watching her there, standing among her glittering display cases in a sky-blue dress that made her skin look brighter and her eyes darker. Anahita was a bit plump, no longer young but still girlish, as if infinite possibilities still lay before her. She'd talked to me about most of the important things in her life, yet I still knew so little about her. When she was silent I couldn't begin to guess what she was thinking. And there was a lot of silence between her sentences; her words often seemed to drown in it. Actually, she knew nothing about the outside world that produced the tourists she despised. She had grown up in Abu Dis on the West Bank when it still belonged to Jordan, an only daughter, unmarried, a servant in her father's house. She had finally rebelled and moved to Jerusalem where a single woman can run a shop and life alone. Not entirely alone, though. She roomed in the Armenian convent.

At five o'clock she set the alarm system, locked the door, and pulled the iron gate closed, solemnly, as if every movement was a symbolic act of great significance. In the Jewish Quarter housewives were doing their last-minute shopping before the Sabbath, baguettes and pale-colored vegetables in their shopping bags.

Anahita led me past the convent doorkeeper and we walked through a labyrinth of corridors and up staircases onto the roof. The two whitewashed cubes jutting out of the flat rooftop were her rooms, each of which was covered with corrugated steel. Their iron doors were shedding chips of blue paint. My bedroom, she indicated, my kitchen. The evening wind caressed the rooftop cupolas. It grew cool as we sat at a table drinking Turkish coffee and eating grapes. Anahita faced the Old City wall behind which the sky had begun to light up in dark flames. I looked out at the Mosque of Omar. Its golden dome drew the waning red glare like a heavenly body illuminating the night.

"Do you think I can still fall in love at fifty-five?" she asked.

"Have you never been in love?" I said.

"Every so often a man would show some interest, but nothing would really come of it."

But her employer had big plans for her. "He trusts me," she said. "He lets me run the business any way I like. Maybe I'll even go to Europe one of these days." Then she looked young, like an overweight girl about to shake off a strict upbringing, eagerly anticipating her future.

"Things are going well for me now," she declared.

I felt close to her and wanted to promise that it was all possible, her own shop, trips to Europe, falling in love. I told her that she had good business sense and that it was never too late. And since we were talking about the future, she turned my cup over and read my fortune in the black coffee grounds, while the long howl of sirens announced the onset of the Sabbath.

"You should stick to West Jerusalem," she said, sounding just like all my Israeli friends. The coffee grounds gave her the occasion to drive the point home. "You see," she said, turning the black rim of the cup toward her, "there's danger lurking in the east, especially down in the valley, in Abu Tor and Silwan. And you shouldn't go to the Muslim Quarter, either."

"That's what everyone says," I protested.

"Visit the Israel Museum," she advised. I laughed. During my first week in Jerusalem I stayed in a kibbutz guesthouse, and every morning an old retiree kept asking me to go to the Israel Museum with him.

We looked out over the railing at the dark street below. Pious Jews and tourists rushed quietly toward the Western Wall. The sky was still holding on to a strip of faded red, but over the Old City rooftops and the Mount of Olives it had cooled down to a clear, translucent green.

"I met a young Armenian," I said, and saw a wariness enter her eyes.

Did I imagine it? Was she suspicious right away, at the first mention of Sivan's name, or did it develop over time, little by little?

"Where did you meet him?"

"In the Jewish Quarter, at the Hurva Synagogue."

She said nothing.

"He said he was Catholic."

She shrugged her shoulders. Possible, but unlikely.

I couldn't read the expression on her smooth face, but the sense of closeness had vanished. Suddenly I felt heavy with loneliness and sorrow. Maybe it was the melancholy of a Friday night, or of the whole city, or maybe Anahita's sadness was contagious.

"Do you have the letter p in your alphabet?" I asked, already knowing the answer.

"Why?"

"Because he cannot pronounce it."

"Then he's Palestinian," she said. "We've even got two p sounds. Palestinians often try to pass as Armenians, so be careful."

"It's too late for that. Would an Armenian drive to Ramallah at night?"

"No Armenian would dare be caught on the West Bank at night. He's lying to you."

I didn't ask any more questions and she wasn't interested in my story. In her eyes, I had just become another dumb, naive tourist.

"Stick to West Jerusalem, where you belong. You don't understand East Jerusalem, you're putting yourself in all kinds of danger."

We sat a while longer looking at the glassy dark sky. A slender sickle of moon hung over the Mount of Olives like a gently curved blade. In two weeks it would be full and a month would have passed since Sivan disappeared. Strangely, when Anahita killed my last hope that he might have been telling the truth, I began to reclaim the affection I'd transferred to her in his absence. She had just become another woman who'd been cheated of her life. We both felt it was time for me to leave.

"Don't go back through the Zion Gate," she warned me. "It's too isolated, something might happen, be careful."

We felt our way through the convent's dark maze of stairways, hallways, and courtyards, finally arriving at Jacob's Church. The gate was locked. "I lived in a convent for a while," Sivan had told me, "but you have to be in by ten o'clock, so I moved out." At least he was well-informed.

The street was deserted and for the first time I felt afraid of walking through the Old City alone.

In the beginning I wasn't at all afraid, not even in Silwan, or Abu Tor or the Kidron Valley, places everyone warned me about. But then things started to happen almost every day, especially at the Central Bus Station, "disturbances," they were called. Suddenly, the lines of people waiting for buses would be herded into a corner by a nervous young woman soldier, or the station would be closed off altogether. The word spread quickly, bomb scare, one of many. Traveling on buses, I could measure the force and size of rocks thrown at the windows by the smudge of splintering glass left behind. Once, I discovered a bullet hole just above my head.

I didn't read the newspapers and trusted the tour guides who, seeing their incomes shrinking, swore you could go anywhere in Jerusalem, no one would touch a tourist. But I'd met tourists whose rented cars had been set alight. I learned to listen for small things, casually mentioned, to interpret the message in people's eyes, and I began to pick up the slight restlessness in a crowd before someone yelled bomb scare, everyone out. More than once, I'd seen uniformed police in vans with barred windows stop in the middle of Jaffa Road and herd young men into the back, slamming the doors shut. No one ever stopped to look, no one ever inquired. "They're suspects, probably Arabs, it's just a fact of life here, you get used to it," people explained. Like everyone else I asked no questions. When the bomb squad closed off a street to detonate a stray package or unclaimed shopping bag I'd simply take a detour, like everyone else. I hardly even winced at the sound of the blast. But still, I became uneasy, edgily alert, as if there were special dangers waiting for me personally.

I had known Sivan for less than a week when I suggested we go up to the Mount of Olives for a view of the city at night, by the light of the moon.

"But it's dangerous," he said.

"Are you afraid?" I asked.

Then he insisted on going, as if the trip had become a test of his courage. He wanted to prove that he wasn't a coward, but he stole down Mount Zion past the stone houses of Silwan as if he were making his way through enemy lines. He dragged me across the stony slope so impatiently that I started to protest. "Keep quiet," he whispered, "it's dangerous here." I didn't know whether we were playing a game or whether we were in real danger. Sivan only loosened his grip once we reached the cemetery in the floor of the valley, where the bony white graves of the prophets and the sinister shadows put the fear of ghosts in you. Then we ran up the Mount of Olives. The cypresses loomed so high and dense in the night sky that I couldn't see the path through the blackness and lost all sense of direction. As we climbed over the rubble of a stone wall, I was startled to see the city spread out below us, moonlit and shimmering.

We sat on a wide stone slab and looked at Jerusalem until I was sure I'd fixed the image in my mind forever – the Dome of the Rock and Al Aqsa, with their gold and silver globes, the black mass of squat stone houses stacked one above the other, the distant glitterings of light which flickered and then died away. The air was sharp and cold, but we still made love in the piercing night wind, naked on our stone slab as if laid out for sacrifice. First, we slid our hands beneath each other's clothing for warmth, then we sheltered our nakedness from the wind with our loving, tender bodies, feeling every touch on bare skin, every downy hair ruffling under searching fingers. We were unpracticed with each other that first time, but every seeking, probing attempt unlocked a new and wondrous intimacy.

Sivan broke the silence when we heard a noise. As we slid off the edge of our stone slab and hunched down in the darkness of a rock pile overgrown with thorny brush and weeds, I thought, this is probably a tomb, we just made love on the grave of a prophet.

I remember the cypresses on the way back and a plain, unremarkable mosque to the right of a sharp bend in the path, and that we ran hand in hand without saying a word to each other. It wasn't until we were back in the Old City that Sivan kissed me, hard, as if I'd just saved his life.

"You think you can go anywhere you want," Frieda said, when I told her I'd been in the Old City, in the Hinnom Valley, or on Mount Zion. I said nothing about my midnight trip to the Mount of Olives.

"Don't you understand that we are at war?" she said. "Why do you deliberately put yourself in so much danger?"

"Come on, Frieda, you're exaggerating," I said. "I've seen plenty of Jews over there."

"It's Channa," she corrected me. "It's been Channa for fifty years."

But she'd always been Frieda to me; whenever my grandmother spoke of her it was Frieda she talked about. My grandmother was related to Martha and so was Frieda on her father's side, but they'd also been close friends. Which brings me to the real reason that I came to Jerusalem – I was looking for Martha. I came because of her.

Frieda-Channa has an open house every Sunday and Thursday. On those afternoons I would take the bus out past the hills of Kiryat Yovel, beyond the shabby apartment blocks built in the fifties, where the slopes covered with thistles and olive trees drop off sharply in the direction of her isolated village, Ein Kerem. Few tourists ever came out this far, but there were usually a few young mothers sitting in the shade of pine trees while their children slid through the giant maw of a plastic park monster, and in the late afternoon, from Frieda-Channa's kitchen window, you could see lovers searching for a secluded spot among the bushes.

At night, Frieda would take me to the bus stop and would never forget, even if the bus was coming around the bend, to point out a rough-hewn stone by the roadside, engraved with the names of four dead commuters and the date of their killing. Pointing her finger, she'd remind me to at least be careful, even if I couldn't bring myself to show some common sense and move into her guest room. "Four innocent people, totally unsuspecting, stabbed on a beautiful spring afternoon by an Arab fanatic. They were doing nothing, just waiting for a bus, and you go walking around East Jerusalem in that getup you're wearing."

"Why don't you move to Tel Aviv, where it's safer?" I asked her

She gave me a horrified look. "I built this city," she said. "The difference with you is that you're reckless. We're careful. We live with the danger, but we never forget it."

There were more and more things she couldn't forget. The house in Vienna from which her parents were deported in 1942. Every single piece of furniture, every household item, the view from the kitchen, the courtyard of linden trees, the wild grape vines, and the flower beds. For Frieda, the details of Vienna in the 1930s grew sharper and more vivid with each passing year. Even I could see her home in Vienna and smell the fragrance of linden here in Ein Kerem. I too could summon up the picture of her parents leaving their house with two suitcases in the damp gray dawn of a cold March day. That's the last image Frieda has of them, or perhaps just the last image she'll allow herself to impose on her visitor. Then followed a long silence in which we both separately traced their journey to its end. "I've never forgiven myself for not getting them out," she told me. "I tried, but not hard enough. If we'd had any idea of what was going to happen, I'd have done anything, I'd have done the impossible."

"What about Martha?" I asked.

The last time Frieda had seen her was in Salzburg, shortly before she emigrated to Palestine. Martha had married an artist, a Viennese man who divorced her later, after 1938, just as Frieda had expected. When they met in Salzburg, they were no longer close; they hardly had anything to say to each other.

"I was a Zionist," Frieda said, "and she was blind, blind and crazy in love with that man. He was a real charmer, anyone could see. But he was only interested in himself and had to be the center of attention. After the Anschluss, after her eyes had been opened, Martha wrote me here in Jerusalem, but her letter took a number of detours before finally reaching me. It was postmarked Prague, but for all I knew, she might no longer have been alive when I read it. She wrote about emigrating. Not to Palestine, God forbid, but to England, Holland, or Switzerland. Me, all I ever wanted was to come here and build my own country. Not Martha. If there's one thing for sure, it's that she never came to Israel."

I said nothing. I was convinced Martha was here, but I didn't want to open up my obsession to Frieda's scrutiny.

Frieda went back to Vienna once, thirty years after she'd left. The city she returned to was strange to her, foreign. It took her eight hours to get up the courage to look at the house. "You can't imagine what it's like," she said, "living for thirty years with those images tormenting me, then coming back to a different city." Frieda found the neighborhood easily enough, even the street, but she circled the house for eight hours, walking around the core of her pain. "I couldn't do it," she admitted. "I could see the house from the end of the street. It was still standing, with the same facade, but I couldn't walk up to it and go in." She spent two days in Vienna and then went to Frankfurt, where her husband was born, and stayed two weeks with friends.

"Forgiveness, reconciliation – I've got no use for those words," she said. "They mean nothing to me."

I visited Frieda twice a week and spent hours sitting with the two pieces of furniture she brought from Vienna, her little art nouveau desk, and a chest of drawers with rococo marquetry. She plied me

with fruits and candy like a long-lost granddaughter and told me
about a Jerusalem that no longer exists: the Old City before the War
of Independence in 1948, the Jewish Quarter where she starved during the siege, Rehavia, the refined German neighborhood where
she lived for thirty years. Some stories she told again and again:
about the old woman holding her last egg in her hand during the
siege, being so careful not to break it; about the cooking stove she
improvised from a window grille; how hungry they had been and
how hard it was for her to watch her child suffer. Her eyes shone
when she described the Old City in those days, the Ethiopian
monks living above the Church of the Holy Sepulcher, the Via Dolorosa, and the Muslim Quarter, "but I don't ever want to catch you
going there," she would add. "One day, when there's peace, we'll
go down there together and I'll show you everything. You haven't
even begun to scratch the surface of Jerusalem. There's always
more, it's inexhaustible – the views, the little hidden courtyards
with their ancient trees and fountains, you have to know where they
are otherwise you can walk right past them."

I didn't tell her that I'd seen more than she knew. Still, she was
right, I hadn't discovered her Jerusalem.

"One day they'll slaughter us all," she said calmly as she put fruit
and sandwiches on the table. She could have been talking about the
siesta she always took between two and four, her voice was so
impassive. "Not yet, though," she went on. "We have the best army
in the region, but it's inevitable."

I didn't tell Frieda that my plane ticket was no longer valid, and
she had no idea about what kind of life I'd been living. I kept
wanting to tell her, sure that she'd understand. But then she'd start
giving me her advice – "Don't go to the souk on Fridays when
they're all wound up after the sermon at Al Aqsa Mosque, and if you
can't manage to keep away from there, wear a longer skirt" – and
she'd show me that rough memorial by the bus stop and I would
feel as if I was the assassin, I the traitor.

Ruth Beckermann

Ruth Beckermann was born in Vienna in 1952, where her parents had moved after the liberation. Her mother, a Viennese Jew, had survived in exile in the British Mandate of Palestine and been a member of the Israeli military; her father, a Holocaust survivor from Czernovitz, Romania, had come to Vienna after the destruction of his culture. Beckermann grew up in Vienna in the company of children of survivors. After graduating from high school, she studied journalism and art history. Beckermann's main themes are central European Jewish culture and the existential choices faced by German-speaking Jews born after the Shoah. The focus of her work is securing the traces of history: the remnants of Jewish life in Vienna and eastern Europe and the crimes perpetrated by German and Austrian Nazis and central and eastern European anti-Semites. Beckermann is a major figure in contemporary Austrian Jewish culture. She is one of the coauthors of *Im blinden Winkel: Nachrichten aus Mitteleuropa* (1985; In the blind spot: News from central Europe) and the author of *Die Mazzesinsel: Juden in der Wiener Leopoldstadt, 1918–1938* (1984; The Matzoth Island: Jews in Vienna's Leopoldstadt 1918–1938), *Unzugehörig: Österreicher und Juden nach 1945* (1989; Not belonging), *Ohne Untertitel: Fragmente einer Geschichte des Österreichischen* (1996; Without subtitles: Fragments of a history of Austrianness). Her films include *Wien Retour* (1983; Return to Vienna), *Die papierene Brücke* (1987; Paper bridge), *Nach Jerusalem* (1990; Towards Jerusalem), and *Jenseits des Krieges* (1996; East of War), a film that documents the reactions and attitudes of visitors at the 1995 exhibition *Vernichtungskrieg: Verbrechen der Wehrmacht, 1941 bis 1944* (War of extermination: Crimes of the German Wehrmacht), which took place at the Vienna Alpenmilchzentrale in the fall of 1995. Beckermann lives as a journalist and filmmaker in Vienna and Paris.

Ruth Beckermann

Youth in Vienna

One could consider it surprising
that the obvious futility
of all of our strange disguises
has so far failed to discourage us.
—HANNAH ARENDT

In conversations with Jews born in postwar Vienna certain sentences occur again and again, sentences such as: "My childhood is
situated in a no man's land"; "We lived here and did not live here";
"Home, that was an extraterritorial site"; "I do not remember that
Austrian politics were ever discussed at home except when they had
a direct effect on Jews. However, we had to be very quiet when the
news broadcasts dealt with Israel or America. Israel was considered
our actual homeland, America the great power protecting the Jews."

No doubt, these memories are not objectively true; however, they
describe a perception. We lived in Vienna, but we socialized almost
exclusively with Jews. With them we celebrated birthdays and Jewish holidays, spent our Sundays and vacations. It was as if in the
midst of the Austria of the 1950s an Austria long past and far away
was transmitted that was featured primarily in the literature of
the "world of yesterday." As far as the present was concerned, Austria represented a place with which one did not want to become
involved.

Only in school did we notice the discrepancy between the interior
world of our family and circle of friends and the "world outside."
There was always this discrepancy. I believe that Jewish children of
the postwar era were confronted with their Jewishness as soon as
they took their first breath. When I see the plain hairstyles and stern
faces of the nurses in the photographs taken at the hospital where I

was born, I think that a Jewish child had to evoke extraordinary sensations in these women who perhaps a few years earlier had been members of the BDM [Hitler Youth] or who at any rate had been nurses and midwives at a time when only Aryan children had the right to live. When I imagine what the nurses thought of the many visitors who wanted to see me at all hours and of the little coral bracelet that was placed around my arm immediately after I was born to ward off the evil eye, I believe that, at the very least, a Jewish child born after 1945 was met with apprehension.

Later, at school, we observed the unwritten law to take nothing that was discussed at home to the outside. We even modified our language. None of us would have dreamed of using Yiddish vocabulary in conversations with our fellow students, including words that had already entered everyday Vienna speech, such as *Ezes* or *Mezie*. Even the word *Jew* was taboo. We were students of the Mosaic faith, who listened every morning in silence to the class prayer and stared at the crucifix where our alleged victim languished. Even if we tried to attract attention by telling the exciting stories about life and death that we had overheard at home, we were unsuccessful. Nobody wanted to hear them. Hardly any Jewish child in Vienna would be able to tell a story like Alain Finkielkraut, who aroused compassion and gained love because he was so exotic.[1]

Nonetheless, the outside world was exciting and alluring. We wanted to belong at all cost and blamed our parents for the difficulties that stood in our way.

We began to rebel against our parents' ghetto existence, as we used to call their reticence at that time. We were embarrassed by the way they lived. On the one hand, we interpreted it as subservience and adjustment to the conditions in Austria and on the other, as soon as they congregated at the synagogue for weddings or charitable events, as a comedy of vanities.

In the mid-1970s our criticism found its artistic expression in the Jewish cabaret skit "For Ghetto's Sake."[2] In it we presented to our parents who were in attendance our protest against business and community, and in particular against the visions and desires they had for our future. We were supposed to find a Jewish spouse to preserve tradition and religion and to prevent the disruption of the domestic harmony. To avoid all possible temptations we were supposed to marry as young as possible. At the same time we were supposed to succeed in the outside world unencumbered by anything Jewish. We should become solid and respected citizens, preferably doctors and lawyers.

Many of us expressed our rebellion by adopting a pioneerlike Zionism in opposition to our parents' admiration and financial support for Israel, which we considered lukewarm. Many of us left Vienna after graduating from high school to study in Israel or America.

For many of us the rebellion against the "ghetto" involved opening ourselves up to the non-Jewish environment and an interest in the country in which we lived; in other words, political involvement.

Our confrontation with the destruction of the Jews occurred in a highly abstract and embarrassed fashion. Everyone knew something, everyone had noticed something strange about their relatives, but no one had any knowledge of a coherent family history. Everything that had to do with the era of the persecution was connected with a great deal of fear and shame. It was a wound no one wanted to touch, a wound covered up and concealed.

On the one hand we devoured the pertinent literature about National Socialism and the persecution of the Jews, on the other we did not dare to ask our parents about their experiences and the fates of our relatives. We were afraid of our parents' answers and even more so of their reactions to suddenly emerging memories. We sensed that we might touch on something we could not handle. We would not be able to console them.

All of us were aware of some incomprehensible reactions on the part of our own relatives. We associated them with that era, and they were frightening to us, but at that time we discussed them with no one. I remember a great-uncle who frequently began crying all of a sudden. Without any provocation, it seemed to me. Once on a beautiful summer day he wanted to take a walk with us after lunch. We left the house and tears streamed down his cheeks. Much later I learned that, and how, he had survived Auschwitz. Only much later did I understand that the memory of the horror is almost impossible to bear in a situation of normalcy. In the midst of beauty and happiness, however, it becomes intolerable.

Peter Sichrovsky describes how he and Arje, whose story he tells

in his book about young Jews in Germany and Austria, enjoyed the
autumn sun somewhere in Vienna. Both men sit on a park bench,
their eyes closed. At this idyllic moment Arje says: "What they did
to our people is sheer insanity. No matter where we are, no matter
what we do and think, it attacks us, imposes itself on us, interrupts
our thoughts and feelings."[3]

Only in the 1980s did we begin talking about such feelings.
Earlier we had accommodated ourselves to the outside world, each
in his or her own way. With aplomb and enthusiasm some of us had
integrated ourselves into Austrian society. The time around 1968
had fostered many different illusions. An alliance with the New Left
seemed viable; after all, it was based on our mutual anti-Fascism. In
an act whose power and determination impressed us, our new
friends broke their ties with their Nazi parents, and we were naive
enough to feel accepted and at home. Meanwhile we failed to notice
that for some time and once again we had cut ourselves off from a
part of ourselves. We did not deny that we were Jews, we just never
talked about it. Of course, we defended ourselves against blatant
anti-Semitic attacks, but we put up with the sharp dissonance, the
Yiddish jokes, the lapses and the silence of our friends when a
person at the adjacent restaurant table said, "It smells of garlic over
there, like in a Jewish apartment." We convinced ourselves that
there were more important things than those. Our common commitment to the liberation of the working class and all the oppressed
worldwide was supposedly more important than ancient history.
Our error had been to assume that if people had such lofty goals
they could not be anti-Semites.

We also failed to reflect why we were suddenly interested, if
in anything Jewish at all, in the Jüdischer Arbeiter-Bund (Jewish
Workers' Association). Was that merely a response to Zionist historiography, which neglected other Jewish movements? Was it a genuine interest in Jewish history? Or did we want to focus on our
Jewish workers' movement at a time of widespread enthusiasm for
revolutionary movements in order to turn ourselves into more authentic proletarians by taking that detour: Look, not all Jews are
intellectuals and capitalists. We also have people like Hersch Mendel in our family.[4] And who was not ashamed of meeting, while
being in the company of his leftist friends, some Jewish nouveaux

riches who, clad in mink coats, descended from their Mercedes (what else?). Not only because they were such obvious capitalists, but because the others might realize that they were Jews and thus forget Hersch Mendel. We were constantly preoccupied with strategies to neutralize the others' explicit and implicit prejudices. Hence we quickly became masters of reading the gaze of the others and of the art of disguise but remained as unsuccessful as Schnitzler's Oscar Ehrenberg.[5]

Because the arrival of the recognizable Jew immediately gives us away; it undoes all our efforts. No medal and no loden coat can divert the others' gaze from our Jewish relative.[6] They look at him, and then at us. And we have no other choice but to follow their gaze with a furtive glance in order to read their thoughts.

The main character in Schnitzler's novel *Der Weg ins Freie* (The path to freedom), Georg von Wergenthin, reminisces about his summer vacations at the Riviera with the Ehrenberg family. He remembers the elegant mother, the daughter, Else, and the son, Oscar. Smiling, he recalls how one day the fifteen-year-old Oscar "appeared on the promenade in a light blue, formal coat, white-and-black embroidered gloves, and a monocle in his eye."[7] He also recalls "how one day the ammunition producer Ehrenberg, a millionaire, took his family by surprise and put an end to the Ehrenberg family's aristocratic airs simply by turning up." As soon as he opened his mouth, "a secret fear began to show underneath the ostensible serenity of his wife's face. As much as he could, Oscar acted as if he did not belong to the family. His features displayed a somewhat bashful scorn for his begetter as if the latter were not worthy of him, and, pleading for understanding, he smiled toward the young barons."

Who does not know the furtive glance at one's classmates when Father and Mother show up? The surprise that one's teacher talks respectfully to a father whom one does not consider entirely worthy? Who does not catch oneself scrutinizing the faces of the people walking toward oneself when an orthodox Jew walks by in the street, in order to assess the way they gaze at him? We need more than a direct reflection, a satisfying answer to our question: how does the other see me. I can disguise myself as an aristocrat, a bourgeois, a farmer, or a proletarian. But as soon as someone "untransformed" or differently "transformed" appears, all of that is in vain.

The disguise is of course not restricted to dress, language, and manners. Once those have been mastered, there is still the name – the Jewish-sounding name. To be sure, certain names are unrecognizable. The author Hans Weigel, for instance, enjoys an Austrian-sounding name. Changing a surname is not all that easy. One can, however, change one's given name or hide it. As much as Salomon Ehrenberg enjoys using his presence and his jokes to interfere with his family's feudal aspirations, he does make the concession of abbreviating his name. Everyone knows him as S. Ehrenberg. After the name has been taken care of, the nose still remains. Some survivors of the mass extermination took haste to liberate their children from the "Jewish" nose.

We went so far as to making distinctions between the dead by emphasizing constantly how many workers and craftsmen had perished, as if their lives counted for more than those of rich persons. We had our reasons for this shabby behavior. For one thing, we had to fight against the deep-seated prejudice that all Jews were rich, and we wanted to gain sympathy and compassion. And those we got only if we adjusted to the anti-Fascist ideology that used the term "victims of Fascism." Secretly we hoped that the others would also think of the Jews just a little bit when they clamored against Fascism. We accepted the fact that the destruction of the Jews was only discussed in conjunction with the persecution of other groups. Moreover, we were the first ones who were more likely to speak about the Gipsies and homosexuals than about the Jews.

We did not realize that our comrades on the Left had as difficult a time to pronounce the word "Jew" as our former classmates. Only when they suddenly talked about Jews with ease and began to use the fate of the Jews as a metaphor for all and every persecution, did we become suspicious. The blacks in South Africa, trees, and women were pronounced "Jews," but most of all the Palestinians. They were termed the "Jews of the Jews." There could be no mistake: anti-Semitism had taken on the guise of anti-Zionism. Very clearly, the solidarity with the Palestinians served primarily the purpose of self-exoneration. Again an underhanded, calculated game began, following the perverse logic that if people do evil, the evil inflicted upon them cannot have been all that unjustified. During that era, so reduced to political categories, the Jews fell into the category of victim, and woe to them if they did not comply with this classification.

Once again, anti-Semitism plain and simple, as we had known it since childhood, showed through the cracks of our view of the world. Blinded by ideologies, we had simply assigned anti-Semitism to the category right-wing and were taken by surprise when it came at us also from "our" side. Only when during the war in Lebanon the remainder of the political Left marched through the streets, rhythmically shouting, "Nazis, get out of Lebanon," only when there was talk about a "final solution" perpetrated against the Palestinians, did it dawn on us that once again we found ourselves on the outside looking in.

The disintegration of the Left and our particular disagreement with it finally brought us in touch with ourselves. For the first time we began to explore the interconnectedness of our relationship with our parents and with the Jewish fate. Not as a rebellion, but as an attempt to comprehend the extent of the break that had occurred before we were born and that patterned our lives. The political disillusionment was merely the catalyst. Our own age and that of the generation of the survivors were at least of equal importance. So was the temporal distance to the events themselves, which forty years after the fact reemerged as memory.

Living in the country of the murderers and in the proximity of the dead appears to offer a paradoxical psychological advantage for the next generation as well, particularly in an anti-Semitic environment. They function as a guarantee not to forget without requiring that the atrocities remain alive as an internalized and thereby accepted memory.[8] It was a fictitious new beginning that the Jews undertook. It is precisely the "normal" anti-Semitism that reminds them constantly of the atrocities without having to actually remember. Remaining here apparently offers the majority of the Jews a chance to achieve a task that they probably cannot achieve: the psychological task of acknowledging what they experienced as factual and to effect a separation from the dead. In a certain way anti-Semitism protects them from having to confront the survivors' guilt and the unbearable question about the meaning of life after having survived. How intolerable it can be to ask these questions is evident from the fact that survivors who could not and did not want to shirk them did not find an answer worth living for. Some of them – Paul Celan, Jean Améry, and Primo Levi – ended their own life many years later.

For the children of the survivors, too, the meaning of their own life is challenged by the memory of the extent and the far-reaching implications of the loss, for the survival of their parents was ultimately accidental. A death sentence had been passed on all Jews, without distinction, regardless of their social class and personality. This was not only the case in the territories under Nazi control; the Nazis had no other objective but to expand their sphere of influence ad infinitum. Only the course and conclusion of the war decided that the Jews were not persecuted in the unoccupied parts of the Soviet Union, in England, and in Palestine.

The fact that the death sentence passed by the perpetrators applied to all Jews and that they had the intention to execute it to the fullest extent is a fact, which we, however, fail to comprehend intellectually and grasp emotionally.

Beyond all that, the event Auschwitz has implications for human existence that are not limited to the historical perpetrators and victims. Technological progress and the abstract character of its social organizations enabled the very country – where Karl Marx had expected the revolution of the proletariat to take place for precisely these reasons – a system of destruction that "banished the faces of the victims"[9] and turned genocide into a job like any other.

Only the most cynical persons can integrate the death factories into their progress-oriented concept of the world. Yet, some of the medical experiments, the psychological insights, the technocratic administrative models that were invented and tested in Auschwitz entered, albeit isolated from the specificity of place and circumstance, into different branches of science, industry, and the thought patterns of the entire Western world.

Human consciousness refuses to acknowledge that Auschwitz ultimately proved "that scientific progress and the rational social patterns shaping society that had been considered the best defense against the fear of death and as instruments to give human life new meaning turned out to be instruments of the ruthless destruction of life."[10]

When someone told Hannah Arendt that after Auschwitz he was ashamed of being German, she replied that she was ashamed of being a human being.

Notes

1. Alain Finkielkraut, *Der eingebildete Jude* (Munich, 1982).

2. Played by the Vienna Jewish Cabaret Company: Albert Misak, Anne Korn, Hermann Teifer (now living in New York), Liane Segall, Peter Stastny (New York), Rafaela Schmidt (Tel Aviv), Robert Schwarcz (Baltimore).

3. Peter Sichrovsky, *Wir wissen nicht, was morgen wird, wir wissen wohl, was gestern war* (Cologne, 1985), 182.

4. Hersch Mendel, *Erinnerungen eines jüdischen Revolutionärs* (Berlin, 1979).

5. Arthur Schnitzler, *Der Weg ins Freie* (Frankfurt am Main, 1961).

6. A loden coat (Lodenmantel) is a specifically Alpine and Austrian regional coat made of gray wool with green elements.

7. Schnitzler, 16.

8. Cilly Kugelmann, "Zur Identität osteuropäischer Juden in der Bundesrepublik," In *Jüdisches Leben in Deutschland seit 1945*, ed. Brumlik et al (Frankfurt am Main, 1986), 180.

9. Alain Finkielkraut. *Die Weisheit der Liebe* (Munich, 1987), 183.

10. Bruno Bettelheim, "Die äußerste Grenze," in *Erziehung zum Überleben* (Stuttgart, 1980), 16.

5. The Generation of the Second Austrian Republic

Robert Menasse

Robert Menasse was born in Vienna in 1954. He studied philosophy, political science, and German language and literature in Vienna, Salzburg, and Messina. His first story, entitled "Nägelbeißen" (Biting one's nails), appeared in 1973. From 1981 to 1988 he taught Austrian literature and literary theory at the University of São Paulo. His essay collection entitled *Die Sozialpartnerschaftliche Ästhetik* (Aesthetics of social partnership) appeared in 1990, followed in 1992 by a second collection of essays, entitled *Das Land ohne Eigenschaften* (The country without qualities). His fictional works include *Sinnliche Gewissheit* (1986; Sensual certainty), *Selige Zeiten, brüchige Welt* (1991; Blissful times, brittle world), and *Schubumkehr* (1995; Thrust reversal). Together with Gerhard Haderer he wrote *Die letzte Märchenprinzessin* (1997; The last fairy-tale princess), a book about the myth making involving the British Princess Diana. Menasse received the literature prize of the city of Vienna (1989), the Heimito von Doderer Prize (1991), and the prize of the Alexander Sacher Masoch Foundation (1994). Both Menasse's culture-critical works and his fiction combine a keen political and historical interest tempered by the awareness that texts of all genres are constructs. Menasse's interpretation of modern Austria, in both his essays and his novels, is based on Holocaust history, which is introduced as a corrective for the historical lies from which contemporary Austria derives its identity. Menasse's most Austrian characters, such as Judith Katz and Leo Singer in *Selige Zeiten, brüchige Welt*, are at home in the exile landscape. Even here, however, they hold on to a vision of prewar Austria, a home that, rather than in the material world, they temporarily find in each other's imagination. Menasse explores Austria as well as its alternatives, the former exile countries of Austrian Jews, revealing that for the post-Shoah generations there is no place of comfort, no real "home."

Robert Menasse

EXCERPT FROM

Blissful Times, Brittle World

On 26 February 1959 Kurt Walmen, who was fifty-two years old at
the time, poured a cup of Universal Paint Stripper over Rubens's *The
Descent of the Damned into Hell*. The corrosive paint stripper disfigured
the painting forever. The perpetrator managed to leave the scene of
the crime undisturbed, but before entering the Art Collection of the
State of Bavaria, he had already sent letters confessing and justifying his act to news and press agencies. He wrote that he had to
"sacrifice" this one work of art to save all the other artistic achievements of mankind, indeed, in order to save mankind altogether.
For the world was headed for a new war. However, he, Walmen,
claimed to have developed a philosophical system that was taking
philosophy to its final conclusion. This system, if it were generally
known to the human race, would fundamentally change the world
and effect permanent peace. Since he was completely unknown,
this act was his only opportunity to attract public attention to himself so that his philosophical theses, which were indispensable for
the world's future survival, would be heard. After all, Walmen asserted, atomic bombs would make a cleaner sweep than a little acid.
He stated his intention to turn his criminal trial into a platform for
presenting his insights.

The next day, Walmen surrendered to the police. During the trial,
however, the presiding judge foiled the defendant's self-portrayal.
Characterized by the media as a "madman" and "charlatan," the
Rubens assailant was pronounced legally competent and was given
a tough sentence; he was forgotten soon thereafter.

Yet, when Leo Singer and Judith Katz met in the spring of 1965 in
Vienna, the selfsame Kurt Walmen was the topic of their first longer
conversation. In great length, Singer told the story of this self-
appointed, misunderstood genius and failed world reformer with

an ardor by which he was amazed himself considering the almost anesthetizing physical attraction he felt for Judith Katz. It left him, as he thought, so mind- and speechless that he himself had no idea where all those words came from. As far as their relationship was concerned – it started that day and with some interruptions was to last for eighteen years – this overture was indeed so fitting as if Singer had deliberately planned it. It was as if he already had been aware of his own ultimate deed, as if one day he wanted to be able to justify himself by saying that it had been the final logical conclusion of something that had been latent from the start.

Imagine, Singer said, expecting this woman to agree and thereby to become his accomplice against the entire rest of the absurd world, nowadays one is already declared insane if all one has is the intention to change the world or if one says that one has taken philosophy to its final conclusion. For example, had Wittgenstein said anything different after he finished the *Tractatus?* He had said precisely that!

I really don't know about that. But this, what's his name, this Walmen, he was not labeled a madman for that reason, but rather for destroying a Rubens painting.

No, he has always been a madman, even before destroying the painting. Even Löwinger always said "that madman!"

Yes, Leo Singer got around to talking about the frustrated world reformer by way of Löwinger. Leo Singer had seen Judith Katz at the university, at the buffet close to the main auditorium. He had imme-diately been spellbound by her appearance, so that he approached her table as if in a trance to strike up a conversation. For a decisive second this had appeared more ordinary to him than, for instance, eating because one is hungry, or to have one's heart race because one is afraid. When he came to his senses with a familiar kind of anxiety that made him expect the usual type of humiliation or rejec-tion, his: "I hope I don't disturb you, may I sit down?" had already been said, and as if through a cloudy glass he had already noticed that Judith nodded her head. Already half an hour later they had left the university together to continue their conversation elsewhere where they would not be disturbed, to tell one another everything, already almost like a devoted couple. No doubt they were meant for each other.

What a wonderful coincidence that we have met.

It was unavoidable, Judith said, sooner or later we simply would have had to meet.

Yes, perhaps every chance encounter is in reality a date! Both were the children of Viennese Jews who had escaped National Socialism in 1938 and finally ended up in Brazil. Singer, born in Vienna, grew up in São Paulo, and Judith was born in Porto Alegre. Finally she had moved with her parents to São Paulo. Now the two were studying in Vienna, Leo Singer because "unfortunately," as he said, had followed his parents in 1959 when they had decided to return home "because everything was all right again." Judith Katz, on the other hand, had realized her desire to study in Vienna, the hometown she did not know, against her parents' wishes. Although, strangely enough, they had always spoken German at home, they had not wanted to hear of returning to Austria.

On their way to the Café Sport they already explored whether they had mutual acquaintances in São Paulo. Leo asked if she knew Löwinger. Josef Löwinger, who was also a Jewish immigrant, was the best friend of Leo's parents and had been like a second father to him. In Brazil he had climbed the professional ladder to success and had become the director of a large bank. He had applied the same dedication and commitment with which he had advanced his professional career to building one of the largest private art collections of his time. In his spacious house in São Paulo he had established a salon that was frequented not only by São Paulo's German-speaking colony but also by Brazil's, even Latin America's, foremost artists and intellectuals. Judith said that her parents, as far as she knew, had been at Löwinger's a few times. However, they had never taken her along; probably she had been too little at that time. He himself, Leo reported, had spent a lot of time with Löwinger, particularly as a child, and not only when there was an open house. Löwinger's house and his big garden had been much more interesting than his parents' apartment, and Löwinger – Uncle Zé – had loved him in an unobtrusive and patient manner. Ultimately he had paid more attention to him than Leo's real father. He had shown him works of art from his collection and queried him about his impressions with a serious curiosity as if speaking to an adult. Together, they had sat in deep leather *fauteuils* in Löwinger's library, which had become so extensive that it required a permanent librarian. With a seriousness that he modeled after Löwinger bent over a book, Leo had hovered over an illustrated volume. Blind to the illustrations in the heavy book lying on his knees he had felt a diffuse sense of awe and a ponderously beautiful shyness. Finally Uncle Zé had placed Leo on his lap and told him a little story, asking him questions to stimulate his imagination and challenging him to respond, with the result that in the end Leo felt as if he himself had invented parts of the story. In the huge garden, Leo recounted, he had romped all by himself, because Löwinger had not been a friend of "the wild," as he called it; he had considered the garden merely a quiet view from the window and a protection against an immediate neighbor. During the two or three strolls they had taken early on through the spread-out gardens Leo's incessant questions as to what this plant or that tree was called had irritated Löwinger inordinately. Responding with absurd or tautological answers ("Those are azaleas, only they are bigger than azaleas, or at least they are something similar!" or: "That bush? Well that's just a bush!"), Löwinger had fallen silent and stopped accompanying Leo into the garden. But Leo took Löwinger's stories outdoors with him. Having absorbed them in the house, sitting immobilized and demure, he enacted them, as it were, and filled them with life outdoors. He recounted how he had marched through the garden, a *bandeirante* forging ahead into the interior of the country, conquering it, and founding São Paulo. Then again the garden had been all of Europe and he was Napoleon, while he had still felt the book at the tips of his fingers. Only a while ago he had held it in his hands and imagined that this book was the *code civil*, and he was taking it to the nations of Europe. And then there had just been people, again and again, many people when there was an open house, or there were individual visitors, important person-alities. When they came to São Paulo, they did not pass up the opportunity of visiting Löwinger. Among them were Otto Maria Carpeaux, who always gave Leo chocolate, or Jorge Amado, Carlos Drummond, Guimarães Rosa, de Cavalcanti, Cândido Protinari, Villa-Lobos, even Jorge Luis Borges had once made an appearance. Even more so than Uncle Zé, the latter impressed Leo as a man who had entered the world already an old gentleman.

He lifted me up on his lap and whispered something in German into my ear, yes, in German. His voice sounded as if it came from far away, around many corners, as if from a labyrinth! Singer lied. And afterward someone said to me: Do you know who that was, little boy? That was Borges! And someone else asked: What was it that Borges whispered in your ear? I'll never forget that!

Once this Kurt Walmen even turned up at Löwinger's; someone from the German colony had probably taken him along. Rumor had it that he had fled from the Nazis to Latin America, had done odd jobs in different places to support himself, and now wanted to settle down in São Paulo. Walmen proclaimed that he was a philosopher. Leo remembered him quite distinctly, not only because he had claimed to have traveled to Latin America as a stowaway, which was bound to engage especially a child's imagination, but also because of the way in which Walmen staged himself: while little Leo was told about Löwinger's other guests only how important they were, Walmen had cultivated, independently from all that, the portentous demeanor of a genius, easy for any child to recognize. In contrast to the stories Löwinger told him, Leo did not understand a word of the heated discussions in the salon, but Walmen's grandiose gestures made a lasting impression on his memory; Walmen had an intolerant and apodictic way of talking, of dismissing counterarguments, of jumping up from his seat and assuming a messianic tone. Leo grasped only individual words of his tirades, such as "undoubtedly," "unmistakably," "completely," "absolutely," and again and again "the world" or "mankind," but they were stated so powerfully as if he had created them.

When he told Judith these things, Leo noticed how intoxicated he was, inebriated by his own words. He transformed and embellished certain details, described Walmen's "shifty eyes" and the "icy dismay" that prevailed among those present. In reality he had learned about those things at a later time when Walmen was discussed. But at this moment Leo enjoyed the process of talking so much that it was a matter of irrelevance whether he kept to the truth in every detail.

In fact, soon thereafter Leo, unable to follow the conversation in the salon anyhow, had run into the garden. A little while later he slipped back into the house through the servants' entrance – now he was a *lampião* fighting against the *coroneis da terra*. He sneaked through the hallway of the mansion and passed by the kitchen. Through a crack in the door he heard strange sounds and peeked inside. There he saw stockinged feet, a pushed-up dress, a man's back, hands tearing at a shirt: There were "the man," Walmen, and the cook, rolling on the stone floor of the kitchen like wrestlers.

Then I ran into the salon, positioned myself in front of Löwinger, and, imitating Walden's gestures and diction, proclaimed: There can be no mistake about the fact that in the kitchen mankind is involved in a life-and-death wrestling match. Everyone laughed, only Löwinger looked at me attentively. He clearly had understood what I had seen.

That can't be true! Judith said.

Of course it is not true in that sense. It is correct that Leo had peeked through the kitchen door and seen Walmen and the cook lying on the floor, and it may be correct that he thought it was a brawl. At the same time it had puzzled him in a disquieting fashion and had seemed shocking to him: He had known immediately that he ought not to have seen that. But imitating Walmen in the salon, that was something that had just occurred to him while he was telling the story. And if Leo were honest, he would not even have been able to say if Walmen had made such a fool of himself because of his behavior in the salon, or his adventure with the cook, or something entirely different. At any rate, he was never again seen at Löwinger's house, even if he continued to be present insofar as heated debates took place about him.

Now Leo remembered how he had arrived at this topic. They had explored whether they had mutual acquaintances in São Paulo, and Leo had asked Judith if she knew Löwinger. In the process it had occurred to him that in 1959, during his last visit at Löwinger's before his departure to Vienna, Löwinger had shown him a news-paper clip with a photograph of Walmen – the paper reported about the Rubens attack in Munich – and said, Do you still remember the madman? Look what he's done now!

Just imagine, Leo said, I really love Löwinger a lot, I love him like a father. And then this sophisticated art collector, one of the most distinguished art collectors of our time, reads a newspaper article about a man who destroyed what is probably the most important painting by Rubens, and some time before that man had been a guest at his house. It is obvious that someone like him cannot understand Walmen. But who knows, Walmen may be right. I mean, maybe he does have a philosophical system that could change the world. No one has ever listened to him. No one has ever discussed it with him. It must have been horrible – no, wait! Just imagine that! – it must be horrible, to know the Ultimate and to see that no one wants to listen; perhaps an oriflamme is appropriate here. What is, after all, a Rubens painting compared to the entire world, I mean, if it had worked out. But afterward they labeled him all the more a madman. That is precisely the problem, they drove him to it so that he would give them proof that he was what they had already conjectured much earlier, namely, a madman. But seen in that light, everyone else is guilty of destroying the painting, not Walmen!

Leo looked at Judith with an urgency that pushed all the sounds in the restaurant against the wall, where they possibly would remain stuck like pictures, and he knew that to entice her and possibly seduce her he would have to continue talking for hours. In a very intense way everything about him was lacking vitality, and again and again this knowing smile that makes it so easy to ally oneself with anyone, while at the same time it produces no clue at all when one looks into a face like Judith's.

But it is completely absurd, said Judith, for a person to believe that the world can be changed simply and exclusively through one's ideas.

Why? That has always been the case! Singer, in spite of his twenty-nine years was unusually innocent and naive. Napoleon, for example, changed the world, and the noise he made while doing it intrudes into Hegel's study. He, in turn, is inspired to create a philosophy that was to change the world, and so forth. History teaches nothing but that the world is changed by individuals. That's what Singer had learned. Judith laughed; the size of her mouth made her laughter appear grand in a figurative sense, a privilege granted only to a select brilliant few. He was a short, slight man of a sharp, one might say, vitriolic ugliness. Everything was about him was sharp: his hooked nose, which dominated his face, his narrow mouth, whose lower lip could suddenly curl forward when he talked, so that it appeared obscene in a carnal sort of way, his thick, black-rimmed glasses, which he would sometimes push backward into his hair when they pressed on the wart on his nostrils. His hair was meticulously combed backward and looked greasy. Judith, however, liked him, she recognized in his sharp features extreme sensibility and kindness along with a glowing, albeit not yet tested, readiness to experience the world. She was touched when she observed the gestures of his small, tender hands and listened to the timbre of his speech, this accent, almost imperceptible to anyone else but immediately familiar to her, a collage of a Brazilian childhood and Viennese parents. Leo would have loved to know everything about Judith, to familiarize himself with every detail, every second of her past life, but she had no chance to speak, because he was talking incessantly out of sheer curiosity about her. He continued to pursue the topic of Walmen, although now in a general way. He talked about the prerogative of changing the world and the reasons supporting it, and the fact that in today's world such a prerogative was considered a symptom of insanity. The Nazis, he said, had destroyed everything, even the most minimal historical knowledge. And because they had destroyed everything, the generation of the victims and rebuilders considered everything insane that pointed beyond that which they were in the process of rebuilding. He said this without thinking, the same way he said everything without thinking. He was delighted about the things that spontaneously came to his mind just because he was inspired by Judith's presence, and that they sounded as if they were the result of extensive thought processes that he was revealing exclusively to her. His theses sounded bizarre in a city that was extremely callous toward each and every idea that implied that something might be different from the status quo, a city whose very being appeared so unusually stultified that even the phrase "Vienna remains Vienna" had to be perceived as a lie. It sounded much too euphemistic because of the mere fact that the verb "to remain" was far too dynamic. They had gone to the Café Sport because at that time this place seemed more liberal than the entire city. It was the only somewhat cosmopolitan place within the place called Vienna. However, Leo did not take notice of space and time any longer, nor of the filth in the Café Sport, which supported a kind of romanticism that would use a spot of red wine on a marble table as a point of departure for meditation. He did not notice the surprisingly urban character of the guests; for the most part they were Arabs, Iranians, or Greeks throwing dice, yes, it was a more urban place than Vienna, the "Sport," even if some of the patrons were Viennese. Those, however, were few in number and had already been abroad and had seen the world. Now they sat there, defiantly cosmopolitan, wearing Canadian fur coats or Peruvian ponchos; the majority, however, consisted of cliques of artists who in the presence of the other guests prepared themselves for the art of barring others from the premises in which they would excel later, after climbing the social scale and becoming innkeepers in their own right. But Leo turned a deaf ear to the Greek or French records from the jukebox, to the people playing a game of Puff or others who debated and yelled, and those who, inspired by the volumes of poetry by Villon and the Kerouac editions scattered about, got drunk and toyed with the thought of giving up reading altogether. He turned a blind eye to the brown wood paneling and the dull mirrors on the walls. Judith noticed all of it very clearly but in passing and casually. She perceived it as details that evaporated before her eyes, blending with the ambiance as soon as she had noticed them. At the same time, she continued to focus on Leo with amusement. She liked the ambiance of this place to which she had just now been introduced by Leo, the run down, yet colorful and boisterous, simplicity reminded her of the Sarado Bar in the Rua Dona Veridiana in São Paulo, where she had liked to sit before the military coup. It had been a meeting place for the students of the nearby Mackenzie University, the place to which Judith owed the first hangover of her life, produced by too much Brahma beer and endless discussions about God and mankind.

Doron Rabinovici

Doron Rabinovici was born in 1961 in Tel Aviv as the son of eastern European Jewish immigrants. In 1964 he moved with his family to Vienna. Following his high-school graduation in 1979 he began studying medicine, psychology, ethnology, and history at the University of Vienna, where he completed his master's degree. In 1991 he started writing a dissertation entitled "Authorities of Powerlessness: The Reaction of the Israelitische Kultusgemeinde Wien [official Jewish community in Vienna] to the National Socialist Persecution, 1938–1945." Rabinovici is the founder of the Friends of the Israeli peace organization Shalom Ashav (Peace now). Since 1986 he has been an executive member of the Republican club New Austria. Rabinovici is a freelance historian and a journalist. From 1993 to 1994 he worked on the topic of the image of Austria in the United States during and after the two world wars. In addition to his independent book publications, a highly acclaimed collection of short stories entitled *Papirnik* (1994) and the novel *Suche nach M.* (1997), his works have appeared in anthologies, journals, and newspapers. Rabinovici is one of the most distinctive young Jewish voices in present-day Austria.

Doron Rabinovici

The Right Nose

Inadvertently Amos had run into a crowd that had coagulated in the pedestrian zone: a mob of people, women and men, mostly older ones, who had gathered here to get rid of their loneliness and to mingle, in order to emit their respective little gas explosions of displeasure. The latter soon began to cloud the atmosphere. Amos Getreider intruded quietly upon the vapors of complacency. Initially he thought that it might be entertaining to stroll by, detached, unconcerned, and unperturbed. He carried a vain smile on his lips.

Only an instant earlier a political event had taken place on this very square. The masses were already disintegrating into individual human clusters, when sounds of dissatisfaction disrupted the universal harmony and opposition made itself heard. A few individuals had tried to distribute flyers with discomforting questions among the people. However, the leaflets were torn from their hands by the angry crowd, and somewhere a sign had been torn from the hand of a counterdemonstrator and smashed on his head. Now he stood there, numb, holding his head, his glasses lying on the ground, and the police had already arrived to take down his personal data. Bewildered, the young man felt his skull and realized that he was bleeding. He did not respond to the inspector who was about to reprimand him. Desensitized, he kept looking at the blood in the palm of his right hand and felt his pain with the left. Two policemen in uniform suddenly twisted his arm behind his back while their superior continued to question him, but the man did not understand, be it that he was a foreigner who could follow the language only when spoken slowly and was altogether unfamiliar with the regional dialect, be it that the pudgy gentleman who had thrashed him yelled at the police officers in a loud voice, demanding the arrest of the counterdemonstrators. The stranger looked around in confusion. Startled, he cried out when his arm was yanked up. He resisted his arrest and had to be forced into the police bus.

In those days the customary unified silence, that perfidious tranquility among people, was disrupted. Those elements that had constituted the basic consensus, the decorum and the "good tone" of society, had degenerated over the years into a cacophony. In order to drown out the scandal the people had gathered here today. However, what spoke out of them revealed the very thing they wanted to cover up.

Amos, who had merely wanted to stroll through the commotion, had soon become involved in the flow of the debates. The majority considered the crimes of the past the decisive issue, a small minority, however, focused on the timelessness of the crimes. A short man yelled at Amos: "If you don't like it here, go to Israel or to New York."

"New York is more fun," Professor Rubinstein of Columbia University was to assert with regard to Vienna a few weeks later when he asked Amos one day if he wanted to stay here – in this city, in this country. "After graduating from high school I want to live in Israel," Amos had replied suddenly and to his own surprise. "New York is more fun," Aron Rubinstein responded with the same sentence and in addition chewed forth the German translation in his American accent.

For several weeks already Susi, Professor Rubinstein's black-haired daughter, had sat next to Amos in class. His mother had been taken with the girl from Brooklyn and had invited the American family to her home for Pesach dinner. The Rubinsteins were neither traditional nor sentimental, but they savored the chale, the kreplach soup, the gefilte fish, and the rest of the traditional dinner menu. Although they did not understand a single one of old Mr. Getreider's prayers, they found the Hebrew songs and other folklore utterly delightful.

Susi spent the few months during which her father lectured in Vienna with Amos and grew increasingly fond of him. As her return to America was drawing near, he became increasingly special to her. Even though his mother had already given her verdict the morning after the feast, "Such a beautiful young girl," Amos, too, had fallen for Susi.

Susi was so little concerned about her grades in a school that she was to attend for only four months that her desk pal Amos too fell hopelessly behind in his achievements – he had never been a diligent student. She tried to see Amos as much as possible, in order to learn German, she emphasized. Maybe the lonely American with the kinky hair hoped to mirror herself in this pale and scatter-brained young man.

Professor Aron Rubinstein said, "New York is more fun," and when Amos wanted to contradict him and come to the defense of the state that had been founded to prevent Jewish suffering, the professor contended, "I love Israel. It represents a process of self-purification for us. All the racist, narrow-minded Brooklyn Jews who hate blacks travel to Israel in order to hate the Arabs over there for even better reasons. I love Israel. It represents a process of self-purification for us. New York is more fun."

"We don't hate the Jews," said an older gentleman in the midst of the crowd. He had a full white beard and smiled pensively. He had spoken in a loud voice in order to make himself heard in the general excitement. He wanted to drown out the noise to return to the main theme of the gathering. He ignored the crowd's shrill attacks against a young woman, a critic. With a glare he reproved insults and, with a gesture of his hand, dismissed any polemic in a conciliatory manner. He spoke very deliberately: "We do not hate the Jews. But the Jews – ja? – the Jews hate us, perhaps not even unjustifiedly, perhaps I would hate us too, but the time has come for this hatred to end."

The counterdemonstrator interrupted him. With an expansive motion of his arms and in a well-modulated voice the older gentleman replied, "But, my dear young lady, I beg your pardon." He jovially folded his hands over his round potbelly and continued, "We do not hate the Jews. All that is a propaganda campaign: Fear aligns itself with hatred in a disastrous alliance." "You may wonder, which fear?" he preempted her question and went on to inform her, pointing his index finger, "The fear of the loss of power. Which hatred? Well, which one could it possibly be?"

For the time being, he kept the answer to himself, but when the young woman still did not understand, he declared, "The hatred of the Old Testament. An eye for an eye, a tooth for a tooth." Now his eyes were wide with meaning, and all of a sudden he had become very quiet.

Now she understood what he had meant, what he had talked about – and against what. He rebuked her succinct objections with an air of kindness: "Listen, my dear young lady, we actually like all races," and while others nodded in agreement, the man with the full beard and a full head of white curls continued, "Isn't it beautiful that our world is so colorful? However, with all of its array of colors, it needs to understand itself as a whole, just as all colors together produce white light. Would it not be stupid if blue and yellow hated one another, or red and green? It is equally stupid when the Jews hate us and we hate the Jews."

After his last words the critic had fallen silent, but the old man, an expert in the theory of harmony, found himself exposed all of a sudden to overenthusiastic agreement. His appeal was complemented by demonstrative statements against a particular person, a politician, a Jew.

Immediately he placated the impassioned gentleman, "Yes, we have to love him too. Ja. Because he is not our enemy, only the hatred is." "Which hatred?" the young woman asked, outraged, but he continued, "Ja, and we must overcome their hatred. There is only one way. We must love the Jews until they stop hating us, regardless of how long it will take."

Amos's mother was hoarse when talking about these things. She said, "I want you to beat him up. Do you hear me?"

Early in the morning she woke him up with her loud singsong, and Father implored her, "Not so loud. The neighbors," but his mother continued trilling. When she yelled at him immediately thereafter for not having gotten out of bed yet, Father pleaded, "Not so loud. The neighbors," and he reassured Amos, "Don't annoy Mommy. Get up."

She wore her tightly woven and twisted abundance of hair meticulously amassed on her head; this is how she sternly looked down at Amos, how she laughed at him, how she beheld her son, her little one, who was precocious and tried to tell jokes at an early age, who asked, "Papa, am I funny?" and whose father decided, "Yes, you are very funny," while she kissed and reprimanded him, "You are a little clown." Already as a nine-year-old he tried to teach her lessons in politics and later asked her: "Mommy, am I smart?" and she would sigh: "You are a little clown."

At the age of four Amos was already in the habit of metrically scanning his opposition: "No, we appest! No, we appest!" a phrase the boy had invented. When his father had told him that he mispronounced the word, he had called out to his mother the next morning when she was about to take him to kindergarten: "No, we protest." Thereupon the dark-haired woman had assured him, "The correct word is appest." "Protest! Protest!" It surged up from within him in despair. "No, appest. Appest," she laughed at him, as she tied his shoes. "Protest! Protest!" he chuckled in resistance, but she insisted, chortling, "Apest! Apest! Apest," and, giggling, they tiptoed down the steps of the stairwell.

She screamed until she was hoarse, "I want you to hit him the next time. You hear?" A fellow student named Helmut had told him during the break that he had been forgotten in Mauthausen. Amos had taken the boy to task and discussed the matter with him, which had been usual practice since he was nine, and he had tried to explain.

"I want you to are you listening? beat up such a person the next time around. Discuss, schmiscuss! No. If someone tells you something like that I want you to beat him bloody. Do you hear me? Bloody! I couldn't care less if you come home bleeding as well. I'll take care of your wounds. But you are supposed to kick him and scratch until blood flows, until his clothes are torn, so that his parents ask him who did that, so that they go to the principal to complain about you. Do you hear me? I want them to go to the principal, and then I shall go to your school and explain that I told you to do that. Don't worry, I'll take the blame. Do you understand me?" she screamed, and Papa, unsuspecting, walked into the kitchen, saw Amos sitting there, his head lowered, and said, "Go ahead, obey your mommy. You know what she has been through."

But Amos did not want to get into fistfights. He trusted the power of his words, the eloquence of his speech. He had never tried to settle for any kind of dialect, any other jargon but the standard language because he was afraid that he would fail to master the local accent. At least he wanted to be in line with the written language.

In Hebrew he was a different person. There his voice and his expression seemed to have a particular sparkle, as if his own timbre resounded in this language of the south, of the summer, and of the shining ocean. Idiomatically this language rang forth from him in deeper registers, and he felt so secure in it as if he were behind tinted windowpanes, as if he were armed with sunglasses, as if he were leaning against an olive tree, a blade of grass between his teeth.

Something within him believed that he would be able to gain access to a more exclusive circle by way of Hebrew, a circle that had nothing to do with W., nothing with his school, nothing with his non-Jewish or Jewish friends, and also nothing with the pious Jews whom he saw occasionally passing through the streets in dark clothes. Regardless of how uniquely packaged they seemed, in Hebrew Amos felt as if he belonged to the prouder edition, the nobly bound luxury edition of the Jewish assortment.

All of a sudden Peter Bach had emerged from the crowd. The muscular, slender youth bent down to the older gentleman with the white full beard and said, "What is that supposed to mean: the Jews. The Jews, you proclaim, hate us. We are supposed to love the Jews. The Jews? All of them?"

Peter, the lanky, giant boy had stood behind the slightly built Amos. A smile twinkled between the two fellow students, while a short gentleman with a brown hat and a black suit began to chatter excitedly.

That day both Peter and Amos had not walked home immediately after school, and they had not, as was their habit, walked toward the subway together with Georg Rinser. In the afternoon, the 150 meters between the neo-Gothic building and the subway that Georg – a habitual latecomer – crossed every morning in a few seconds took the three friends at least half an hour. Actually, Peter Bach was only an accompaniment for the duo, whose antics amused him and whose pranks he let go on with delight. Amos and Georg, on the other hand, had to admit with envy Peter's head start regarding amorous adventures. Amos even asked his advice when thinking about Susi Rubenstein and the apartment that would be available for a late-night rendezvous with Susi during the few days when his parents were going away.

Peter Bach said to the stout little man with the hat, "Listen, what you are saying is clearly anti-Semitic." But the short man merely sniveled, "I am no anti-Semite, I just don't like the Jews." "But that precisely is anti-Semitic," Peter explained, but he was put in his place by a fat adult: "So what? A little more tolerance, young man. Let the gentleman have his opinion."

Amos: The name was a billboard. As soon as it was mentioned, there was enough material for a two-hour conversation. Because of it there was no denying his descent; on the contrary: He learned to enjoy the alienation he caused others by being exotic. He had a potentially imposing attitude concerning these matters, but it came across as a pose, a production, because his righteousness had little to do with character, and he could always be certain of his parents' support.

"He talks a good line, our little Amos," Peter asserted, but Georg added, placing his arm around Amos's shoulders, "He sure does. Incessantly. Without listening. What he likes to do best is to listen to himself talk." Amos smiled, and at home he told his mother, "Peter says that I have a good way of talking, and Georg thinks that he is right in a way." However, she just looked at him sternly and sighed, "You are and always will be a little clown."

A few people were still standing on the square in small, scattered groups. The conversation rustled on and soon congealed once again. It crackled and then flared up high again, as if the square in the Inner City, close to the cathedral, had been seized by a turbulence. All of a sudden a swarm of pigeons fluttered up into the air. The birds circled close above the crowd and ascended in an arrowlike formation.

An older lady in a dark dress and white lace gloves reaching up to the middle joints of her fingers and leaving her fingertips exposed, an umbrella tucked underneath her arm, had forced her way into the front row of the dispute. A little hat was attached with a pin to her bluish gray hair. She was excited, her hands fluttered swiftly through the air, and Amos was reminded of the rapid and diligent movements of Flemish lace makers. Gesticulating, she seemed to be spinning, while airing her indignation in the nasal sounds of a highbrow accent tinged with status consciousness.

Amos talked himself into a passion during the debate, and now articulated his countercharges in a penetrating staccato.

"How can you possibly say that I am anti-Semitic," the lady erupted. Amos: "Because what you say is anti-Semitic." "But," the woman smiled piquedly, "One can smell anti-Semites." She had placed a particular emphasis on the word "smell" and turned up her nose. Amos followed up by asking her in a friendly and encouraging tone, "And Jews probably too?" For an instant the old woman stopped the movement of her hands and her words. Musing, she said, "Yes, Jews probably too."

The crowd panted, be it that it dawned on some of the people that the old lady had given herself away, be it that some of the others were tickled by a statement that resembled a dirty, forbidden joke. Then a man in his mid-fifties bent forward and proclaimed, "Please, that is not true. One cannot smell Jews, except for the Polish ones."

Peter jerked forward, but Amos Getreider simply said in a very low voice, "My mother is a Jewish woman from Poland."

For a moment there was silence. Then the man hastily seized the hand of the seventeen-year-old and said, "Oh, I'm so sorry."

Amos, shaking his head, could not but laugh out loud.

The conversation had petered out. Amos looked at the Plague Column towering over the pedestrian zone. The monument had been erected as a warning and a reminder of the black plague. It was a prayer of gratitude made of stone on behalf of all those who had been spared by the epidemic.

In the final decades of the seventeenth century the pestilence was again making its rounds through many parts of Europe; it mingled with the people and infected thousands. The disease divided the population into those who were still counted among the living and those who had already fallen ill and, there being hardly any hope for recovery, were counted among the dead. Whoever was seized by the plague was quarantined. The clothes of the infected were burnt.

Their bodies were interred in mass graves. Only the money – the coins – was saved from destruction. It had to continue circulating despite the epidemic.

The borders of the country were closed off, and it was decreed that henceforth they were to be crossed only with a health certificate. It was the task of the army and the government to drive the disease away. The Jewish people, who had been suspected of poisoning the wells since the Middle Ages, had been expelled from the city many years before.

Amos looked at the Plague Column as dark figures dressed in old-fashioned attire walked past it. The group of people dressed in black crossed the square where a little while earlier the event had taken place and crowds of people had hollered and screamed.

Peter Bach followed his friend's glance and gasped all of a sudden: "You know, anti-Semitism is of course inexcusable, but when I see the orthodox Jews: Why do they always have to isolate themselves like that? There is actually no reason for them to run about like that. And besides: Why do they only accept circumcised people? Considering all that, one can understand in a way why resentments arise. I mean, they are not particularly adept, not even when it comes to politics, for example those gentlemen . . ."

That was precisely the moment when both a friendship of long standing and Peter's nose were broken.

Peter's face was to take a conspicuous turn after this right hook: The classical straight line that had characterized his olfactory organ up until that time was gone and bent. As for the problems that arose as a result of this incident in school, Amos did not have to worry about those; his mother, of course, took care of them. Amos had become the family hero with a single blow.

Doron Rabinovici

Foreigners

The office, a corner shop behind dark-tinted windows, was located on a vast square adjacent to a broad avenue lined with palm trees. The travel agency Nimrod Guttmann worked for had been established here twenty years ago. Nothing was left to call to mind the old café that had been at this location before, nothing to remind one of the waiter by the name of Hermann and his black tie.

Every day Nimrod's grandfather, Jakov Guttmann, had sat at his usual table. Occasionally he had taken his grandson along, ordered a piece of nut pastry for the boy, and said, "This coffee, Hermann's small espresso, is the only compensation from Austria that will ever reach me."

Jakov Guttmann had been dead for a long time; Hermann Heller, the waiter, a refugee from Vienna, lay in a retirement home, and every night, when the nurse tucked the old man in, he slipped his dentures into her hand and said, "Thank you very much, young lady, you may keep the rest."

Whether it was coffeehouse or office, this location built a bridge across time and to faraway places. The people in this square no longer went to the café. Instead, they hurried to the falafel stand or to the bar. They got a little something from the fast food place and met at the espresso place, a branch of a world-famous chain. For the most part, the surrounding houses had remained unchanged. Architects, exiles from Europe, had planned the buildings in a style of simplicity. The concrete façades and their balustrades curled around the square and contained it like hollow hands.

The lawn at the center of the traffic circle was situated underneath a barrage of water throwers. Nimrod Guttmann crossed the street. He fought his way through the traffic jam. The air above the blacktop glistened in the summer heat. The sunlight reflected by hundreds of high-rise windows blinded him.

At the office he was inundated by a wave of cool fresh air. The air conditioner was humming, and Nurith called in a husky voice, "Nimrod! They finally let you go." He had been gone for a month. The army reserve service had torn him away from his everyday life. Every time he returned Nimrod Guttmann felt as if he were a different person. He looked at the plastic belts with which the cables under Nurith's desk were strung together. They were identical to the ones he had used two days ago to tie a man's hands.

Nurith said, "Nimrod, it's about Chaim. We don't know what to do. He's losing it."

All of a sudden the speakers began to crackle. Someone had turned the radio on to listen to the news. The names of two killed soldiers resounded through the room, blending with the ringing of the telephone, the rattling of the keyboards. In Lebanon a unit of soldiers had come under fire. Today, the speaker announced, it had been a year that Yitzhak Rabin had been murdered. The Knesset would commemorate him. In Jerusalem, in front of his tomb, a ceremony would be held and a rally in Tel Aviv at the erstwhile scene of the crime. Rabin's party, now the opposition, demanded a state memorial day for their murdered leader. The new government denied their request.

Nurith repeated, "Nimrod, are you listening to me? Chaim is losing it. What are we supposed to do?" Pushing back her blond permanent-wave curls, she took a sip of coffee and a drag of her cigarette.

Chaim Stein was the senior tour guide at the travel agency. He had initiated the younger ones into their duties and taught them how to guide foreigners through the country. Nimrod felt as if he recognized in Stein the esprit of his uncle and the assiduousness of Hermann, the waiter. Stein appeared like a relic, a regular of the old café who had been overlooked after the very last closing time and left behind. In his conversations with Chaim Stein, Nimrod Guttmann rediscovered the fragments of German that his grandfather had taught him.

Chaim Stein, born in Berlin, knew the history and nature of Israel. He could tell stories about every kibbutz and every village. He was of a short, stout build, but no tourist could lose sight of Chaim, because even at frequently visited places crowded by masses of people his white, rich hair shone like a guiding light ahead of all the others. His voice was able to fill big halls and vast squares; its timbre forced people to pay attention. Chaim not only talked about the beauties of the country, he rhapsodized about them. When he raved about Masada, his voice covered the range of two octaves.

The collar of his short-sleeved shirt was open, turned up on top of his jacket. On his feet he wore sandals. His watch crystal was protected by an old leather flap attached to the wristband.

Lately Chaim had become peculiar. His associates were convinced that the tour guide was hardly able to see any longer. And yet he recognized every place in the country. All he had to do was to touch the earth and his face lightened up immediately.

A young colleague asserted that Chaim, totally blind, had run between the hind quarters of a cow. Afterward, he said, Chaim merely wiped his face, put on a smile, and informed the bystanders from which moshav the animal came and when this particular Zionist settlement had been founded.

Nurith said, "I don't know what is to be done. You are the only one, Nimrod, who is able to talk with him. I don't have any strength left for him." They were interrupted. Next door an employee argued with a customer who wanted to cancel a flight reservation. Nurith was asked for advice, but before she could answer, her daughter called asking her permission to go to a party. Nurith was running all over the place, a cigarette between her fingers.

Nimrod Guttmann listened to the radio announcer. A leading representative of the opposition party had been attacked in Hebron. "Do you want some tea?" a settler had asked him. "With pleasure!" The boiling fluid, poured into the politician's face, left second-degree burns. On his neck and chest. Not a single person in the crowd, neither a passerby nor a policeman, had stopped the perpetrator.

Nurith returned. "Nimrod, where are you? Listen to me! Chaim has lost hold of himself and is out of control." Stein, Nurith said, had begun to tell stories that had nothing to do with the country. Tourists complained about him. The tour guide was leading them astray and made fun of them. When they arrived at the sights, he told them completely different stories than those that could be read about them in the books for foreigners.

"You must set him straight," Nurith said and hurried away to take care of other problems. Alone, Nimrod stood in front of her desk. At this time many customers were in the office. They crowded around the employees and asked their advice. Nimrod crossed his arms, shifted his torso to the side, ran his left hand up to his head, across the black, stubbly hair, all the way down to the nape of his neck. Self-absorbed as he was, he still towered over almost everyone in the room.

He did not know how to proceed. How was he supposed to subdue Chaim? Who could expect Nimrod to stop Chaim Stein if no one in Hebron had been willing to stop a violent criminal, at least to fend him off or arrest him? Why should he be concerned if Chaim deviated in some of his explanations from the usual legends made for tourists? What understanding did some German foreigner have of this country, or Nurith Elassar of Chaim Stein? The old man had firsthand experience and knowledge of the reversals of reality, of the transformation of many a popular legend, and of the upheavals of history. To take the role of a tutor toward such a man, his former teacher, was the last thing Nimrod Guttmann considered doing. Particularly since the wickerwork of anecdotes and legends that they served their guests on their sightseeing tours hardly corresponded to the historical theories that Nimrod had studied at the university. They served whatever seemed palatable, and occasionally Nimrod would spice his words to the point of driving tears to the eyes of the central Europeans. For the most part, however, they merely digested what was to their liking to begin with.

An hour later Nimrod sat in a minibus with the driver and nine tourists, waiting for Chaim Stein. He wanted to participate in the sightseeing tour to check the old man out in the process. The foreigners did not talk.

The chauffeur turned the radio on. Except for him, only Nimrod was able to follow the news in Hebrew. Every hour on the hour the population of this country performed this particular devotion. They listened with half an ear to the announcer as if a preacher, a muezzin were calling upon them to congregate in front of their

radio sets. Voices were lowered. At times all sounds died down, and
index fingers were pressed to the lips. How many had died and
what were their names? Nimrod Guttmann knew that the common
silence no longer contained unanimity. Two persons might listen to
the same words, but they heard different things.

The announcer discussed the progress of the negotiations. The
occupied territories had been closed off. All the youth organizations wanted to honor Yitzhak Rabin in a collective memorial service, but certain associations, it was said, refused to intone the song
of peace, the popular song into which the statesman had joined
during a big mass rally. A few minutes prior to his assassination.

All of a sudden Chaim Stein came rushing in, asked, if everyone
was there, welcomed the group, sat down, and began his commentary while pointing his eagle's profile in one or the other direction.

Nimrod noticed that his friend had changed. Stein did not recognize Nimrod. He did not seem to see him. The glass blue eyes of the
tour guide looked straight through him, stared into empty space,
and did not focus on anything. Although Chaim had probably gone
blind, he was still able to talk about every sight at which they
stopped, just as if he were able to perceive everything distinctly. Yet,
his commentaries met with disbelief. Some people laughed out
loud, others nudged each other, others shook their head about
Stein's presentations.

For example, in Jerusalem they were standing before the western
part of the Jewish temple ruins, and the old man related that right
here a new luxury hotel was under construction. He praised the
simplicity of the architecture. He claimed that the orthodox Jews in
their black clothes, praying, dancing, singing, or leaning against
the hewn stone were workers. He fantasized that they were diligent
work details, masters of their trade. He turned the different Hasidic
sects into guilds, carpenters, plumbers, or masons. He changed
the religious services into trade union meetings. The rabbis were
turned into big shots. Pilgrims hauling their crosses through the
Via Dolorosa, Stein alleged, were furniture dealers.

Nimrod remained silent and tried not to attract attention even
though after a little while he had realized that Chaim would not
discover him anyhow. Their bus had to be rerouted on account of
the memorial service for Yitzhak Rabin. Stein did not say a word

about the assassination or the most recent acts of violence. He praised the Masada, the ancient fortress in the desert, alleging it was a modern stadium.

One of the Germans, a heavyset guy, burst into laughter. The man, wearing tennis shorts, shirt, sports shoes, and a soft sun hat on his head, snorted, elbowing his fat little wife and his son, a lanky youth. His revelry proved infectious to almost everybody. He stamped his feet, yelling, "That's super! That's Jewish humor. What a great old guy!"

The group ran after Chaim and seemed to be delighted by him. Even Nimrod Guttmann had to smile when he listened to Stein. He crossed his arms, shifted his torso to the side, his hips gently swaying. He ran his hand up to his head and across his hair all the way down to his neck. Off and on he groped for his notebook, opened it, and wrote a few sentences. He tried to suppress a smirk, the quiver around the corners of his mouth. It felt good not to be forced to hear any longer the things that Nimrod Guttmann had to tell on every tour, to hear any longer about the hardship and the terror that the journalists in this country knew how to report so well.

Only a young woman wearing glasses was annoyed about Chaim Stein. Narrow, almost emaciated, she stood in isolation, leafing relentlessly through her guide book, shaking her head and sometimes rolling her eyes. No one paid attention to her.

They spent the night in Jerusalem. The next morning they took the long way back to Tel Aviv and drove to the center of the city. All of a sudden the bus slowed down at a traffic light and came to a stop at the vast square in front of city hall. Chaim began to stare with excitement. He clenched his fists, pressed his face against the windowpane, and then ordered the driver, "Stop! Pull over! Let us off!"

He stumbled to the exit, and the entire group followed him. Seventy meters from a gigantic graffito, a portrait of Yitzhak Rabin, they stopped. A crowd had gathered here. Some individuals held posters in their hands, others carried banners. Children lit candles and placed them on the ground. Some people were singing. The song of peace. Chaim did not move, all he did was blink his eyes in their direction. The group of tourists became restless. No one knew what was going on.

Nimrod went over to Stein and asked, "What's the matter?" The old man stared, seemingly lost, and all of a sudden he said, "All this reminds me of the past. It looks like a square that I once knew. A long time ago."

"You mean a place in Berlin?"

"But no," Chaim answered. "Much later. Decades after I left Germany. I lived there. A different country."

"But this is that very country. Listen, this is that country."

Stein dismissed the remark; he extended his hands above his head. "No! You really don't know what you're talking about. That can't be it. All of this is strange! Just take a look! Don't you see? That's where he was shot. That can't be it. Everything here is strange!" Tears were streaming down his face.

The tourists whispered among themselves. On the opposite side of the street a few people had congregated around a speaker, an adolescent. Behind him was a woman holding a microphone, which looked like a feather duster on a long stick. In front of the speaker was a man shouldering his camera. Nimrod hugged his older friend, whispered, "Chaim, it's me. Nimrod. Don't you recognize me?"

"Nimrod," Stein murmured into his ear and put his forehead against the younger man's chest. Then he whispered, "I must tell you something, Nimrod. I have lied to all of you. I have gone blind."

"I know, Chaim."

Stein lifted his index finger and cleared his throat. "No, I have been for a long time. I guided all of you young people across the country, I taught all of you, but I have been blind for years. . . . Yet I felt that I knew everything. Only now do I see that I saw nothing at all."

Nimrod Guttmann did not want to let Stein leave. He held on to Chaim, studied his face. He wanted to say something, wanted to pick up something consoling, but he had lost his words. In the course of time the old man had become hard of seeing; gradually his lenses had become cloudy as if frosted glass were rising all around him. In the beginning, Nimrod thought, Chaim had probably wondered where those shadows came from that accompanied his every glance.

Nimrod's arms fell off Stein's shoulders. He looked up and all of a sudden it seemed to him as if he himself no longer recognized this city, as if his vision too had become obstructed in the course of the year. Or had something blinded him earlier? Had staring at an enemy, having those foreigners in their sights, deprived all of them of their senses? Why had they overlooked the one danger, not recognized the assassin, not accosted him, pushed him away, or stopped him?

Chaim Stein kept repeating, "Only now do I see that I saw nothing."

The German tourist in tennis shorts, who had appeared so jolly during the entire trip, had become impatient. He shrugged his shoulders, craned his neck, nudged his little wife, and walked up to Chaim Stein, "What's the matter? What's the meaning of this?"

Chaim turned toward him. At this point the fat guy and the other foreigners shrank away from the man with the white mane and the dead eyes. Then Stein stumbled off, and for the first time Nimrod noticed that at every step the old man took he felt his way – why had it escaped him until now? – like a blind person. Chaim disappeared into the crowd, and with him Grandfather Jacov and Hermann the waiter seemed to fade away too.

Matti Bunzl

Matti Bunzl was born in Vienna in 1971. The son of
an Austrian-Jewish father, the historian John Bunzl,
and an Israeli mother, a physician, he graduated
from a Viennese high school in 1989. In 1990 he enrolled as an undergraduate at Stanford University.
Following his graduation in 1993—he received a master's degree in anthropology – he continued his studies at the University of Chicago to complete his Ph.D.
in anthropology and history. In 1998 he joined the
Department of Anthropology at the University of Il-
linois at Urbana-Champaign as an assistant professor. Bunzl's academic interests range from the
anthropology of contemporary Austrian Jewry and
the culture and literature of fin-de-siècle Vienna to
the history of anthropology and issues of gender and
sexuality. His work has been published in such journals as *History and Memory*, *City and Society*, *Cultural Anthropology*, *History of Anthropology*, *The German Quarterly*,
and *Austrian Studies*. He is working on a dissertation
entitled "Technologies of Modernity in Late Imperial
Vienna: A Historical Ethnography and Cultural History of Jung-Wien."

Matti Bunzl

From Kreisky to Waldheim

Another Jewish Youth in Vienna

I was born in Vienna in July of 1971, and my childhood coincided
with a peculiar moment in Austrian-Jewish history. In April of 1970,
the Social Democrat Bruno Kreisky had assumed the country's
chancellorship as the head of a minority government. After over a
year of ruling against a conservative parliamentary majority, he
cemented his position by capturing over 50 percent of the vote in
elections called in the fall of 1971.[1] For the next twelve years, Austria's most powerful political post was held by a "racial" Jew, a fact
hardly lost upon the country's Jewish citizens, many of whom rev-
eled in Kreisky's enormous popularity. Notwithstanding conservative Jews' repeated quibbles with the chancellor's progressive
Middle Eastern politics, Kreisky's ascendance to the helm of the
republic suggested an effective normalization of Austrian-Jewish
relations, seemingly evidencing that anti-Semitism no longer constituted an operative factor in the country's social fabric.

In my left-leaning family, Kreisky was revered with little equiv-
ocation. My father, born in London in 1945 as the son of upper-
middle-class Austrian Jews who returned to Austria shortly after the
war, not only shared Kreisky's social background but also his rejection of the bourgeois values that had dominated his upbringing.
Instead of embracing a Jewish upper-middle-class existence, my
father had opted for the transethnic left-wing political orientation
available to members of the student movement of the late 1960s. It
was a delocalizing move not unlike that of Kreisky, who had re-
invented himself as an ethnically unmarked Socialist of Austro-
Marxist persuasion when entering Austria's political stage in the
1930s.[2]

But while such Socialist identifications potentially transcended any overtly Jewish identities, a distinct sense of ethnic specificity continued to lurk in the background. In Kreisky's and my father's cases, this constellation surfaced as a hybrid subjectivity that merged profound concerns for Jewish and Middle-Eastern politics with a sense of Austrian national belonging (although my father's Austrian sentiments never reached the heights of Kreisky's genuine affection for the country).[3]

Insofar as a sense of political and ethnic identity existed for me during my early childhood, it was a product and mirror of the dynamic underwriting of Kreisky's and my father's identity politics. In principle, I felt very Austrian. Sure, the *Klassenbuch* at my elementary school identified me as "mosaisch," as did the transcripts I was handed at the end of each school year.[4] Certainly, I had to leave the classroom when my school mates were instructed in (Catholic) religion. And, of course, I was silent during the daily Lord's Prayer that commenced instruction at my public school. But while I had a keen sense that the man on the cross in the classroom had not died for my salvation, none of these markers of difference detracted from my sense of feeling like a more or less genuine Austrian.

Perhaps the best way of characterizing my ethnic identity during elementary school in late-1970s Vienna was one of diffuse but welcome difference, the kind of difference that saves a child from feeling all too ordinary. I certainly knew that I was Jewish. In fact, I was quite happy to volunteer that information to anyone who seemed interested. I was similarly happy to divulge details about the global dissemination of my family, proudly recounting the curious fact that the sisters of my father's mother lived in such exotic places as New York, London, and Tel Aviv. That it was the horrors of the Holocaust that had uprooted these relatives from their Viennese surroundings may have been apparent to me, but the fact neither conflicted with the identification I felt with Austria, nor did it negatively implicate the country or its citizens.

If anything, Austria's seemingly unproblematic relation to the Nazi past was continually reinforced to me. This had to do with my mother, who, having grown up in Israel as the child of Polish survivors, often told me of the wonderful things she had heard about Austria while still living in Israel. Indeed, in the eyes of most Israelis, Austria was regarded as an "island of the blessed" as late as the 1970s. I remember well a number of occasions when on visits with my grandparents in Israel my speaking German would elicit anxious comments by acquaintances or passersby. In such situations, my explanation that I was Austrian, not German, would invariably assuage any concerns. While most Israelis were unable to fathom how Jews could live in post–World War II Germany, the possible presence of Jews in Austria occasioned no such sentiments.

Moreover, I always felt confident in assuring my Israeli interlocutors that Austria was indeed different from Germany (or at least the Germany I imagined as the place where the Holocaust had been perpetrated). Especially on the question of anti-Semitism, I was very certain that, if at all existent, it was the absurd credo of a tiny minority and enjoyed no currency in Austrian society at large; and I remember several situations in which I pointed to Kreisky's chancellorship as the ultimate proof for my assertions.

It was in that context that I grew up as a rather fervent Austrian chauvinist. The concerns of the national image were my own concerns. While I may have been too young to fully comprehend the magnitude of Franz Klammer's triumph in the downhill at the 1976 Winter Olympics in Innsbruck, I remember my own excitement in the face of the cathartic moment of Austria's victory over the then reigning champion Germany in the 1978 Soccer World Cup, an event whose historical overtones quickly established it as a constitutive part of postwar Austrian national mythology.[5]

In rendering me such a committed national, my early childhood would seem to provide evidence of the utter effectiveness of the Second Republic's foundational *Lebenslüge*.[6] If it allowed "ordinary" Austrians to effectively externalize the Nazi past as an episode of German, not Austrian, history, it also invited Jews to imagine the country as a genuinely anti-Fascist state that had overcome anti-Semitic prejudice and welcomed its Jewish citizens into the symbolic fold of the nation.[7] I wasn't even fazed by repeated skepticism regarding my citizenship, occasionally voiced in such questions as, "You are Jewish. Doesn't that mean that you are an Israeli citizen?" Chalking up such inquiries to mere ignorance, I would happily educate my interlocutors about the possibility of living as an Austrian Jew, always noting my proud belonging to that category.

So strong was the sense of security emanating from my willed belonging to Austria's anti-Fascist national community that in 1985 in the context of awakening political interests and consciousness I took to the streets to protest Friedhelm Frischenschlager's official welcome of the convicted Nazi war criminal Walter Reder.[8] Having myself produced a large poster with the slogan "Verteidigungs-minister verteidigt Naziverbrecher,"[9] I joined my father and several Jewish and non-Jewish friends in publicly demonstrating against this breach of the Second Republic's anti-Fascist consensus. Look-ing at it now, this willingness to take part in such a protest not only suggested my belief in the viability of that consensus but the fact that I as a young Austrian Jew presupposed my compatriots' accord with my grievance over Frischenschlager's affront. Indeed, save for a vocal defense by Jörg Haider,[10] Frischenschlager's handshake with Reder was universally condemned, confirming my sense that the overwhelming majority of Austria's populace was indeed com-mitted to an anti-Fascist credo that could underwrite the nor-malization of Jewish-Austrian identity. Or put differently, when I marched in protest of Frischenschlager's faux pas in 1985, I was certain that the people lining the street respected and ultimately agreed with my condemnation of the incident.

All this changed a scant year later, during the months of the so-called Waldheim affair in the spring of 1986. To be sure, the affair had started in similar fashion as the Frischenschlager/Reder alter-cation. When documents disclosed by the New York–based World Jewish Congress revealed Austrian presidential candidate Kurt Waldheim's former membership in Nazi student organizations and his involvement in previously unacknowledged activities in the *Wehrmacht*, I, for one, was quite certain that public opinion would sway against the former UN secretary general. But in the face of Waldheim's reaction vis-à-vis the forthcoming documents (which sought to effect an identification with a wartime generation that had "only done its duty"), his case readily came to stand in for the problematic dynamics of Austrian *Vergangenheitsbewältigung* (pro-cess of coming to terms with the past) at large. In particular, it was the party supporting Waldheim's candidacy, the Christian, conser-vative People's Party (ÖVP), that had a palpable interest in exploit-ing the situation, quickly figuring the election as a referendum on

Austrian national identity. The party did so by taking a defensive stance, effectively construing any inquiries into Waldheim's past as an organized onslaught on the candidate's and Austria's "good name in the world."[11]

What was so shocking to me at the time was the ÖVP's ready recourse to patently anti-Semitic tropes when articulating this position. In the discourse of the leaders of a party that had underwritten the anti-Fascist consensus of post–World War II Austria, efforts to shed light on Waldheim's past were equated to a "campaign," a notion that was substantiated through allusions to Jewish conspiracies and the hegemony of the "East Coast press" (a term indexing both the New York Times and stereotypical figurations of a Jewish-controlled press). It was clear to me that the discourse of ÖVP politicians and other Waldheim backers deliberately blurred the boundaries and distinctions between the World Jewish Congress, Austria's Jewish community, and the country's Jewish citizens, thereby effectively constructing "the Jews" in crude anti-Semitic fashion as the essentialized opponent of Waldheim qua Austria.

More than anything else, it was the choice of political posters that conveyed to me this not so subtle message. On the one hand, the ÖVP had reacted to the forthcoming revelations about Waldheim's past by encouraging the electorate to vote for the candidate "now more than ever."[12] I distinctly remember my consternation at the extremely hostile logic, which suggested that Waldheim's now questionable wartime past could actually be figured as an asset rather than a detraction in the competition for votes. On the other hand, Waldheim's party mounted placards displaying the following sentence as if scribbled on the wall by an angry passerby: "We Austrians vote for whom we want."[13] Left unwritten by the purported author for lack of space, the sentence nevertheless implied a clear afterthought: In the overtly anti-Semitic context of the Waldheim affair, I could not but read the poster as: "We Austrians vote for whom we want, not for whom the Jews want."

More immediate for my life than the public display of anti-Semitic sentiments, however, was the profound change I felt in the social climate of my own surroundings. Whereas I had never been the target of overt anti-Semitic hostilities, I was now confronted with repeated charges by classmates who, much like the politicians they were aping, readily confused the actions of the World Jewish Congress with my own, entirely passive political stance. Usually, such disputes would culminate in accusatory questions like, "Why don't 'you' stop attacking Waldheim?" figuring me as part of that seamless whole of world Jewry haunting Waldheim and Austria.

More generally, however, I was made to feel profoundly different. While my entire early childhood had been marked by a happy Austrian-Jewish symbiosis, the Waldheim affair effectively undermined my nationalist inclinations. How, after all, was it possible to feel genuine allegiance to a country whose second-largest political party had taken ready recourse to anti-Semitic sentiments and whose population had endorsed that course of action at the voting booth? And how, after all, was it possible to think myself part of Austria's national collectivity if I was so readily figured as its hostile other?

If such considerations made me feel extremely vulnerable about my position as a Jew in mid-1980s Austria, an event in the fall of 1986 brought my new situation into extremely sharp relief: One evening, I was waiting for the subway with a Jewish friend of my own age. He was wearing the kind of beret many observant Austrian Jews wear to cover their yarmulke in public. After a few minutes on the platform, we were spotted by two older youths, who proceeded toward us. Apparently drunk, they started to talk loudly about our appearance, and when the subway rolled into the station, they made it a point to follow us into the car. As the train began to move, they accosted us, pushing us repeatedly while making a number of anti-Semitic remarks. As other passengers looked on without intervening, my friend and I tried to deal with the situation by ignoring the thugs' actions as well as we could. Finally, when the subway arrived at the next stop, we made a quick escape, ran up the escalators, and sought shelter in a restaurant, still hearing the taunts of our attackers.

While the event, which had occurred just days after Jörg Haider had taken over the leadership of the Freedom Party (FPÖ),[14] left me visibly shaken for a few days, I eventually came to regard it as part of a larger lesson, a lesson painfully learned in the wake of the Waldheim affair and its concomitant circumstances. Ultimately, it was less the fear of random physical assault and manifest anti-Semitism that stuck with me than the realization that Jewish existence in Austria remains highly contingent and can just never be taken for granted. While progressive social forces may have made earnest strides in extending Austria's national imagery to accommodate the country's Jews, political expediency and hostile motivations always allow the figuration of Jews outside Austrian nationness. In the final analysis, the Kreiskian Jewish identity that had dominated my early childhood has been superseded by a sense of ethnic difference. In Schnitzler's dictum, Waldheim has taught me that in 1980s Austria it was once again impossible for "a Jew . . . to ignore that he was a Jew."[15]

Notes

I would like to thank Dagmar Lorenz for posing the challenge of writing this short autobiographical piece. While my work has repeatedly addressed questions of Austrian-Jewish identity (see Matti Bunzl, "On the Politics and Semantics of Austrian Memory: Vienna's Monument against War and Fascism," *History and Memory* 7, no. 2 [1995]: 7–40, and "The City and the Self: Narratives of Spatial Belonging among Austrian Jews," *City and Society* [1996]: 50–81), I usually refrain from the use of extended first-person narrative. At the same time, there is a well-established genre of reflexive anthropology, and the present piece, a hybrid of autobiography and reflexive, native anthropology, owes much to the conventions established there (see Paul Rabinow, *Reflections on Fieldwork in Morocco* [Berkeley: University of California Press, 1977]; Anna Lowenhaupt Tsing, *In the Realm of the Diamond Queen: Marginality in an Out-of-the-Way Place* [Princeton NJ: Princeton University Press, 1993]; and Jack Kugelmass, "Bloody Memories: Encountering the Past in Contemporary Poland," *Cultural Anthropology* 10 [1995]: 279–301). For his keen comments on this text, I would like to thank Billy Vaughn.

1. In April of 1970, Bruno Kreisky formed a Social Democratic minority government after winning 48.4 percent of the vote in federal elections. In the fall of 1971, new elections resulted in an absolute majority for the Socialist Party (SPÖ) at just over 50 percent of the vote. After four years of sole governing authority, the SPÖ increased its share of the vote to 50.4 percent in the 1975 elections and topped out at just over 51 percent in the 1979 vote. Kreisky headed the Socialist cabinets established after each of these votes until the election of 1983 when he resigned after the SPÖ had

dropped to 47.6 percent of the vote (Volker Lauber, ed., *Contemporary Austrian Politics* [Boulder CO: Westview Press, 1996]).

2. On Kreisky's life and career, see the three volumes of his memoirs: Bruno Kreisky, *Zwischen den Zeiten: Erinnerungen aus fünf Jahrzehnten* (Berlin: Siedler, 1986); *Im Strom der Politik: Der Memoiren zweiter Teil* (Vienna: Kremayr and Scheriau, 1988); and *Der Mensch im Mittelpunkt: Der Memoiren dritter Teil* (Vienna: Kremayr and Scheriau, 1996). See also H. Pierre Secher, *Bruno Kreisky, Chancellor of Austria: A Political Biography* (Pittsburgh: Dorrance Publishing, 1993). For a critical analysis of Kreisky's Jewish identity, see Robert Wistrich, "The Kreisky Phenomenon: A Reassessment," in *Austrians and Jews in the Twentieth Century: From Franz Joseph to Waldheim*, ed. Robert Wistrich (London: Macmillan, 1992), 234–51.

3. This hybridity is reflected in my father's academic work, which ranges from analyses of Middle-Eastern politics to studies of anti-Semitism and Austrian Jewish history. See John Bunzl, *Klassenkampf in der Diaspora: Zur Geschichte der jüdischen Arbeiterbewegung* (Vienna: Europaverlag, 1975); *Israel und die Palästinenser: Die Entwicklung eines Gegensatzes* (Vienna: Braumüller, 1983); *Der lange Arm der Erinnerung: Jüdisches Bewußtsein heute* (Vienna: Böhlau, 1987); *Juden im Orient: Jüdische Gemeinschaften in der islamischen Welt und orientalische Juden in Israel* (Vienna: Junius, 1989); and John Bunzl and Bernd Marin, *Antisemitismus in Österreich: Sozialhistorische und soziologische Studien* (Innsbruck: Inn-Verlag, 1983).

4. The *Klassenbuch* is a register of the students in a class. It has the character of an official document and is treated as an item of great importance. Although under the control of the teachers, it is usually also accessible to students who wish to inspect it.

5. To this day, the winning moments of this match are replayed on Austrian television with great regularity. More generally, the country's sports rivalry with Germany (a decidedly one-sided affair, for it is not perceived as such by the German side) occupies Austria's national imagination. Soccer bouts with Germany on the club and national level arouse enormous interest and arc invariably figured in terms of asserting Austrian national identity vis-à-vis the stronger, more powerful neighbor. More recently, tennis matches against Germany, especially in the Davis Cup competition, have similarly stirred national sentiments.

6. Austria's Second Republic was founded on the myth of the country's victimization at the hands of Nazi aggression. In the Moscow declaration of 1943, the allies had officially deemed Austria the "first victim" of Hitlerite expansionism in order to stimulate Austrian resistance against the Third Reich. The formulation was mirrored in Austria's declaration of

independence, signed on 27 April 1945, where the representatives of the three anti-Fascist parties, SPÖ, ÖVP, and the Communist Party (KPÖ), interpreted the years between 1938 and 1945 as the violent imposition of a foreign regime. That declaration in turn formed the conceptual basis of postwar Austria's anti-Fascist consensus, a consensus that presupposed the externalization of the Third Reich as part of German (not Austrian) history, as well as the neglect of the high percentage of Austrians supporting the Nazi Party.

7. For a memoir exposing the darker ramifications of Austria's *Lebenslüge* for postwar Austrian Jewry, see Ruth Beckermann, *Unzugehörig: Österreicher und Juden nach 1945* (Vienna: Löcker, 1989).

8. The Frischenschlager-Reder affair occurred when then secretary of defense Friedhelm Frischenschlager, a liberal member of the FPÖ, who has since joined Heide Schmidt's Liberal Forum (LIF), officially welcomed the convicted Austrian war criminal Walter Reder on the occasion of his deportation from Italy to Austria. In particular, it was Frischenschlager's warm and friendly handshake with Reder that provoked outrage, having been extended, as it was, by a high-ranking member of Austria's government.

9. The slogan translates as "Secretary of defense defends Nazi criminal."

10. When the Frischenschlager-Reder affair occurred in 1985, Jörg Haider was more than a year away from taking over the leadership of the FPÖ. In the course of the affair, Haider ridiculed Frischenschlager for bowing to "Jewish pressure" when the latter apologized for his action after the World Jewish Congress considered canceling a conference scheduled to be held in Vienna. At the time of the affair, the FPÖ steered a liberal course under the then party leader Norbert Steger, who served as vice chancellor in a coalition government under the Social Democrat Fred Sinowatz. Within the FPÖ, Haider had been the most vocal critic of Steger's course, advocating a return to the right-wing, nationalist position that had characterized both the FPÖ and its predecessor, the Independent Party (VdU), which had been founded in 1949 to accommodate former members of the National Socialist Party (NSDAP).

11. The original slogan for Waldheim's presidential campaign, "Der Mann dem die Welt vertraut" (The man the world trusts), had played on his former position as UN secretary general and, by extension, on Austria's role as an important site for international diplomacy in the 1970s and early 1980s. On the anti-Semitic politics of the Waldheim affair, see Richard Mitten, *The Politics of Antisemitic Prejudice: The Waldheim Phenomenon in Austria* (Boulder CO: Westview Press, 1992); see also Ruth Wodak, Peter Nowak, Johanna Pelikan, Helmut Gruber, Rudolf de Cillia, and Richard Mitten,

"Wir sind alle unschuldige Täter": Diskurshistorische Studien zum Nachkriegsantise-mitismus (Frankfurt am Main: Suhrkamp, 1990).

12. The German original read, "Jetzt erst recht!"

13. The German original read, "Wir Österreicher wählen wen wir wollen!"

14. Haider gained control of the FPÖ in the fall of 1986 in a hotly contested party referendum between himself and Norbert Steger. A few days after the coup, the Socialist chancellor Franz Vranitzky, who had succeeded Franz Sinowatz when the latter resigned in the wake of Waldheim's victory in the presidential election of July 1986, terminated the coalition between SPÖ and the FPÖ and called for new elections.

15. The quote is from Schnitzler's famous memoir, *Jugend in Wien* (*My Youth in Vienna*). See Arthur Schnitzler, *Jugend in Wien: Eine Autobiographie* (Frankfurt am Main: Fischer, 1981), 322.

Acknowledgments

All translations are by Dagmar C. G. Lorenz unless otherwise specified.

Excerpt from Albert Drach, "M.T.": That is the meantime, is a translation of "Z.Z." das ist die Zwischenzeit: Ein Protokoll (Munich: Carl Hanser, 1990), 320–38. Copyright © 1990 by Carl Hanser Verlag München Wein. Translated by permission of Carl Hanser.

Excerpt from Elias Canetti, The Secret Heart of the Clock: Notes, Aphorisms, Fragments, trans. Joel Agee (New York: Farrar, Straus & Giroux, 1989), 100–15. Reprinted by permission of Farrar, Straus & Giroux, Inc. and Andre Deutsch Ltd. Originally published as Das Geheimherz der Uhr: Aufzeichnungen, 1973–1985 (Munich: Hanser, 1987). Translation copyright © 1989 by Farrar, Straus & Giroux, Inc.

Veza Canetti, "The New Guy," is a translation of "Der Neue," in Geduld bringt Rosen (Munich: Carl Hanser, 1992), 67–72. Copyright © 1991 by Elias Canetti Zürich; copyright © 1992 by Carl Hanser Verlag München Wein. Translated by permission of Carl Hanser.

Friedrich Torberg, "Aunt Jolesch in Person," is a translation of "Die Tante Jolesch persönlich," in Die Tante Jolesch oder Der Untergang des Abendlandes in Anekdoten (Munich: dtv, 1977), 13–21. Copyright © 1975 by Alber Langen Georg Müller Verlag in der F. A. Herbig Verlagsbuchhandlung GmbH, München. Translated by permission of Langen Müller Herbig.

Hans Weigel, "The Draped Window," is a translation of "Das verhängte Fenster," Plan 1, no. 5 (1946): 397–99. Translated by permission of Elfriede Ott. The excerpt from It is impossible to speak about it dispassionately is a translation of Man kann nicht ruhig darüber reden (Graz, Austria: Styria, 1986), 117–41. Translated by permission of Styria.

Simon Wiesenthal, "The Waldheim Case," in Justice Not Vengeance, trans. Ewald Osers (London: Weidenfeld and Nicolson, 1989), 310–22. Reprinted by permission of Orion and Editions Robert Laffont.

360 Acknowledgments

Hilde Spiel, "I Love Living in Austria," is a translation of "Ich lebe gern in Österreich," in In meinem Garten schlendernd (Munich: Nymphenburger Verlagsanstalt, 1984), 17–21. Copyright © 1984 by Nymphenburger Verlagshandlung in der F. A. Herbig Verlagsbuchhandlung GmbH. Translated by permission of Langen Müller Herbig. "Aura and Origin" is a translation of "Aura und Ursprung," in Die hellen und die finsteren Zeiten (Munich: List, 1989), 15–31. Translated by permission of Verlagshaus Goethestrasse.

Jean Améry, "Antisemitism on the Left," in Radical Humanism, trans. Sidney Rosenfeld and Stella P. Rosenfeld (Bloomington: University of Indiana Press, 1984), 36–51. Reprinted by permission of Maria Améry. Originally published as "Der ehrbare Antisemitismus," in Weiterleben (Stuttgart, Germany: Klett-Cotta, 1982), 151–84.

Excerpt from Elisabeth Freundlich, The soul bird, is a translation of Der Seelenvogel (Vienna: Paul Zsolnay, 1986), 9–22. Copyright © 1986 by Paul Zsolnay Verlag Ges.m.b.H., Wein. Translated by permission of Paul Zsolnay.

Michael Hamburger's translation of Paul Celan, "Death Fugue," appeared in Paul Celan: Poems. A Bilingual Edition, trans. Michael Hamburger (New York: Persea Books, 1980), 50–53, and in Poems of Paul Celan, trans. Michael Hamburger (London: Anvil Press Poetry, 1995). Copyright © 1972, 1980, 1988, 1995 by Michael Hamburger. Reprinted by permission of Persea Books, Anvil Press Poetry, and the translator. John Felstiner's translation of "Death Fugue" appeared in Paul Celan: Poet, Survivor, Jew, trans. John Felstiner (New Haven: Yale University Press, 1995), 31–32. Reprinted by permission of the translator. Both versions are translations of "Todesfuge," in Mohn und Gedächtnis (Frankfurt am Main: Suhrkamp, 1952).

Ilse Aichinger, "A Summons to Mistrust," is a translation of "Aufruf zum Mißtrauen," Plan 1, no. 5 (1946): 588. Translated by permission of the author. "Rahel's Clothes" is a translation of "Rahels Kleider," in Schlechte Wörter (Frankfurt am Main: Fischer, 1976), 52–58. Copyright © 1976 by S. Fischer Verlag GmbH. "My Father" is a translation of "Mein Vater," in Verschenkter Rat (Frankfurt am Main: Fischer, 1978), 19. Copyright © 1978 by S. Fischer Verlag GmbH. Translated by permission of Fischer.

Erich Fried, "To Austria," is a translation of "An Österreich," in Frühe Gedichte (Hildesheim, Germany: Claassen, 1986), 78. Copyright © 1986 by Claassen Verlag, Düsseldorf. Translated by permission of Claassen. "My Girlfriends," in On Pain of Seeing: Poems by Erich Fried, trans. Georg Rapp

Acknowledgments 361

(Chicago: Swallow Press, 1969), 38, was originally published as
"Verwandlung," in *Anfechtungen* (Berlin: Klaus Wagenbach, 1967), 42.
Reprinted by permission of Klaus Wagenbach. "Is Anti-Zionism Anti-
Semitism?" is a translation of "Ist Antizionismus Antisemitismus?" in
Anfragen und Nachreden (Berlin: Klaus Wagenbach, 1994), 158–165.
Translated by permission of Klaus Wagenbach.

Georg Kreisler, "Bundschuh the War Criminal," is a translation of
"Bundschuh, der Kriegsverbrecher," in *Worte ohne Lieder: Satiren* (Frankfurt
am Main: Ullstein, 1986), 120–21. "The Unknown Nation" is a translation
of "Das Unbekannte Volk," in *Worte ohne Lieder*, 289–91. Translated by
permission of the author.

Excerpt from Eva Deutsch and Brigitte Schwaiger, The Galician woman, is
a translation of *Die Galizianerin* (Reinbeck, Germany: Rowohlt, 1984), 79–
90. Translated by permission of Brigitte Schwaiger and Robert S. Deutsch,
stepson of Eva Deutsch, living in the U.S.A. Mr. Deutsch has reviewed the
translation and provided valuable comments on the context and English
phrasing of Eva Deutsch's account.

Jakov Lind, "The Story of Lilith and Eve," was originally published in *The
Stove: Short Stories* (New York: Sheep Meadow Press, 1983). Reprinted by
permission of the author.

Ruth Klüger Angress, "Halloween and a Ghost" (1960) and "An
Admonition" (1963) are printed from the manuscript versions by
permission of the author. "Vienna Neuroses," is a translation of the 1997
manuscript version of "Wiener Neurosen." Translated by permission of
the author. "Lanzmann's *Shoah* and Its Audience" was originally
published in *Simon Wiesenthal Center Annual* 3 (1986): 249–60. Reprinted by
permission of the author.

Excerpt from Peter Henisch, Stein's paranoia, was originally published as
Steins Paranoia (Salzburg: Residenz, 1988), 76–91. Translated by
permission of Residenz.

Robert Schindel, "Double Lamb," prologue to *Born-Where*, trans. Michael
Roloff (Riverside CA: Ariadne, 1995), 1–9. Reprinted by permission of
Ariadne. Originally published as *Gebürtig* (Frankfurt am Main: Suhrkamp,
1992).

Excerpt from Elfriede Jelinek, *Wonderful, Wonderful Times*, trans. Michael
Hulse (London: Serpent's Tail, 1990), 94–112. Copyright © Elfriede
Jelinek, 1989 trans. Michael Hulse, 1992. Reprinted by permission of

Serpent's Tail. Originally published as *Die Ausgesperrten* (Reinbeck, Germany: Rowohlt, 1980), 98–115.

Nadja Seelich, "Film, State, and Society in Eastern and Western Europe – and I," is a translation of the 1992 manuscript version of "Film, Staat, Gesellschaft in Ost- und Westeuropa und ich." Translation by permission of the author. "Farewell to Jana Cerna" is printed from the 1992 manuscript version by permission of the author.

Anna Mitgutsch, "Farewell to Jerusalem," is an excerpt from *Lover, Traitor: A Jerusalem Story* (New York: Henry Holt and Company, Metropolitan Books, 1997), 3–17. Reprinted by permission of Henry Holt and Company. Originally published as *Abschied von Jerusalem* (Berlin: Rowohlt, 1995), 7–22.

Ruth Beckermann, "Youth in Vienna," is a translation of "Jugend in Wien," in *Unzugehörig* (Vienna: Löcker, 1989), 117–29. Translated by permission of the author.

Excerpt from Robert Menasse, Blissful times, brittle world, is a translation of *Selige Zeiten, brüchige Welt* (Frankfurt am Main: Suhrkamp, 1991), 7–18. Translated by permission of Suhrkamp.

Doron Rabinovici, "The Right Nose," is a translation of "Der richtige Riecher," in *Papirnik* (Frankfurt am Main: Suhrkamp, 1994), 60–74. Translated by permission of Suhrkamp. "Foreigners" is a translation of the November 1997 manuscript version of "Fremde." Translated by permission of the author.

Matti Bunzl, "From Kreisky to Waldheim: Another Jewish Youth in Vienna" is printed from the manuscript version by permission of the author.

In the *Jewish Writing in the Contemporary World* Series

Contemporary Jewish Writing in Britain and Ireland
An Anthology
Edited by Bryan Cheyette

Contemporary Jewish Writing in Austria
An Anthology
Edited by Dagmar C. G. Lorenz